No One
Wants You

No One Wants You

A True Story of a Child
Forced into Prostitution

Celine Roberts

EBURY
PRESS

5 7 9 10 8 6 4

Published in 2008 by Ebury Press, an imprint of Ebury Publishing
A Random House Group Company
First published in Ireland by Merlin Publishing in 2006

The Random House Group Limited Reg. No. 954009

Addresses for companies within the Random House Group can be
found at www.randomhouse.co.uk

A CIP catalogue record for this book is available from the British Library

The Random House Group Limited supports The Forest Stewardship
Council (FSC), the leading international forest certification
organisation. All our titles that are printed on Greenpeace approved
FSC certified paper carry the FSC logo.
Our paper procurement policy can be found at
www.rbooks.co.uk/environment

Printed in the UK by CPI Cox & Wyman, Reading, RG1 8EX

ISBN 9780091922702

To buy books by your favourite authors and register for offers visit
www.rbooks.co.uk

Dedicated to all the silent survivors of abuse
of any kind who feel trapped and unable
to raise their voice in protest.

Acknowledgements

To Gerry Ledwith, my agent, whose literary skills and endless gentle patience kept my aspiration to write alive.

To Chenile, Aoife and Julie, at Merlin, for believing in me and taking the risk.

To Charlotte and the team at Ebury for accepting my work and for being so caring to me personally.

To Peter Davin for my promotional photos.

Contents

My First Communion

My emotional future was determined by a life-changing event that happened in May 1956. At age seven, I was to make my First Holy Communion.

There was quite a lot of excitement among the children at school in the weeks leading up to this day. Even my foster-mother made sure that I would not miss out on this grand occasion. At least she would be seen by others to be looking after my religious education.

We had to learn certain new prayers. On a practical level, we had to go to the church to practise walking up the aisle, kneeling at the altar rails and sticking out our tongues at the priest, to receive the Communion wafer into our mouths.

Everybody would be dressed up.

There was great talk among the girls about what kind of dress they would wear. Of course all clothing for the day was to be in white. Bearing in mind that my clothes were always second-hand rags and never ever having had a school uniform, I asked my foster-mother with cautious expectation if I would have a white dress. 'Course ya will, Child, course ya will,' she assured me in her lilting Cork accent. I didn't really believe her. I usually had to go and pick up second-hand clothes and shoes for myself from a shop in Limerick. I was afraid to say anything and just prayed that I would get a white dress so that I didn't look different from all the other girls.

First Communion was to be at early mass on a Sunday morning. After mass we were to go to the school for breakfast and to play among ourselves for a few hours in the schoolyard. I was also looking forward to breakfast as I had heard that we were going to have rashers and sausages. I had never eaten them before but I had smelled them cooking. My foster-mother used to cook them on very rare occasions. They used to smell lovely and my mouth would water when they were frying, but I was never given any to eat. 'They'd poison ya, Child,' was what I was told, as she chewed them all up. They were always accompanied by several slices of fried bread, oozing grease that dripped on to her ample bosom.

A few days before Communion Sunday, the parish priest arrived at the house with a large box. I was called in to meet him. He opened the box in front of my foster-mother and myself and took out the most exquisite, spotlessly white Communion dress and head-dress that I had ever seen. He handed it to me.

'This is from your auntie nuns in Cork,' he said.

I had no idea what he meant by my 'auntie nuns'. I did not know any nuns except the teachers at the convent school which I attended on an irregular basis. The remark went right over my head. The dress was brand new. I had never seen anything so beautiful in my life.

'Is this mine to keep?'

'This is your First Communion dress. It's yours.'

I was overcome with excitement. I would have my own new dress for the big day.

Sunday dawned. I was up early and washed in a pan of water from the water barrel, as best I could. The water was freezing and there were insects floating in it. I dried myself off with a rag that was left hanging on a nail in the kitchen.

We were fasting before Communion so there was no need for breakfast. My foster-parents stayed in bed.

A pair of white shoes had arrived a day after the dress. They were lovely but they were about two sizes too big for me. I stuffed paper in them to make them fit snugly. I was used to doing this as all my shoes were second-hand and never fitted properly anyway.

When I was dressed, I felt like a princess.

I walked to the church with my foster-mother and when we arrived I joined the other children in the front row of the pews.

The ceremony went according to plan and then we went back to the school where we all had breakfast. I was starving at that stage but I was used to no breakfast. I can still remember how delicious the rashers and sausages tasted. The nuns had laid the table and the hall looked really white and nice, with long tablecloths on all the benches. To this day I love the smell of bacon.

After breakfast it was out to the schoolyard to play. After a couple of hours the bell rang and everyone joined their families who had come to collect them. I remember thinking that everyone else had their father with them, except me. I was told to go home on my own because no one turned up for me. That was normal and I didn't mind.

It was a two-mile walk home and on the journey I met a number of people. They all said that I looked lovely and a few of them gave me money. One gave me a sixpence. Others gave me a threepenny bit. One man had a camera and asked me to stand beside the gate of his house and he would take my photograph. He said he would give me the print when he had it developed. I was thrilled.

I was so happy by the time I reached home. The sun was shining. It was a lovely day in May. A few of the usual visitors, mainly adult men, had called at the house. There were about three or four of them. I had met two of them when I was out working in the fields, picking potatoes. I didn't like working with them because they made fun of me and were always poking me. They used to say that I looked like a little tinker. They said that they were calling especially to give me a present of money for my First Communion. Some tried to give me a sixpence or even a shilling, but when my foster-mother saw the coin she berated them into making a larger donation.

'Ah ya stingy divil ya, give her a half-crown, at least,' she said, as she stood over them while they dug into their pockets once again.

When they had given the money, which I handed to my foster-mother, out came the bottles of stout. It was to be a party in the middle of the day on a Sunday.

One man told me that he had no present with him. He said that he had half a crown at home and that I would have to go with him across the fields to get it. I didn't really want to go but, with my foster-mother's blessing, I set off with him. He was holding me by the hand as we went across the fields to get my First Holy Communion present.

As we were walking through the fields on that sunny May afternoon to collect the present that he had promised me, he suddenly grabbed me and threw me on the ground.

While he pinned me on the ground, with one hand over my mouth so that I could hardly breathe, he snarled, 'Ya dirty little tinker ya. Ya won't need this anymore,' as he ripped off my Communion dress. His words still haunt me to this very day.

I choked silently as I desperately gasped for air through his rough, foul-smelling fingers. I felt something snap and tried to scream. My hand was killing me. I couldn't move it. With his one free hand he ripped away my knickers. He then unbuttoned and lowered his trousers. He pulled my legs apart and tried to force something hard inside me. He kept pushing and pushing. It was agony. He was leaning over me and muttering and grunting. I tried to turn off the pain from my lower body. He continued to push into my body, with thrusts. It felt like it went on forever. He eventually collapsed on top of me. He was so heavy.

I went dead inside. I shut down.

I was suffocating.

When he had got his breath back he rose up, fixed his trousers and just walked away in silence.

He just left me there on the ground.

I was seven years old.

I was covered in blood.

Trembling uncontrollably, I made my way home, injured and alone. I could barely stand up. I could only walk a few steps at a time. The pain was excruciating. I was weak from loss of blood and felt dizzy.

I made it as far as the pond where I tried to wash the dirt, the blood and the sticky stuff off me. I was crying because the beautiful First Communion dress sent to me from my auntie nuns was destroyed. It was torn and covered in blood and muck, and I thought my foster-mother was going to kill me.

I stumbled on to the house and tried to open the front door to go in but I was in such shock that I collapsed unconscious on the front doorstep.

I woke up in my foster-mother's bed. I have no idea how I got there or when I was put there. I was there for about five days. I was drowsy most of the time, but I was aware of a beautiful, tall, well-dressed lady in the room who talked to the others but not to me.

My injuries were bandaged up and I was left alone to recover. Nobody said anything to me about what had happened. I was too scared and sick to say anything. The wounds became infected and I was very sick for many weeks afterwards.

My torn skin eventually healed.

My mind never did.

That day, my First Holy Communion day, I was damaged, utterly. Every other little girl who made her First Communion on the same day as me, in 1956, got nice presents from her loving parents and relatives. What present did I get on my special day? I was brutally raped by a monster who left me injured with a broken wrist and three broken fingers in a muddy field. I will never forget what should have been one of the happiest days of my life, but for all the wrong reasons.

I never saw the Communion dress again.

What must have been many months later, my foster-mother and I were coming out of Sunday mass in Kilmallock Church. The churchyard was packed with people but I saw her catch hold of a man tightly by the arm. When he turned and saw who was gripping him, he tried to escape. Her grasp tightened. I moved behind my foster-mother clasping the folds of her long woollen coat, as if for protection. I peered out around her, staring up at him, sick with fright.

It was the man who had raped me.

'Ya never gave this little girl the First Communion money that ya promised her.'

'Eh, eh, I have no change on me now at the moment. I gave my last few coppers to the collection at church.'

'It's not change she wants!' she spat venomously at him, as her grip tightened painfully.

'I've only a pound note on me now, for a few pints, later,' he winced.

'That'll do grand,' she said, as she leaned threateningly closer to him.

'Aw, shag ya, there yar' so,' he said, with anger in his voice, as he grudgingly handed her a crumpled green-coloured pound note.

He pulled his arm from her vice-like grip and disappeared in the throng of people. She compressed the note in the palm of her hand and smiled to herself.

'Let's go home, Child,' she said, as she marched off, with me shuffling close behind.

That day I was traded for a pound note.

ONE

My Foster Family

I was born, at about 6 pm, in the Sacred Heart Home for Unmarried Mothers at Bessboro, Blackrock, County Cork, Ireland, on November 14, 1948. I was premature by three weeks and my weight at time of birth was 4 lb. 12 oz. My name was registered as Celine Clifford.

In Ireland in the 1940s, when a young unmarried girl was found to be pregnant, it was impossible for her to keep living her normal life. She could not have her baby and rear her child as a single mother. The culture of the time prevented it. It was considered shameful for any young girl to get pregnant while unmarried. If one was a good Catholic parent, it was considered a slur and a disgrace on the entire family if one's daughter became pregnant. A pregnant girl's own people would have put her out.

To take care of such situations in the Ireland of saints and scholars, homes for unmarried mothers existed. These were institutions where a girl could have her baby, and then have it fostered or adopted, usually by Americans. Then she could rejoin some part of Irish society, but usually not in her original position, as if nothing had happened. These homes for the unmarried were places of detention, more like prisons than homes. They were a source of income for the order of nuns that lived there.

In my case, Cork Corporation paid the home £1. 2s. 6d. per baby, per week, as a maintenance fee. Bessboro was owned and run by nuns of the English Order of the Sacred Heart of Jesus and Mary. Mostly Irish women entered this Order. It was their proud boast that 'the girls' spiritual lives and the future of their babies were well taken care of'. I am an example of the latter and 'my future' was not taken care of by anyone.

Entrance to this home, was usually arranged by the clergy, at the behest of the girl's mother. Once the pregnant girl entered through the doors she was not allowed to leave, unless strict conditions were met. After her baby was born, each girl had to stay and work for a period of three years, to help with the running of the home and self-supporting farm. During this time the babies were breastfed for 12 months. After three years, the babies were sent out to foster homes or orphanages or adopted.

The homes earned a lot of money if a baby stayed there for three years. If a girl could arrange to pay the nuns £100, which was a huge amount of money at the time, she was free to leave the home, ten days after the birth. Their babies were then immediately made available for adoption.

There was one other way of escape without the baby. If a girl's family could arrange payment of £50, her baby would be sent to a foster home in the city, and the girl would be free to go. No girl could keep her baby or go home with her baby, no matter what her family paid.

While researching my history, a nun told me that my mother walked out the gates with me in her arms on April 18, 1949. This seems to go against the rule that no mother was allowed to leave with her baby. I have to accept that fact, but I don't know how true it is. It is very difficult to get any valid documentation from these organisations, even now.

At that stage I would have been almost five months old.

I have no idea who paid for my mother's liberation from that place. On that same date I was fostered or 'boarded out' as it was known in those days. That day, my mother who had breastfed me for five months, gave me away to someone else.

As she walked away, she closed her heart to me, for ever. Every baby smiles when being held by its mother. I wonder if we ever bonded as mother and daughter.

As a total coincidence, on that same November 14, 1948, another young mother was giving birth to her first child, in somewhat better circumstances, at Buckingham Palace in London. Her name was Princess Elizabeth Windsor. The Princess named her precious newborn son, Charles Philip Arthur George.

For two people who were born on the same day, we would be fated to lead vastly different lives. His to be one of absolute privilege, mine to be one of utter deprivation.

An extremely poor, old-aged, childless couple, who lived in a remote area of County Limerick, fostered me. The fostering arrangement was made through Limerick County Council as my foster-parents had already done a bit of fostering. I had a foster-brother living in the house with me. I don't know what age he was when I arrived, but he had a terrible time. My foster-father used to beat him so hard, for no reason at all, and they would lock him in a room for days. I remember trying to hide bread and give it to him because he was starving. I felt so sorry for him. When I got a bit older I didn't see him so much because he was working.

We lived in what was then called a cottage, but would be better described as a shack. It consisted of two rooms, a large central room with a small bedroom at the end. There was a tiny porch-sized area, attached at the rear of the building, where turf for the fire was kept and through which access was provided to the backyard. The roof of the main building was rough slate. From inside you could see the rough wooden beams, holding sods of clay that were packed close to the stone as soundproofing against the monotonous din made by the incessant Irish rain. The central room had a large fireplace, and this was where almost all of the daytime and night-time social gatherings took place. The house was built on about an acre of land.

I later discovered that a Catholic priest, a nun and a medical doctor, who were all close friends of my grandmother, on my mother's side, were instrumental in making arrangements for this fostering. I was now to be called Celine O'Brien.

By the time I arrived, my foster-mother was in her sixties and her husband was perhaps ten years older. They were a totally unsuitable couple to foster a five-month-old baby girl. But nobody cared. If abortion had been available, I would have been a prime candidate. Everyone wanted me out of his or her world. Alive, I was an embarrassment to everyone.

At an early age, I was told by my foster-mother, that she was paid £300 to keep my identity secret. In 1949, £300 was a huge sum of money and would have purchased a large amount of secrecy. The reason for such secrecy, I was later told, was that my father had two sisters who were nuns. As my existence could cause serious scandal to this very important family, and particularly to the two nuns and the Catholic Church, my fate was sealed.

One of my earliest memories is being told, 'No one wants you.' It seemed that this piece of information preceded almost every conversation that I had with both my foster-parents until I was 13 years of age.

I got the message early on. I believed that it must be true; I thought whatever adults said was the truth. I considered it normal that nobody wanted me, but I could never understand why.

I always felt afraid.

My foster-mother ruled the household. Physically, she was of medium height and looked like a man. She was very overweight and had a double chin that seemed to rest on her chest and wobbled like a jelly as she spoke. She even walked like a man.

One of my earliest memories is of hiding when I heard her coming. I could always anticipate her arrival, as I would hear her before I saw her. On her good days she always whistled or hummed a lively tune; on her bad days she was completely silent. When she was walking, her heel hit the ground first and the large flat sole of her foot followed on remarkably quickly. To me it always sounded like a sharp slap. She always walked quickly, with urgent short steps, as if she was in a rush to tell someone some important news. When I heard the distinctive whistling or humming and 'slap slap' sound of a pair of shoes, at any distance, a chill would run through my body.

She was not an intelligent woman, but she made her living by being cunning. One time when neighbours of ours, an old brother and sister, died, I was sent to the house to steal the pillows from their beds. I was scared to go but I was more afraid of what would happen if I didn't come back with the pillows. When I came back and handed them over, my foster-mother ripped them open. She thought there might be some money hidden in them but there wasn't, so she slapped me in the face.

Rationality is supposed to be what distinguishes human beings from the animals of the world, but my foster-mother could not be described as in any way rational. I don't think she had any brain cells. She could not think and could only react to situations. But because she was a stupid person she thought she was intelligent.

She was also a bully and she could always detect other people's vulnerability. She bullied all of us at home, but even when she met a stranger she knew immediately whether they could be bullied or not. If they were confident and assertive, she was very polite to their face and was over-helpful in every way. I think these people thought she was a bit of a 'lick-arse' but they put up with her because she could be useful.

With no education, she was virtually illiterate. I never saw her read a book or paper. The only thing she knew how to do was count money. She never bowed to anything or anyone though, except someone whom she deemed to have 'book learning'. If she thought somebody was educated, she avoided them. She did not engage with the local teachers or bankers, as she considered them to have 'the better of her'. The local parish priest was also a challenge to her but, while he was educated, he was half afraid of her. She was a big woman and had an awful loud voice that she was not afraid to use. She had an obsession about physical size. Her husband was small and the parish priest was also no giant. She could not understand, and this was a complete and utter blank with her, how any man who was smaller than her, could be more intelligent. This was the cause of many rows in the house. If she was trying to explain her version of an event or when she wanted something done, if my foster-father asked a question or suggested something different, he usually got a punch on his head. This would be quickly followed by a dismissive verbal lashing, 'Ahhh, for Jaysus' sake, Bie, you're only a little ludramawn, how would you understand anything?'

She never called anyone by their name. Everyone was called 'Boy', whatever their sex, but being originally from Cork and using the vernacular, mixed with a Limerick lilt, it sounded like 'Bie' (rhymes with pie) or in the plural 'Bize' (rhymes with size).

'Come here, Bie.'

'I'll tell you now, Bie, you do what I say or you'll be trun' out.'

''Tis only a load a bollix, Bie.'

''Tis tenne paz seven, Bie, you shoulda been up ages ago.'

She had one advantage as far as the parish priest was concerned. She was at the centre of the local sex scene. She knew everything and anything of a sexual nature that happened in the area. The personalities involved gravitated towards her. When I was very young I remember standing in the back room staring at my foster-mother's bed, which looked like it was moving. She just said that 'foxes had got into the bed'. The parish priest used her to find out information about certain individuals. It was a control thing. As long as he knew who was involved, he was prepared to allow her to continue about her business.

She also knew where the priest was vulnerable. If she was talking to someone, and the priest approached, she would say in a voice loud enough for everyone to hear, 'Backs to the wall, Bize, the Mallow bus is comin'.' It was her way of letting him know that she had discovered that he was homosexual.

Someone once asked her what she meant and she explained, 'All dem educated bize in Mallow, is queers, you know.'

As far as she could figure it, anyone male and educated and who also embraced the Church, acted as if they were homosexual, because they always had 'certain airs and graces about dem'.

I was to find out that she was also ruthless and evil.

My foster-father was a grumpy, small man. He worked for local farmers, on a casual basis, as a farm labourer. He was totally dominated by his wife and was also illiterate. He had no status in life other than that which he was allowed by his wife. As I got older I began to think that it might be why he got drunk as often as possible.

When he got drunk, it gave him false courage and he would try to beat anyone who was less powerful than him. In that part of the country, it was common to have a bellows to get the fire burning. This bellows had a strap, which my foster-father used to beat me with when he was drunk. Once he had sated his drunken anger, he would usually go to bed and fall asleep.

From as far back as I can remember, I was always afraid in that house. At first it was the little things. Like when the community nurse called, to bring vitamin pills for me, I was told to say that I slept in a room of my own. I felt uncomfortable telling lies to the nurse, as I never had a bed of my own, never mind a room. My foster-parents slept in the bedroom at one end of the kitchen.

From the first day, my bed or sleeping space was a tea chest. The tea chest was positioned in the corner of the tiny lean-to room at the rear of the house. Made from a lightweight balsa wood, it measured about two feet wide by about two and a half feet deep. In front of the tea chest was a one-foot high log. As I grew and was able to move and run, I could hit that log with one foot, spring up over the edge of the box in a somersault and land on the soft turf mould at the bottom.

When in my tea chest, I was generally left alone. I was considered to be asleep. Even if I were not, I would pretend to be asleep.

Out of sight was out of mind.

Our family had a little dog, called Spot. He was a type of Jack Russell terrier. He was lovely. I shared my tea chest with Spot. Spot and I became great friends. I don't know if I slept in Spot's bed, or he in mine.

We seemed to share the same fate in that household. If he offended somebody, or was in somebody's way, he got kicked or hit with a stick or whatever was handy at the time. If I did something bold, or was in somebody's way, I suffered the same punishment.

Most mornings I would wake up, cuddled close to Spot in what was our box. Most times, if I was told to go to bed, I headed to the box, climbed in with my 'Blankie', lay down and went to sleep. It was the most normal thing to do. If I wasn't in the chest, I was left wherever I fell asleep.

Food always seemed to be in short supply and I was always hungry. Breakfast was always the same, porridge. If my foster-mother was drunk on the previous night, there was no breakfast on the following day. If she was sober, a bowl of cold porridge was your lot for the day, as the fire had likely burned itself out during the night. I ate the porridge every morning that it was available. But the type of porridge changed often. Sometimes it was an inedible yellow mixture, which even Spot would not eat. If neither me, nor the dog, ate what we were given, we were both put outside as a punishment.

I had the same status in the hierarchy of that household as Spot.

Occasionally Spot and I spent a long, wet or freezing cold day or dark night outside, at the mercy of whatever the elements decided to throw at us. If we were thrown out after dark, we spent the night in a small rickety shed, about 20 yards from the house. It was home to about ten hens. This shed also had some hay and straw stored in it. When Spot and I snuggled down in the hay, we were warm and dry. The hens slept high up on horizontal wooden poles and never objected to our presence. They probably thought we were their security guards.

One morning a neighbour saw us emerging from the chicken coop. I could see he was mystified. Before he got a chance to say anything, my foster-mother jokingly informed him, 'We keep herself and the dog in there at night, to protect the hens from the foxes.'

I was not yet four years of age.

I remember washing the stone floor and making sure that the fire was on. I was terrified if the kettle wouldn't boil. I knew it was my fault. If the hens didn't lay their eggs

I didn't know what to do. One day, when I was about six, I broke an egg. I didn't dare tell them. I knew I had to get another one. I ran across the fields and stole one from the neighbours. I was so afraid they'd catch me as I ran back, but they didn't.

Dinner was only ever a bit of boiled bacon, cabbage and potatoes, and somehow I learned how to cook them. I don't remember how. I'd be sent to get a quarter pound of bacon and maybe four sausages in the shop. I might get the rind to eat. There was one shop in town where she used to leave money and I'd have to go in and get the food.

The house had no running water, no electricity, and of course, sanitary conditions were terrible. I was never taught how to wash myself. I was filthy but my foster-mother wasn't interested in cleanliness – except on Sundays. A basin, filled with heated water, appeared as if by miracle, on a Sunday morning. My foster-mother bathed her face, and some other parts of her body in it. My foster-father then used the same water to shave with, for the only time in a week.

Sometimes, perhaps once a month, my foster-mother caught me by the hair, saying something like, 'Come here, ya dirty little cunt, till I give ya a scrub.' My face was plunged into the already well-used water, and scrubbed. That was the full extent of my personal hygiene, while a member of the O'Brien family.

Then after that Sunday morning ritual, we all walked the two miles to the local Catholic Church, to attend mass. Whatever happened during the week, it was obligatory to attend mass on a Sunday morning, come hail, rain or shine. The Catholic Church decreed that it was compulsory to go to mass on a Sunday; otherwise it would be a mortal sin. If someone died, while in a state of 'mortal sin', their soul went straight to hell.

My religious education was taken care of every Sunday and the rest of my education began at the age of four. This is when I started school. On my first day I wore a red jumper, a tartan skirt and brown boots. They were second-hand and given to us by a charitable organisation called the St Vincent de Paul Charitable Trust.

From the first day, I loved school. The first thing that I noticed was the great number of children, together in one place. I had no contact with other children before my first day in school. I had seen other children at mass on Sunday or on the occasional visit to the nearest town, but I had never met children of my own age.

I was shy in the beginning and I also felt different. Almost all of the other children had a uniform. About five children and myself did not wear a uniform. I once asked my foster-mother for a uniform to wear like all the other children. She replied that she was being paid nothing to keep me, so how could I expect her to feed me and clothe me, as well.

School brought unexpected pleasures. Every lunch-time a nun called Sister Claude would take the six of us children who did not wear uniforms to the back kitchen of the convent, and give us hot cocoa, along with bread and butter, or bread and jam. I was so glad to get any food that I did not care about standing out. I gulped down the warm cocoa, and ate as much bread as I could, as fast as I could. I had never tasted jam before I went to school, so if there was jam on the menu, it was a special treat for me. I used to think I'd love to be like some of the children who brought their bottles of cocoa from home and left them at the fireplace to keep warm. I never had one.

While I became friendly with the girls who did not wear school uniforms, I was made to feel different by the other girls. It did not take me long to realise the difference. All or most of the other children had something which I did not have – they had parents. All the other children had a mother and a father.

I somehow thought that I had parents too, until some of

the other children began to tease me about not having a mother and father. They used to call me a 'dirty bastard'.

I had heard the word 'bastard' being used by my foster-parents and their friends about me, but I did not know what it really meant. I just thought that it was not a good thing to be a bastard. The other children soon explained the word to me. At once I resolved that I would somehow, someday, become a 'non-bastard'.

Of course, as I didn't wash myself, I didn't smell nice. I was often ridiculed at school by the children who called me all kinds of names, but then one day we were in the middle of a class when the teacher, who was a nun, just stopped talking. She came down to where I was sitting at my desk, caught me by my ear, and pulled me roughly towards the front of the class. Then, in front of all my classmates, she showed them how dirty I was. I was terrified but I didn't dare say anything. I remember just looking at the floor and feeling so ashamed. When she had finished I was in tears. She ordered me out of the classroom and the school. I was told not to come back until I had learned how to wash myself. To me this meant that even the nun thought I was a 'dirty bastard' so it had to be true. When I finally got home I repeated the nun's message to my foster-mother, who promptly caught me by the hair and threw me out the front door. Accompanied by a stream of foul language, I was made to understand that if I wanted to I could wash myself in the filthy pond at the side of the house.

To this very day, I am extremely diligent, about my personal hygiene. I wash my hands so many times a day that people remark that I must have a guilt complex. I always deny it, but still think to myself, 'If they only knew.'

Some evenings, when I got back from school, my foster-mother would send me to a neighbouring farm, called 'the Farmers', for milk. To get to the dairy, I had to go through the vegetable patch where they grew cabbages, potatoes, onions and other vegetables for their own use. My foster-mother used to tell me to steal some cabbage from their garden on the way home. I grew to dread having to go for the milk. Sometimes the cabbages were very well secured to the ground by their roots and I couldn't pull them up. All I could do was pull bits off the leaves. The bits were probably no larger than the palm of my hand, which wasn't very big. When I returned home with these, my foster-mother would scream at me and follow it by a slap of her hand across my face.

Depending on the time of year, when I was able to pull up a few heads of cabbage, the owners or people that worked for them would often catch me stealing. I was called 'a dirty little thief' or worse. I feel they used to watch me and wait until I had pulled at a vegetable, and then shout at me. My memories are of hearing a loud angry shout of 'Get out, ya little thief.' Immediately, I was off and running. I remember sprinting through endless drills of potatoes, whose long green stalks had pretty white flowers on top. I can still remember the distinctive smell of the tubers. But there was no time to enjoy the potato blossoms; I was running for my life. I was running, terrified of getting a severe beating. I was only about the same height as the potato stalks and as I ran, I could feel my little heart thumping so hard, that it was about to explode out through my chest.

They always caught up with me. They used to grab me by the arm and follow up with a severe whack of a hurley stick on my bottom. They enjoyed dishing out the punishment and used to laugh out loud at me, as I ran scampering or limping up the lane in pain and distress.

By this time in my life I was immune to physical pain.

My foster-father was older and mellower than his wife. He sometimes seemed kinder to me than she was. He certainly was not as aggressive or violent towards me, when he was sober. He ignored many of my perceived indiscretions. If my foster-mother had known about them she would have punished me, without misgiving.

In the summer of 1955, when I was just 6 years old, my foster-father was taken ill. It was considered serious enough that he had to go to hospital. I did not know what particular illness he was suffering from, but I was instructed by my foster-mother to pray for his healthy recovery.

One evening, a few days later, we all had to kneel down in the kitchen, and say the rosary together for him. We had never before recited the rosary as a family. My foster-father died the following day. We never recited the rosary afterwards.

I felt sad because of his death, but there was such drinking and carousing at his wake, I was confused. There was such merriment for two days and nobody else seemed to feel sorry, I remained in a state of confusion. When he was taken to the church, and later to the cemetery for burial, the mood of everyone concerned became sombre and sad, when in public view.

His presence, while alive, was a protection to me of a sort, although difficult to understand at times. When I realised what the finality of his death meant, my feeling of fear, of living in that house, increased unimaginably.

Little did I know how my life would turn after he died.

TWO

A Commodity

In the months after my foster-father's death, local men began to call on my foster-mother. My foster-brother was working for the local farmers as a labourer by then, so I didn't see much of him. In February, farmers would pick out labourers for a six-month contract and the boys and men picked would go off and live on the farm. They were treated like slaves really. The following year he went off to another part of the country and was living there, sleeping in the lofts of the outhouse. I only met him once after that.

The men's visits were few and fairly sporadic at first, but it soon seemed that there were always men in the house in the evenings. There were usually other women present, whom I did not know. They used to come to the house to 'ceílídh', the Gaelic word for party, pronounced as 'kayley'.

The numbers were always low, as few as two and seldom more than four. If too many people turned up, she would arrange for them to return on some other night. She used to tell them that she did not want to 'attract attention'. Playing cards, singing and drinking stout, porter, whiskey or poteen were the main ingredients of this 'ceílídh'. But there was an extra element to this ceílídh that I did not understand until later.

My foster-mother and some of the other women used to provide some form of sexual servicing for these men, in return for financial payment. This could happen at any time during the night's ceílídh. A man and woman would disappear outside. After a bit of time had passed, they would return, usually in good humour, laughing and joking. The money would always be paid to my foster-mother.

Some nights, after the men had left, my foster-mother would tell me to get into bed with her. She told me to touch her 'thrush'. I just remember doing what I was told. There was no cuddling or kissing. There was nothing like that. I just followed what she said. I was afraid not to do it. I always did what I was told otherwise I'd be put out.

As time went on, the number of men increased and their visits became more regular. Late evening to early in the morning became the favourite calling time of this growing retinue of men of all ages.

I was now seven years of age.

I became the object of their amusement and entertainment. I had always been used to local men touching my body. They always touched me in places that made me feel uncomfortable, but they never did it blatantly while my foster-father was alive. Now that he was dead, my life was being made a misery.

When my foster-mother began to entertain these local farmers, she used to send me to Meade's pub for whiskey, porter and bread. She used to tell these men that she took me in because nobody wanted me. On these visits when they used to play cards, I would have to bring them drinks.

When I brought their drinks, they would put an arm around me, and touch me on my chest and between my legs. I always seemed to be trying to escape from being held by some part of my body, by somebody that I feared and who got too close for comfort. These men would fondle me and touch me. Sometimes they would lift me up in the air and hold my legs apart so they could all see under my legs. I was constantly trying to avoid their grabbing hands.

They teased me. I had to justify my existence as they pestered me with questions that they knew I would have to answer. It was a kind of test.

'What is your name?'

'Celine.'

'What sorta name is dat?'

'We never heard dat sorta name 'round here before.'

'You must be from England?'

'I'm not.'

'You must be an American then?'

'I am not an American.'

'You must be from Russia so?'

'I'm not from Russia.'

'You must be a boy!'

'I am not a boy!'

'What are you so?'

'I'm a girl!'

'Girls don't wear trousers.'

'I'm not wearing trousers.'

'You are so!'

'I am not, they are knickers.'

These kinds of verbal preambles always led to me being caught and fondled. If that wasn't happening, they were taking place as I struggled to escape the imprisoning grasp of a pair of large, strong, cow-dung stained, agricultural hands.

During their thinly disguised attentions, these men were not rebuked by my foster-mother, so they took it as acceptable to continue with their behaviour, despite my protests. If I objected, or ran away, they would make fun of me. The next time that they got the opportunity, they would touch me more aggressively, or invade my body internally with their fingers. If I objected again, my foster-mother would condone their behaviour by saying to me, often while

I was in the grip of a large rough farmer, 'Sure, he's only having a bit of fun with you.'

With all the late night visits, I was not able to go to sleep at night. I was afraid to go to sleep, but I was also encouraged by my foster-mother to stay awake, to pander to the drunken antics of these nocturnal visitors. Consequently, I was not always able to get up in the morning for school.

I found that my reputation was not confined to the house. One afternoon, as I was returning home from school, I realised that a car was travelling slowly, close behind me. As cars were a rare sight on this part of the road, I turned to look at it. It passed me on the road and stopped about ten yards farther up.

A local man that I knew got out of the car and came up to me. He asked, 'Will you come into that field with me?'

'Why?' I asked.

He grabbed my body in the area between my legs and said to me, 'That's why.'

I swung around in his grasp, in an attempt to escape, but he grabbed me tighter, and tried to lift me. At that moment, a man with a horse and cart appeared a short distance away. The man who was holding me was distracted, and dropped me on the ground. He ran to his car, opened the door, jumped in, started the engine and sped away.

As soon as I was free of his grasp, I stood up and ran to a house nearby. Three sisters, the Misses O'Mahony lived there together. They often greeted me as I passed to and from school. I knocked and knocked on the door. I thought that they would understand my dilemma, and rescue me.

The three of them came out to the door together, to see what the commotion was about. They did not invite me in, but I told them the full story of what had just happened to me. Almost in unison, they laughed heartily. One of them said, 'Ahhh shure Mr Murphy is our friend.'

The other two ladies agreed with their sister's opinion.

As far as they were concerned, that was the end of the matter. They said 'goodbye', turned, and with short little steps, went inside together, one after the other. I was left standing on their doorstep, alone. I walked home dejected, but on guard. I was now aware of dangers that I previously did not expect or know existed.

At school, some of the children began to call me 'whore'. When they said it they pronounced it, as 'you're a hoor'. I got used to hearing this regular chant of abuse.

During the day young men in their early twenties used to spend a lot of time around the house. They used to engage my foster-mother in friendly banter, mostly tinged with a sexual flavour. She did not discourage their visits.

While relatively young, these fully grown adults were always touching me and doing horrible things to me that made me so scared of them. They used to catch me and hold me down on the ground and poke my private parts with their hands, bottles, sticks and anything that they could find. I used to complain to my foster-mother about their behaviour, but she just used to say, 'I'm not getting any money for looking after you, so you will just have to look out for yourself.'

I was not going to school very often at this stage. I had certain chores to do around the house every day. One of these chores was to clean the ashes out of the grate, where the fire had been the previous evening. I had to leave it clean for my foster-mother to set the fire again. I put the ashes in a metal bucket and I then had to dispose of them by a wall at the bottom of the garden. This area of the garden was where all the household rubbish was dumped. It was considered unsightly and was therefore not visible from the house.

On September 4, 1956, I was out in the garden, putting out the ashes. As I bent over to empty the bucket of ashes, I felt somebody rushing towards me.

It was a man.

It was one of the group of younger men that used to hang around our house.

He pushed me against the wall.

He raped me.

He so brutally raped me.

It was the speed with which it happened. It was so unexpected. One minute I was turning a bucket upside down, the next minute I was completely overpowered by him.

I did not have time to react.

I did not have time to think.

He pinned my right hand on the ground with his heavy hob-nailed boot. He ripped my knickers away from my body. He pushed my face into the ground. Then he tried to push his erect penis into my body. I was seven years old.

Blood spurted everywhere.

He grunted and groaned, and finally withdrew himself.

My nose and two fingers on my right hand were broken. I felt it when they snapped. It was extremely painful. I endured the pain and did not complain, as I was afraid of the consequences.

My nose causes me untold trouble to this very day. Today it is still very obvious, as the unset bone protrudes at an odd angle.

As I grew older, and under the toll of negative comments regarding my entire existence, I began to consider myself entirely ugly in every way. The broken bones in my fingers have never been set or repaired by a doctor. They were never examined by anyone and the breaks were allowed to set as they were left.

In fact they have caused me much embarrassment, as I now work within the medical profession. My colleagues are often dismayed by my injuries and the obvious absence of any proper treatment. My excuses, which are always lies, do not entirely satisfy them. They are very sympathetic but they usually don't ask me any more questions. I think they know that I am not telling the truth.

As he left me lying on the ground, I heard him say, 'You can't tell anybody about this, because they won't believe you and because nobody wants you anyway.'

I was completely in shock.

I was unable to move.

I may have been unconscious for a while.

When I realised what had happened to me, and where I was, I rose shakily to my feet. I stumbled my way down the garden, towards the house. Covered in ashes and blood, I collapsed in a heap on the ground outside the back door.

I was shaken to my feet by my foster-mother, who yelled at me, 'What happened to you? What the fuck happened to you?'

I told her the story, as best I could. Incredulously, she berated me for telling lies about the man. She must have realised that I was in a poor condition, as she did not beat me physically on this occasion, as she would normally have done. I was undressed and put in my bed.

My bed was by now two railroad sleepers resting on top of each other, as the tea chest had long since disintegrated. I whimpered in pain, all through that day and the night. Although I was haemorrhaging badly from my vaginal area and my broken bones were extremely painful, my foster-mother did not take me to a doctor.

After that rape of my young body, at the age of seven, I came to believe that I was there, because nobody ever wanted me, and whatever happened, it didn't matter, because no one cared. So, I believed it was entirely normal that whatever bones were broken, or tissue torn, they would remain that way. I believed that medical help was not an option for me. I was not good enough to receive it.

As I healed up after this rape, my foster-mother felt that

I had been initiated into the world of sex. But because of my injuries, infection set in. This was extremely painful and it was often itchy.

The same man, who still came to the house most nights, would watch me. If he caught me scratching my vaginal area he would say to me, 'You are scratching there because you want it again, don't ya?'

I hated him saying things like that to me.

I hated him.

* * * *

Men continued to visit the house on most nights. But now, instead of serving drinks, I became the attraction. Word got around the area that anybody who wanted to have sex with a very young girl, who had not yet reached puberty, could come and pay money to my foster-mother. She ensured they would all be accommodated. They would pay her money and then she would tell me to go out into the field with these men.

They had their pleasure with a young girl and then left me there in a heap on the ground.

It was all done in silence. I was told, 'If you tell anyone, the purple prick will hurt you more.' They had the power. I thought they could actually kill me.

I cannot count the number of times that it happened to me. It happened in fields, in cow barns, in hay sheds, anywhere that presented an opportunity. An unknown number of faceless men, with forgettable names, in hidden places, for what seemed like an eternal number of years. There was no one to rescue me. I was born in the wrong place at the wrong time, to the wrong parents. It could have happened to anyone, but I was the unlucky one.

As I write this, I am distraught just thinking where and how often it happened to me, at such a young age.

You cannot breathe.
You cannot think.
You cannot scream.
You cannot see.
You cannot struggle.
You cannot escape.
I cannot escape the memories.

My life continued. I was ten when I made my confirmation. I went to the church alone that time and there was no breakfast or fuss. I was wearing a white dress, with black shoes and white socks. When I went up to the bishop I said my name was Celine O'Brien, but the nun corrected me and said Celine Clifford. I didn't think anything more about it at the time. I just went home after the ceremony and it was just like any other day.

I spent most days looking after my foster-mother and doing everything in the house. I was the skivvy, but it was better than the night-time. At one stage I was taken to hospital. I'm not sure when. I think I was nine or ten and I was terrified. When the nurse came around with the doctor they leaned over my cot-style bed, which had bars on either side. I must have got myself into bed because I had left my knickers on. She told me to take them off and I remember looking at the light-shade, with the rays of light dancing off it, and I was so frightened. I took them off and felt embarrassed. I didn't know why I was there and there was nobody to tell me. I had no one to help me. On the night I was taken away in the ambulance I'd been wearing a royal blue coat and I was bleeding. When I was taken back to the house a week later I had different clothes on. They had to stop the ambulance on the way home because I got sick. I still don't know why I was there. I never will know why I was there.

Years later, when I went back to try to find out, I did see a copy of my chart. All it listed was my date of birth, my

pulse rate, my temperature and the words 'it is small for its
age'. There was nothing else. I was sure that it would all be
written down. It wasn't. There was no reason to explain why
I was bleeding. They may have spoken to the police but
nothing happened and there are no other records.

The district nurse did visit every year and she had to
write a report. I remember I was cooking dinner one time
she came and was ill another time. I found out later that all
she ever said on the reports was that I was 'underweight'. It
was always the same vague note.

I get flashbacks of these gruesome events. They bring me
to a place that nobody else can come with me. They bring
me down within myself. They bring me so low that I can be
there for days on end. I find myself reliving those awful
thoughts alone.

My attendance at school fell to almost zero. Nobody from
the school seemed to notice. I don't think the nuns ever said
anything to the local policeman, who would be called for
truancy, as he didn't try to catch me out. The parish priest
did call in but all he said was that I should go to mass more
often. I missed school terribly. But by then I lived in my own
little world, isolated from other people, all emotions, all pain
and all feelings. I accepted the sexual abuse as normal
behaviour. I thought that I was being punished. I actually
came to believe that I deserved it.

THREE

Liberation

I have always believed that after my years in hell, God came to my rescue.

I was low, without solace, and I needed help from somewhere.

The torture seemed like it would go on forever and I felt desperate. I believe that God made my foster-mother ill.

One day she could not get out of bed. I was sent to get the local doctor to call and examine her. The doctor finally arrived and made a diagnosis. She was seriously ill. She was so ill that she had to be transferred to hospital immediately.

As the doctor left the house he said that he would arrange for an ambulance to collect her. He told me to make arrangements to stay somewhere else. He suggested that I should stay with somebody who would be able to keep me for possibly a few weeks or months. He said that my foster-mother might be incapacitated and unable to care for a 12-year-old child. I remember thinking that if only he knew how much care she was capable of supplying for me.

I thought I might have to go to one of my foster-mother's sisters. She was called Nonie. I had visited her once before when I was about eight years old. They had something I had never seen in my foster-parents' house — books. They had shelves and shelves of books. There was no reading material of any kind in my foster-parents' house. I remember I was allowed to look at the books in Nonie's house. That is all I wanted to do while I was there.

I had spent very little time at school, but when I did manage to go I enjoyed reading lessons the best. I was very bad at spelling but I was able to follow the meaning of the words. I was also able to understand the story in a book, but with difficulty. I secretly hoped that I would go to stay with these people who had so many books. I thought that I would be able to read all the time.

But in all the confusion of my foster-mother being taken away to hospital, no arrangements were made for me. Later that night, I was taken to the parish priest. I asked him not to send me back to that house and I told him why I was afraid to return. He seemed to ignore my complaints but he did take me some distance away to a family where I could stay, just for that night.

I felt so relieved. I did not have to return to that dark, dismal house that night. I had been afraid that when I went back there all the usual men would call in. I felt a bit uncomfortable with the family but I thought if I helped with the work they wouldn't send me home. When one of the sons asked me to go down the field with him to help with the pigs I got up immediately. I set off in front of him and I didn't say a word on the way down. I was scared of him because he was so big and older than me. It was dark as we got further from the house. I couldn't see the pig-shed but I knew we were nearly there. His hand pushed me from behind and I fell on the ground. He turned me over and pressed his hand into my tummy to stop me moving. He pulled my dress up and fumbled with my knickers, trying to get them off. I couldn't move. I didn't make a noise. I knew what was happening. He had piercing eyes. I froze as he glared down at me. He grunted and twisted and pushed himself inside me. I bit down on my lip so that I wouldn't cry out with the pain. Then it was over and he rolled off me. I didn't move. He got up, pulled his trousers up and was walking off when he turned and said, 'You're only 11 aren't you? You can't have babies yet?' I was still lying on the ground, with my bare legs spread out on the wet grass. I was shivering from cold. I still didn't dare move. I was afraid to get up. He was wrong about my age but I just mumbled 'yes' and then there was silence as he walked off.

The next day, the priest arrived to collect me. He told me that I was going to stay with a niece of my foster-mother. He said that I would be staying with her for the duration of my foster-mother's stay in hospital. In the end I stayed there for about six weeks.

I liked it there.

I was well fed. I never felt hungry. I was allowed to take food from the cupboard, whenever I wanted some. At home, I was never allowed to eat unless I was given the food by my foster-mother. When I realised that I could eat whenever I wanted, I was not shy about it. I ate more and more, at every opportunity. They had such lovely food. The woman of the house was a very good cook. She baked all sorts of sweet cakes. She baked apple and rhubarb tarts. I had never tasted such wonderful food. But I know that they never expected a young girl to eat so much or so often.

They used to say prayers at night and they wanted me to join in. At first, I could not recite the prayers, as I did not know the words. But they taught me the words. Through nightly repetition, I learned them all.

I really enjoyed being included.

The prayers were said out loud and everyone knelt on the floor, facing a chair. Everyone had his or her head bent down, and you weren't supposed to look around. I often sneaked a look, just to see what everybody else was doing, while praying. They were always earnestly involved in their recitations. Everyone took turns to say certain prayers.

When it came to my turn, I used to shout them out loud and I was never shouted at for shouting.

I was enrolled at their local school in Knocklong, County Limerick. The teacher there was very kind to me. She spent some time teaching me some different prayers, and she started to teach me some reading and arithmetic. I also made my first attempts at writing. I was 12 years old before I wrote my first word. That first word was my own name, Celine. It was very scratchy, but I had written it myself. I felt so proud that I could write. I knew that I wanted to continue going to school. I wanted to learn lessons in school.

I gradually began to realise that there was a better life to be had, than the life that I was leading. I also began to realise that what was normal in my life, was not regarded as normal for other people.

One day I was told that my foster-mother was being discharged from hospital. The lady of the house said that I would have to go back to her house to look after her. She said that my foster-mother was recovering, but that she would need constant care and attention.

I was devastated.

I could not believe that I would have to return to my foster-mother. There was nothing I could do about it. I was powerless.

I was delivered back to the house that I hated, by bicycle, the very next day. I did not have a chance to say goodbye to anybody at the school.

When I saw my foster-mother, I saw a frail old woman in the bed. She was only a pale shadow of her former self. I now find it difficult to understand why, but at the time I felt sorry for her. But I soon found out that she was in no way remorseful. She may have been ill, but while she was confined to bed, she remained her usual grouchy self, especially in her attitude towards me.

She felt that it was my place in life to cater to her every

need. Considering that I had been told so often that I was unwanted by anyone else and useless, I just did what I was told. I started to look after my foster-mother, with as much motivation as I could muster.

When my foster-mother came home from hospital, her male friends did not call as often as previously. She was not able to drink alcohol or to remain out of bed for more than one hour at a time. Once out of the bed, she quickly became exhausted. She had no stamina and her breathing was troubled. While I had to wait on my foster-mother all the time, it was much better than having to satisfy the sexual desires of the men who had called to the house for the previous six years.

My foster-mother remained bedridden and towards the end of 1961, she was taken into hospital again. This was to become my salvation. Although I did not know it at the time, I was never to see my foster-mother again.

I was never to return to that house of horror.

It was the end of a period of my life that contained no laughter. I thought I might also be able to stop crying, even though I shed most of my tears in private. If I cried in public, there was always somebody to scream, 'Stop crying', at me. My usual response to this was, 'I am not crying, they are just tears dropping.'

It was an end to a period of which I have a dominant memory of 'torn clothes and a torn body'. The clothing was always 'second-hand', always dirty and never washed afterwards. If it was not torn when I received it, somebody else ripped it, usually a man, trying to get me out of it.

I was taken to stay with a different niece of my foster-mother. Her name was Kit. She was happy in her life and she lived with a lovely compassionate man, her husband Tony, outside a small market town called Buttevant, in County Cork. They had no children of their own. She became the nearest thing to a mother that I could have had.

The first thing she said to me was, 'You are never going back to that house of shame.' From this moment on, we formed a sort of bond between us.

They had a small bungalow, which was spotlessly clean and nicely decorated. It had all the modern conveniences, which I had never been used to previously. It had electricity, piped running water, a bathroom and a Rayburn cooker, which seemed to keep the whole house warm.

It was in this house that I learned to wash myself properly. There was hot water, heated by the Rayburn cooker and piped to all the taps. That first evening, Kit tut-tutted as she cleaned places on my body that I am sure had never seen water before. She showed me how to wash my body thoroughly. I still feel that I will never cleanse myself fully of the filth from those dark days.

It was late December and Christmas was only a matter of days away. The first time I walked in the front door of their house, I was stunned by what I saw. I was stopped in my tracks with amazement. With my mouth wide open, I inhaled deeply. I had never seen anything so beautiful in my life.

What I saw before me was my first Christmas tree. It had all kinds of decorations on it. There were many little silver and gold balls. There were little silver bells attached by silver chains. The best part of all was the set of about a dozen Christmas-tree lights, which flickered on and off. I thought it was just magical.

After being fed, they put me in a large double bed, which I had all to myself. I expected someone else to turn up, to sleep in it also, but it was all for me.

That first night, I did not sleep a wink. I was so excited. I thought I was in heaven.

Kit and Tony were very kind to me.

The next day, they brought me to Limerick City in their car. They brought me to a large department store and bought me new shoes and new socks. The shoes were coloured cream and the socks were blue. This was the first time that I had ever had shoes and socks that were bought brand new and had not been used by somebody else. Up to this time in my life, my clothing, shoes and socks had been supplied as charitable donations and were always somebody's cast-offs.

I loved the fuss that the sales lady in the store made of me. She called me 'a little lady' and made me try on so many different pairs of shoes, until I found a pair that I really liked and wanted.

I felt overwhelmed. It was the first time I'd ever been given a choice. Nobody had ever asked me what I wanted before. My wants or needs had never been considered. It was a difficult gesture for me to appreciate. While such a consideration was rare in my life up to that time, it was a concept that was to remain elusive in my life, right up to the present day.

That Christmas, Kit and Tony had a television installed in their house. I had never been to the cinema and consequently had never seen a moving picture. The introduction of a television into the house was frightening at first. I treated it with suspicion. I could not feel at ease with a box, with live people in it, in the same room as me. But I got used to it very quickly. I soon wanted to watch it all the time. But there were no programmes until about six o'clock in the evenings. They used to turn it on an hour beforehand, and we would all sit around it, watching the unmoving test card, while it played the same music. It was all very exciting.

On Christmas Eve we all went to midnight mass in the local church. When we came home I stayed up for a while, helping to make stuffing for a turkey, which we would have for Christmas dinner the next day. I had never seen so much food for three people.

I went to bed that Christmas Eve night, as happy as I had ever been before. Early the next morning, the three of us assembled around the Christmas tree, and Kit gave out presents to Tony and me. Tony only got one present and all the rest were for me. I must have got about seven presents.

There was a skirt, a blue one.

There was a set of handkerchiefs.

There was a pink cardigan.

There were different bars of chocolate.

There were some sucky sweets.

There was a hat, a beret type.

But my favourite of the whole lot was a handbag. It was fairly small and brown in colour, but in one corner, in gold letters was my name, Celine. I cherished that brown bag with my name on it.

Once again, I thought I was in heaven.

These people gave me so many presents, and made me feel so welcome in such a short space of time. Both of them were very kind. Even when I did something wrong like one time when someone gave Kit a lovely hairbrush and I sat on it and the handle broke. She was angry and snapped, 'Nothing good ever came out of that place', meaning my foster-mother's house. I was scared but I knew she would forgive me and she didn't hit me.

But the experience of my short life had already taught me not to expect very much from anybody. Unfortunately I was right and my world was to be dashed again.

About three months after Christmas, Kit and Tony said that they wanted to talk to me. The three of us sat down around the table in the kitchen one evening. I was drinking a mug of Kit's strong sweet tea and just beginning to tuck into a jam sponge cake that she had made earlier. I had just taken a bite of cake when they told me that they could not keep me with them any longer.

My world collapsed.

I could not swallow the piece of cake. The mug of tea

crashed to the table, as my arm was no longer strong enough to hold it.

All energy drained from me. I was unable to speak. I could not even ask, 'Why?'

They told me that my foster-mother had died. I didn't go to her funeral. Kit hadn't told me at the time. I remember her saying, 'Sure she's no loss to you anyway.' Even though in a strange way we would both call her 'mother' as she had also brought Kit up.

They said that I had missed too much school. They said that I had to go to school again and that it was the law of the land. They said that they had no choice. They could not let me stay with them. They said that a neighbour of my foster-mother's had complained to the ISPCC (Irish Society for the Prevention of Cruelty to Children) months ago about the 'goings-on' in that house and that I had to be sent away. The cruelty officer from the ISPCC had called earlier that day and told them that he would collect me and take me away to a school the next day.

As they said the words, I could sense myself closing down. I had known that feeling of hurt before. My protection was to close down all sense of pain. I did not cry, and neither did I say anything in response. I went to bed and lay there. As I tried to sleep, I was aware of Kit ironing my clothing and packing my few possessions. Eventually I fell asleep.

The next morning, I got up and washed myself thoroughly. Shortly after we ate breakfast in silence, the cruelty officer from the ISPCC came and collected me. Despite tears all round, he took me away from the only people who had shown me any kindness in my life.

Years later, I learned that Kit was the illegitimate daughter of my foster-mother's sister. She was a kind woman who had her fair share of stress, from carrying the stigma of illegitimacy all through her life. On learning that Kit herself was illegitimate it dawned on me that she was either unwilling or unable to adopt me herself, because of her own birth status. She couldn't have adopted a bastard because it would have raked up her own life history and all her neighbours would then know about it. She would not have been able to cope with someone like me bringing her whole world crashing down on top of her. I would have attracted too much attention.

As we drove away from Kit's house, I felt very fearful. I had only been told that I was going to a school. I asked the cruelty officer, 'Where are you taking me?'

'I am taking you to appear at the court in Kilmallock,' he replied.

I began to cry.

The cruelty officer was a well-dressed man in a sports jacket and light-coloured trousers. He was a cold, serious type of a man. I felt that he did not like me. He did not try to reassure me in any way.

I had never been to court before, but as far as I was concerned, nothing good ever came out of having to appear at court. I thought I was being sent to jail. Whenever I had heard the word 'court' before, it meant that somebody had to go to jail. My little knowledge of courts came from the many men who used to visit my foster-mother. Some of them were shady characters, who often talked about the world of judges and courts of law and being sentenced to jail.

For the entire duration of the car journey I sobbed my heart out. I knew that if a person did something wrong, then they went to court. I knew that if you were sent to jail, you had to be sent by a judge of the court.

I was in a panic that morning. I could not figure what I had done wrong. All sorts of bad things that I had done during my life flashed through my brain. But I thought that it must have been something terrible that I had done recently. If I was being taken to court for something bad that

I had done a long time ago, why wasn't I taken at the time it happened?

'No,' I thought, 'it must be something bad that I did recently.' But I hadn't done anything.

Kit had dressed me up in all my new clothes. I was wearing my new cream shoes and blue socks, which they had given to me before Christmas. So I knew that it could not be anything to do with my new clothes. I also had my new leather handbag, with my name embossed in gold on the outside, so that everybody could see that it belonged to me.

Then it occurred to me. The only bad thing that I could possibly have done to merit being sent to jail was committing the crime of being too happy at Kit and Tony's house. For the remainder of the car journey I prayed to God, between long racking sobs, to forgive me for what I had done. If he did not allow the court to send me to jail, I promised him that I would never be happy ever again.

We finally reached Killmallock and the cruelty officer drove the car as close as possible to the front door of the courthouse. He got out from behind the steering wheel, slammed his door shut and rushed around to my side of the car. He opened the door and caught me firmly by the upper arm. His grip was so tight that it hurt me. He roughly pulled me from the seat. My sobbing became screams. Tears streamed down my cheeks.

There were four or five small groups of people standing outside the courthouse and I can remember them all turning in my direction, to see the cause of the commotion. I was half dragged, half lifted up the courthouse stairs, by a vice-like grip on my upper arm, screaming and sobbing at the same time. I felt that I must be the worst living person in the whole world. I felt that I deserved any punishment that I was given. I thought, 'Only the worst can happen to me now.'

The grip was tightened on my arm, and I was lifted entirely off my feet, as we went inside the courthouse.

'Will ya stop crying on me?' shouted my attached cruelty officer, 'You'll come to no harm.'

This was the first and only tiny inkling of reassurance that I was to receive from him. But there were many policemen in and around the courthouse, and all I could foresee at this time was a long period in jail. That was to be my punishment for the crime of being happy.

I was hurriedly yanked back downstairs and out around the side of the courthouse. We entered again through a side doorway that turned out to be an office. Inside there were four policemen standing around a desk. Behind the desk was seated a man with a large book in front of him. I had never seen a book with such large pages before.

The cruelty officer pointed to a vacant chair behind the man at the desk. He said, 'Sit on that chair and do not move one inch and do not let me hear one sound from you. If you as much as move a muscle or squeak, the four policemen will arrest you, and put you in jail and throw away the key. Isn't that right guard?'

'That's right,' said one of the policemen, supporting the cruelty officer.

I was left sitting in that chair for about four hours. I never moved a muscle or uttered a sound. I wanted to go to the toilet but dared not ask. Eventually I could not hold out any longer. I allowed the contents of my bladder to trickle silently down my leg, over the edge of the chair and away from me. I was terrified that somebody would notice.

My cruelty officer had disappeared and the policemen were busily immersed in intense discussions with the man with the large book. As they talked about grievous bodily harm, public house licences, bicycles without lights, lorries without road tax, tractors without white lights, as well as drunk and disorderly conduct, none of them noticed a long thin stream of urine appear from under the desk and gently meander its way across the floor, out the office door. It escaped undetected and away to freedom.

It must have been sometime in the afternoon when my cruelty officer reappeared back in the office. He came over to me and said, 'Come on you, hurry up, you're on shortly.'

To be addressed in such a manner was a normal everyday occurrence for me, so I tried to hop down off the chair. As I had not moved a muscle for so long, the back of my bare legs felt as though they had been glued to the chair. When I stood up, the chair came with me. It was attached by dried sweat to the back of my legs. The back of the chair hit me between the shoulders and both the chair and I fell forward on to the ground. As I fell forward, I dislodged a pen and inkstand at the edge of the man's desk. A large and heavy cut-glass inkwell, full of blue ink, fell on the cruelty officer's nicely shined brown shoes and the bottom of his beige coloured trousers.

He jumped two feet in the air with shock. It was as if somebody had poured sulphuric acid over his feet. 'Me shoes are ruined and look at me trousers,' he shouted.

Two policemen and the man with the big book laughed heartily at the fate of the cruelty officer. 'Awww, Aww come on lads,' he moaned with outstretched arms, as if appealing to the policemen.

This comic interlude had lightened their day considerably. For me, I thought this would surely see me consigned to jail for ever.

When the commotion had died down, the ink-stained and embarrassed cruelty officer dragged me roughly out of the office and pinned me against the courthouse wall.

I began to cry again.

'Shut up, and listen.'

I sobbed harder.

'If the judge asks you a question,' he emphasised, 'you reply, "Yes, your Honour". Do you understand?' he queried.

I tried to say yes, but I could not utter any sound, due to my distressed sobs.

'Do you understand?' he yelled.

'Yes, your Honour,' I replied, in innocence.

'Don't get smart with me, young one,' he snapped.

I nodded, as I still could not raise any sound.

'Now stop crying because we are going in for your case.'

I gulped back my sobs, and climbed the stairs to the courtroom. The size of the room amazed me. There were men everywhere; men in suits, men behind desks and a great many policemen. There was a man dressed in a black robe sitting on a raised platform. He seemed to be wearing a small curly wig on his head.

I sat beside the cruelty officer, behind a desk, facing this man. As I sat down, the cruelty officer said to me, 'That's the judge.'

I sat mesmerised by my surroundings.

A man stood up and in a raised voice announced, 'State versus Clifford.'

At the time it meant nothing to me. It was only the second time in my life I had heard the name Celine Clifford. I was Celine O'Brien.

The cruelty officer took me by the hand and brought me to the judge. I had to stand in the dock at the judge's right-hand side, facing the crowd in the main body of the court. I could barely see over the edge of the dock. I was facing everybody in the room. They were all looking at me. I was mortified. I tried to stay down under the ledge so that nobody could see me.

Years later I got a copy of the Substance of Complaint which was under the Children Acts 1908–1941. It read: 'Application to commit to a certified industrial school Celine Clifford who appears to the court to be a child under the age of fifteen years, having been born so far as has been ascertained on the November 14, 1948 and who resides at Ballyculhane, Kilmallock, having been found having a parent or guardian who does not exercise proper guardianship.'

As I was still gingerly peeping around the courtroom, I realised the judge, the cruelty officer and many other men were discussing me, my foster-parents, my school and many other aspects of my life. I did not really understand what they were talking about. I really wished I didn't have to be there.

In those days there was no such thing as previously taped interviews or videos, so children do not have to go through the trauma of giving evidence in court.

When I heard, 'And now young lady, what is your name?' I looked at my cruelty officer, praying for some guidance.

He nodded back at me, as if telling me to answer the question.

'Yes, Honour,' I gulped.

The cruelty officer threw his eyes up to heaven.

'What is your name, young lady?' the judge bellowed. The sound of the judge's voice echoed around the courthouse. He sounded so stern. I was petrified.

'Celine O'Brien,' I ventured in a tiny, barely audible voice.

'Speak up, I cannot hear you,' the judge said, sounding angry. I was so frightened, my throat felt tight. I couldn't get any words out.

I looked again to the cruelty officer, hoping he might help me. He had his mouth covered with his hand and was looking at some distant point on the ceiling. I realised that he would be no help to me.

'Celine O'Brien, sir,' I yelled back at the judge, in the loudest voice that I could raise.

'What's the meaning of this?' the judge demanded, looking around the courthouse.

The cruelty officer jumped up from the desk saying, 'No, no, your Honour, her name is Clifford, Celine Clifford. Her foster-parents' name was O'Brien.'

Again commotion erupted. I thought it was all my fault for shouting at the judge and I was sure I was in for some terrible punishment.

During all the arguing, I noticed a tall, thin woman in a beige coat, standing at the back of the courtroom. She was the only woman in a room full of men. She seemed to be following everything with great interest. I tried to catch her eye but she stared fixedly ahead of her, avoiding my occasional gaze. Only once, when we made eye contact, did she allow herself to smile briefly at me.

Did I know her? Did she know me? Who was she? Why was she there?

My attention was brought back to the proceedings in hand before I could even think about answers to these questions. It was established that my name was indeed Celine Clifford. As far as I was concerned, they were changing my name in case anyone would know about me being in jail. I thought it was the right thing to do as I had brought enough scandal on my original family, simply by being alive. I did not want to shame my foster-parents' good name, so that all their friends would know that I had to be put in jail, for being bad. I felt as if I was to blame for everything that had happened in my life.

I had to answer many questions about intimate parts of my body. Sometimes the same person, sometimes others, repeated these questions until I gave them an answer that satisfied them. I had to describe some of the awful things that men had done to my body, over the last six years. To have to tell people, in public, especially a roomful of men, was horrible.

There was quite a lot more talking around the court and

then everything went quiet. I looked up to see what was happening.

The judge addressed me directly. 'Stand up, Miss Clifford.'

I rose from my seat and the lower half of my body began to tremble.

'I want you to say after me,' the judge instructed.

I began to cry once again.

'I swear to remain at Mount St Vincent's Industrial School for as long as is deemed to be necessary, or as long as directed.'

I burst out in loud, anguished sobs. I couldn't remember all the words that the judge had said. So he said the sentence again, in groups of two words at a time and I repeated them. As I finished repeating the words, I felt very alone in the world. There was nobody there for me.

The cruelty officer gripped me tightly by my upper arm and I was led reluctantly from the court. Once again, I was crying, deep racking sobs.

So that was it.

I got a chance to see the Justice's Memorandum many years later as the Justice's Minute Book was in the National Archives. It read: 'Ordered that Celine Clifford be committed to the certified industrial cchool at Mount St Vincent's, Limerick, to be there detained as and from this date up to but not including the November 14, 1964. County Council notified. No order as to contribution.'

In those days, the Substance of Complaint, under the Children Acts 1908–1941 was a common method of dealing with children with behavioural problems. It was used to commit children to industrial schools for all sorts of petty crimes, from theft of a loaf of bread, to stealing a bicycle. Some of these children had very abusive upbringings and were full of anger. Some of them were out of control.

Perhaps this might explain the rough treatment I got from my cruelty officer.

On March 2, 1962, at 13 years of age, as I was led from Kilmallock Courthouse, now called Celine Clifford, I thought I was beginning a life sentence in jail. The well-dressed lady had disappeared. She had not made any contact with me. I was taken back to the same office where I had earlier spent most of the day.

I entered the office with my head held low. I was looking at the ground, with my hair falling all around my face. It was wet with my tears as they fell, uncontrollably.

I would have been grateful for any human comfort at that time, but none was forthcoming. I would have loved a drink of water even but I was too afraid to ask. In the court world of men I felt I was even the wrong sex and even that was my fault!

I felt that I could not trust anybody. I still believed I was going to jail.

'You're coming with me to the orphanage. You'll be well looked after there,' the cruelty officer said to me.

I stopped sobbing almost at once. I had distinctly heard the word orphanage. If it had been said before, throughout that long day, I had not heard it.

'Does that mean that I am not going to jail for ever?' I asked in a low voice.

'Of course you are not going to jail. Whatever gave you that idea? You'll be better looked after there, than before now. You were very lucky that woman made a complaint to the ISPCC.'

'What complaint? What woman? What is the ISPCC?'

'What went on in that house was disgusting. The whole world knows about that house. I just have to sign some papers here in the office and then we're off,' he said.

I had a million questions to ask. But I was afraid to open my mouth, in case I got into more trouble.

'Of course, my shoes and trousers are ruined because of you,' was the last statement I heard from the cruelty officer.

Before I left, while nobody was looking, I checked for any evidence of where I had wet the office floor earlier that day. Horror of horrors, it was still visible. I silently prayed to God that nobody would notice the stain. I felt so guilty about it.

FOUR

Safe in Prison

The cruelty officer wasn't as rough after the hearing. He came back to the office and took me gently by the hand this time and led me away. We were going to the orphanage so I had stopped crying. The journey took about half an hour by car. The time passed quickly.

We got out of the car and walked to a heavy wooden door. The officer rang a bell and a nun opened the door and she invited us in. She took us into what seemed to be a large waiting room. It was warm and comfortable and smelled of lavender floor polish.

It was lovely.

'This is Celine Clifford. She is coming to stay with you, Sister,' said the cruelty officer.

'We are expecting you, Celine. You are most welcome to the Mount Orphanage. This will be your home. I hope you will be happy here,' said the nun.

I was still clutching tightly to the cruelty officer, as I looked cautiously around the room.

The nun said that the other children were saying the rosary and that I might like to join in. As I knew how to say the rosary, I said, 'Yes, please.'

She led the way down some long corridors. A faint murmur of sound became a choir of children's voices chanting the responses to the familiar leads of the rosary. The nun said that she would come and get me as soon as the rosary was over. I was then silently introduced to another nun who was leading the prayers, by a system of nods between the two nuns.

I was put kneeling down, between two other girls at a long bench seat. As I looked at the girl on either side of me, each in turn smiled a greeting. As the rosary drew to a close, a large number of the children surrounded me. There were so many of them asking me questions, I could barely raise a voice in reply. Some of them wanted to touch me. I recoiled slightly. But they were all good touches.

A surge of emotion overwhelmed me. I could feel the blood rise to my cheeks. I realised for the first time in my entire life that I felt safe.

I thought to myself, 'I am going to love this place.'

The nun came back to collect me as promised. She asked me if I had been fed. As I had not been given any food during the day, I suddenly felt hungry. In truth, I was always starving but in the past months I'd gotten used to being fed so I was now hungrier than ever. The nun said that I should join the other children for supper, and afterwards they would bath me and show me where I would be sleeping.

She took me down to the refectory, where all the other children were already noisily ensconced at the various long tables. It smelled of sour milk. I never heard such bedlam. Everyone seemed to be shouting or talking at the same time. Each one wanted me to sit at her table. It was so exciting.

Supper consisted of bread and jam, washed down with cold milk. There was a plate piled high with bread and jam. I wolfed down as many slices as I could. The menu for supper was always to consist of bread, margarine, jam and cold milk. But there were rules about the bread, margarine and jam.

You could have bread and margarine for supper. You could have bread and jam for supper. But you could NOT have bread AND margarine AND jam together for supper. This little rule did not bother me.

After supper, two different nuns took me to the washing area. They told me to fill a bath and I did not know what they meant. They showed me how to turn on a tap. With two inches of water in the bath, I turned off the tap. The nuns laughed at me. Some of the orphan girls heard the laughter and came to see the fun. They began to tease me. It did not feel nice to be teased about being dirty and not knowing how to fill a bath for myself.

One nun took charge. 'Get out of here the rest of you, and Sister and I will show Celine what we mean by clean,' she said. Then they filled the bath full of clean warm water. They asked me to take off all my clothes and get in and sit down in the bath.

As I undressed, I laid my pretty suit on a nearby chair, together with my cream shoes and blue socks. On top of these, I laid my precious brown leather handbag, with my name Celine embossed in gold for everyone to see.

When I was in the bath, the two nuns rolled up the sleeves of their habits. They gave me a cleaning all over that I will never forget to this day. Every piece of flesh that was reachable was scrubbed clean. They used some vile foul-smelling potions on my hair and the rest of my body. When the bath was finished, the nuns wrapped me in a huge towel, and partially dried me off.

As I was rushed out the door of the washing area, between the two nuns, I glanced over my shoulder at the chair that held my jealously guarded special possessions: my pink cardigan, my blue skirt, my cream shoes, my blue socks and my beloved leather handbag. These few items represented all that I owned in the entire world.

I was never to see any of them again.

I asked the nuns where they were many times, but my questions were always dismissed lightly. They disappeared into thin air. I had just learned that if you get an unexpected present and you become attached to it, be careful because it may not be yours to keep for ever. It was a lesson that I was to learn many times in life.

When I was dry, I was given a nightdress to put on. I was then shown to what was to be my bed for the months to come. It was in a dormitory where there were about sixteen beds, lined up in two rows. The nuns smiled at me, as they reassured me about staying at the Mount Orphanage and put me to bed. The bedclothes smelled so clean. As I drew up the covers around my neck, I felt comfortable and warm.

I felt safe.

After such a long, stressful, exhausting day, I quickly fell asleep.

Sometime, in the middle of the night, I was woken up with a jolt. I screamed loudly as something hard hit my entire body. I had no idea where I was. I had felt so safe before I went to sleep, so I could not understand what had happened. I had fallen out of the bed. I had never slept in a single bed before!

I was gradually introduced to the other children in the orphanage and I made some friends for the first time, which helped me. I also met the nuns who were responsible for its efficient, disciplined daily routine. I only met the nuns on a need-to-know basis. On the day of my arrival at the orphanage I had almost felt special but on the days following my introduction, I was let know, in no uncertain terms, that I was not in any way special. I was, in fact, only a small cog in what the nuns perceived to be a large and very important wheel. The nuns actually believed that they were providing an essential and valuable service to the Irish public at large. The public face of the nuns showed that they were providing a caring service, for poor unfortunate children, mainly the product of unscrupulous, unmarried mothers.

The other non-public face of the nuns was the reality that they were barely providing shelter, with a very basic diet, for children whom they believed were paying, by their very existence, for the sins of their mothers. According to the Catholic Church in Ireland, the sin that their mothers had committed was that they became pregnant and had a baby, while unmarried. This sin was unacceptable before the eyes of God, everyone involved in religious life, and the decent people of Ireland. And so the vast majority of people shunned girls who admitted to such a sin. And worse, the children of these unmarried mothers were also shunned and considered to be an embarrassment. Industrial schools, often known as orphanages subsidised by the state and run by charitable orders of nuns, became the solution to the problem. Some of the children in the orphanage felt like they were in the army, others felt like it was prison.

There was a timetable for everything and there were rules for every little thing. If the rules were broken, each broken rule had its own merited and rigorously meted out punishment. I remember that we had to clean all the skirting boards in the orphanage. It took hours and if you got even a tiny mark on the wall above, you were beaten. A lot of the nuns had a leather strap that used to hang beside their rosary beads and they would beat you immediately. You were afraid to cry. If you did, you were beaten more. You had to keep quiet all the time, like you were choking. You had to hold it in. You could never scream. Some of the girls couldn't help it and the nuns would hit them with the strap again and again. There was high dusting as well, which was over the picture rails and then we would have to scrub all the floors. There was never a bit of dirt in the orphanage.

I have not been able to banish from my memory the screams and suffering of small children who were punished for breaking some very flimsy and unjustifiable rules. Watching a punishment being carried out on another girl, particularly if she was younger than you, was very difficult. Sometimes there was a very fine line between a rule being broken and not being broken. Many children were punished for nothing and often too harshly. If a girl wet her bed, she had to stand at the end of the dormitory with the wet sheets and then wash them herself. Your hair was sometimes cut as a punishment so that everyone would know. Otherwise we all looked the same, with the one haircut, in the same second-hand looking clothes. If a nun shouted at you to 'Halt', you stopped dead in your tracks – obedience to the nuns was absolute.

The nuns weren't all evil. Some of them had a bit of compassion but they were afraid of the stronger nuns. We were told again and again that we had to suffer for the sins of our parents. I was told that I was damaged – 'ruined for life' – because I wasn't even a virgin. I was used goods and I had to suffer for it. They all knew about my past.

Some of them wanted to humiliate us. You would have to stand still for hours on end or you wouldn't get any dinner or you weren't allowed outside. Some of the special children, who had families outside the orphanage, got to do Irish dancing or to be in the choir, but I was never allowed. There was a press where children who had relatives on the outside were allowed to go to buy sweets if they had been given some money. They'd never share the sweets. I think they were told not to. I remember one time a girl was walking in front of me and she dropped the sweet paper. I picked it up and licked it until there was nothing left on it at all.

An uncanny punishment I used to receive was the nuns' attempts to make me feel guilty by asking, 'What would your auntie nuns think of you now?' If I heard this once, I heard it a hundred times. I had no idea what this meant as I did not know any 'auntie nuns'. Consequently, in my ignorance, I escaped the punishment of the guilt complex they were trying to force on to me.

But everything is relative. As I had come from hell, I thought the orphanage, with all its rules and regulations, was heaven. I loved it. The sister-in-charge of the entire orphanage was a responsible person. Some of her line managers were also fair, but others were obsessed and tough. I quickly worked out that if you caused trouble, you got into trouble, so I caused no trouble.

On my second day at the orphanage, I was told to go to the office. I was given my number. From now on, I was to be known as 1797. I also had to call at the sick bay unit for a routine medical check-up.

The local doctor visited me in the late afternoon. The check-up was the usual inspection of hearing, sight, teeth, nose and breathing. When he asked about my private area, I sat on the chair, crossed my legs and my arms. I hung my head.

He asked me, 'Have you been interfered with?'

I could not raise my voice to answer him.

He qualified the question, 'Have men had sexual relations with you?'

All I could do was nod my head, and burst into tears.

He murmured to himself, 'Oh, my good God.'

He then called the nun in and said to her, 'She will have to be seen by a gynaecologist. She will need a full gynaecological examination. I will give you a letter of referral and you should make an appointment as soon as possible.'

I wondered what they were talking about but understood none of the medical terms. The doctor told me that I was fine and then said that I was dismissed.

On the morning of my third day at the orphanage, the sister-in-charge sent for me and told me that I would have to go to school. She said that they wanted to assess my education to date. She put me in fifth class. While living with my foster-parents, my attendance at school was practically nil. Years later, I went back through the attendance records at my primary school. I found that out of a total of eight years of primary education, my total days at school amounted to less than one academic year. I still don't understand how the school let this happen without reporting it.

So after three days in fifth class, in the orphanage school, the nuns felt that there was no point in me spending any more time in school. I heard the nun in school say to another nun that I was pure stupid, knew nothing and understood nothing that was being taught in class. I do not really blame them for this assessment. It was not their fault that I was 13 years of age and had never received a basic education.

On the other hand, I very much regret that I was not given the help to try to learn. But then I was part of a group of people that were an embarrassment to the community at large. I, along with my fellow inmates, merited only the absolute minimum assistance of any kind.

As my academic future was deemed to be a non-runner, it was there and then consigned to the educational dustbin. I was to stay in the orphanage proper and look after the younger girls, help in the kitchens and clean the toilets. Any skills that I could learn while I was carrying out my duties, I was to consider my education.

Once a week we had to scrub the cement yard and the drains with a deck scrubbing brush, on our knees. It was hard physical work. Needlework was also encouraged as a skill to be learned. There was always a mountain of torn or ripped clothing to be repaired. Every morning at least two hours were devoted to sewing the never-ending amount of torn clothing. I became quite adept at this chore. As part of our needlework training, we were encouraged to actually make the clothes that we would need, when we finally left at age 16, to join the real world and work for a living. Over a period of two years I managed to make a set of pyjamas, a skirt, a dress and a blouse. While I enjoyed the peacefulness of the sewing sessions at the orphanage, afterwards I was never able to do needlework, for pleasure or as a business. Forty years later I have only managed to make one pair of curtains. They were made under duress, to cover a bedroom window of an apartment that half the population of London could see into.

Cookery was another skill that I was to acquire as part of my orphanage training. Again, in reality, this meant acting as a servant, a skivvy, peeling carrots and potatoes in the kitchens attached to the orphanage. I was being trained for a career as a housemaid. In comparison to sewing, cookery at the orphanage was hard work. It required long hours and physical fitness. Breakfast for the following day had to be prepared on the previous evening, before going to bed. Two huge pots of oatmeal porridge had to be brought to the boil and then simmered for about 45 minutes. The pots were so large and contained such a large volume of water, they took hours to boil. The stove was heated by solid fuel, mostly turf. It was part of my duties to keep this cooker alive and burning.

One perk of working in the kitchens was that I always had something to eat. While living with my foster-parents I was always starving. Even though the nuns kept a strict control on the stock of food and waste was not tolerated in the kitchens, there were always bits and pieces to eat. There were never any leftovers but some children might not eat their allotted food on any particular day, for a variety of reasons. The one reason that never applied was that they were given too much to eat. The food was always stews and the cheapest type of potatoes. We used to get a pudding on Sunday that was slimy and a dirty-pink colour. It always made me think of my past life and I never ate it. I used it give it to one of my friends on the sly. At least working in the kitchens, I could always steal a choice piece of meat or hide a piece of prepared food in a safe place. I would eat this at a later time, to replace a less appetising meal. Everyone in the orphanage stole food at one time or another. They had to or they would have starved.

This was not gourmet cooking for a small number of people. This was catering on a large scale. Around 220 mouths had to be fed, three times a day. The refectory tables had to be set with plates, cups and cutlery each time. All the plates, drinking cups and mugs were made from metal. This was to prevent breakages. All the eating and cooking utensils had to be washed after use.

The orphans, overseen by a nun, did all this manually. The nun's role was entirely supervisory. She did not do any of the cooking or washing up. Neither did the nuns ever eat with us in our refectory. They had their own dining room. We were never invited or allowed to visit this area of the nuns' community. It was in a separate building, on the opposite side of the compound.

But after I had been there a few months I did get an inkling of how the system worked. The supplier, in the same van, often delivered the food for both eating areas. Bread deliveries were always eagerly awaited. The orphans had to help carry in all the loaves of bread and the other girls told me how to hide food under our long knickers. We only got two deliveries per week and our bread was what the bread man called 'returns'. This was bread that was returned from shops that had bought it from the bakery. If it was unsold or still in the shop when the next delivery of fresh bread arrived, the bakery took it back. It was always hard and mostly covered with blue mould. When it arrived at the orphanage kitchen, we had to cut off the mould before serving it at mealtime.

The nuns' dining section got a fresh bread delivery every day which included a delivery of fresh pastries and confectionery. We called them buns.

No One Wants You

Our delivery days were Tuesday and Friday and were eagerly awaited by whichever two orphans were on kitchen duty. The delivery man would nearly always manage to give the two girls a bun each for themselves to eat. What a treat that was. Sometimes he had whipped cream on pastry, sometimes jam and cream doughnuts, and sometimes buns with icing on them for us. They tasted so sweet.

We had to swallow them down as fast as we could. If we were caught eating buns, both the delivery man and ourselves would have been in severe trouble. He never asked for, or expected, anything in return, or payment of any kind. I will always remember him as a special person who did not discriminate against us orphans, at a time when most people saw us as human detritus.

Working in the kitchens also included working in the nursery where milk was the staple diet. Every second day a man with a horse and cart delivered the milk to the orphanage, in huge metal milk churns. They were stored in the pantry. There were no refrigerators in those days, so the milk was stored in the coolest part of the pantry. It used to turn sour very quickly, particularly during the warm summer months. It also contributed to the persistent smell of sour milk throughout the entire orphanage buildings. Of course we never noticed the smell, but visitors often commented on it.

Looking back, the bad condition of the milk was probably why there were so many cases of enteritis suffered by the younger babies and children in the nursery area. The smell of diarrhoea was often overpowering, but was drowned out by the incessant crying of the suffering children, possibly infected by contaminated milk.

Another life-skill that I inherited from my time in the orphanage was lace making. The older orphans had to learn lace making. If you were found to be proficient at it, you were encouraged to do it all the time. The nuns sold it as decorative Limerick lace on the lucrative American market. I became quite proficient at it. However, once I left the orphanage, I never did it again. But I did collect decorative pieces of lace, done by others, as a hobby and have quite a few pieces of antique lace in my collection to this day. I suppose it serves to remind me of days spent safely absorbed in lace making.

When I had been at the orphanage for about four months, the sister-in-charge called me in to her office one Saturday morning. She told me to expect a visit from a nun from a different convent. She said that a Sister Bernadette would arrive the following day.

The mystery nun arrived as promised, on Sunday afternoon. I was waiting in the assembly area. She introduced herself to me as Sister Bernadette. She told me that I was her 'case' and that she was going to be a special friend to me. If there was anything that was bothering me, I was to contact her. If there was anything that I felt that she should know about, I was to contact her even faster. She promised that she would look after me. Even after I left the orphanage, I was to regard her as my confidante or special friend. She would leave her address with the sister-in-charge of the orphanage. It was a pleasant sunny day, so she suggested that we should take a walk around the convent grounds.

She started asking me some questions, like how I was settling in at the orphanage. As we walked through the rose garden, she sneezed and said that she might be getting a cold. The comment meant nothing to me but she used it to introduce the topic of changes to my body. She described to me how I would begin to get a cold every month from now on. She said that all girls of my age get a cold every month.

I told her I had often had a cold before.

'Oh no,' she said, 'You have never had a cold like this.'

She told me that I would bleed every month. She did not

tell me which part of me would bleed. I assumed that I would bleed from the nose if I were going to have a lot of colds. As I had had colds and nose bleeds for as long as I could remember, I was not in the least bit concerned. When I talked this interview over with some of my friends at the orphanage during the following week, I was to learn that Sister Bernadette had being trying to tell me that I would soon start getting my period. In the orphanage when girls had their periods, they had to queue up to get sanitary towels. The first time I saw them I thought they were getting white socks. I was jealous and thought why do I never get them? Soon after my chat with Sister Bernadette I had to start queuing myself. When you had heavier periods you had to turn the pad upside-down as the nuns wouldn't give you any more. You'd wrap it in the toilet paper but you were only allowed two squares of toilet paper at a time so it was very difficult.

Sister Bernadette went on to tell me that the 'monthly cold' led on to the 'things boys do to girls'. She started talking about babies. Her description of what happened in such situations was couched in prissy, descriptive names. When I joined in, saying men at home did that to me, she looked shocked and horrified. I told her about the 'purple prick' and how it could hurt you, and she began to realise that I knew many words to describe in detail what she was having trouble talking about. She visibly flinched at some of the words that I used. As far as I was concerned, they were all normal words, used every day in my foster-family home. By what I was saying, Sister Bernadette learnt a lot about the goings-on in my foster home but she chose to do nothing about it.

In a low voice, she finally said to me, 'I think that you already know what I am trying to tell you.' I could not tell by the tone of her voice whether she was disgusted by my knowledge or concerned for my future. I thought that the

interview was coming to an end. But I was wrong. All the
previous talk was just leading up to what she was about to
tell me next. What she said next began with a very simple
statement. But it was to upset me for the remainder of my
stay at the orphanage. Up to this point, in comparison to the
life of abuse and degradation that I had lived with my foster-
parents, my stay at the orphanage was bliss. But I was to be
unsettled emotionally for 30 years by what Sister Bernadette
told me next.

She told me that I had a mother and father. She also told
me that I had a grandmother.

I was shattered. When my foster-parents said that
nobody wanted me, I had not really understood the exact
meaning of that statement. But it became clear to me very
quickly on that sunny afternoon, in the rose garden with
Sister Bernadette.

She said that my father's family lived in Limerick City,
close to where I was presently living. The other family,
which included my maternal grandmother, lived in County
Limerick, but not too far from the city itself. I immediately
became excited. I was jumping up and down with joy. I had
always envied some of the other children at school, as they
seemed to have the one thing that I did not – parents. Quite
a few of the children at the orphanage had either one or
both parents. Sometimes the parents even visited their
children. I was always envious of them, as I never had even
one visitor, never mind a parent.

I asked the nun, 'When can I see them?'

She did not answer my question directly. She told me
that my father could not be told of my existence. She said
that he did not even know I was alive. She said that two of
his sisters were 'Mercy nuns' in Cork and that they would be
embarrassed beyond belief, and would be sent to the
missions in Africa, if it became public knowledge that I was
related to them.

The mystery of my 'auntie nuns' was now finally becoming clearer to me. I began to realise that they were part of my family. They were my father's sisters. It was a concept that I had never allowed myself to explore. It dawned on me then that I really did have a family.

There were also three priests in my father's greater extended family and if the scandal of my existence were to become known, they would suffer untold consequences from their respective bishops.

She said that my father was a lawyer, and was highly respected in the community, as well as in, and far beyond, Limerick City. She also said that my father was now married and had a large family. If my father found out about me now, it would break up his marriage and his large family. He would be disgraced.

In Sister Bernadette's opinion, it was best left alone. She advised me to put it behind me, and get on with the rest of my life. That was a piece of advice that I was to hear many times over the next 40 years of my life. It is a very easy piece of advice to give to somebody, especially if you have not endured hardship or pain. While I would have loved to accept that particular piece of advice, many times over, it is just not possible to do. A person can block many things out of their life, such as pain or emotions, but one cannot block out the memories. From that Sunday afternoon, when Sister Bernadette told me about my family, I knew then that I desperately wanted to meet them. I knew that I would not rest until I did.

That same week I had more bad news, although at the time it did not particularly bother me, as I now had the news of my parents to distract me. This next bit of bad news was very final, and it was to remain with me, at the back of my mind, for many years to come.

My appointment with the gynaecologist was the next big occurrence in my life. One evening after the recitation of the rosary, the sister-in-charge came to me and told me that I was to be excused my duties in the kitchens for the next day. She said that as soon as I got out of bed I was to have a bath. Hot water and soap would be provided for me, and she said that I was to wash myself thoroughly, everywhere, inside and out. I was to be ready and standing by the back door at ten o'clock. A sister would then take me by taxi to my appointment with Dr Leahy, the gynaecologist.

I had no idea why I was being taken to a gynaecologist.

I had no idea what a gynaecologist did for a living.

I had my bath the next morning. It was cold, as usual. Neither the hot water nor the soap appeared so, as usual, the time spent in the freezing water was minimal. I dried, dressed and presented myself at the door to await the taxi. It duly arrived and the nun and myself sat in the back seat.

As the taxi drove us through the open gate and we left the orphanage behind us, I realised that there was another world outside the confines of those walls. I realised that people lived a different life out there. People lived a normal life outside. I had been inside the orphanage for approximately seven months, without ever leaving, or wanting to leave it, even once.

Dr Leahy was an old man. He was a real gentleman and really nice to me. The nun waited outside as he explained what he was going to do to me during my examination. He made sure that I understood everything as best as a 13-year-old child could understand, under the circumstances. He emphasised that he was not going to hurt me or perform any surgery on me. He said that he merely wanted to examine me internally.

He told me to get undressed and get into the white smock, which he had given to me. I did this behind a screen in the corner of the room. He put me up on the examination table, in his examination room. There were many strong lights there. Some of the lights were on wheels so that he could move them around.

He told me to lie on my back and put my legs up in what he called the stirrups. He warned me that he was going to put an instrument into my vagina, and that it might be a bit cold for a few seconds. He inserted an instrument called a speculum into my vagina, which he stretched wider, so he could examine me. He probed deeper towards my uterus with different instruments, sometimes tut-tutting as he met unexpected resistance. He then withdrew all the instruments, loosened the speculum and turned off all the high-powered lights.

He came up to my face and said, 'There you are, young lady, that wasn't too bad, was it?'

As he pulled me to an upright position, I croaked a weak 'No'.

He told me that I could get dressed and go home with the sister. As I was getting dressed behind the screen, I heard him tell the nun that he would write a report and post it to the sister-in-charge of the orphanage.

The nun said, 'That is fine Doctor, but is there anything serious that would affect her daily routine work in the orphanage kitchens?'

'No. Nothing to be worried about in the short-term, but long-term, it is most unlikely that she will ever have children,' he said.

That piece of information was filed in my memory in the folder labelled 'sad', for thinking about at a later date. I then tried to forget about it. I left Dr Leahy's rooms that day, feeling unconcerned about my gynaecological future. I just wanted to enjoy the feeling of freedom, on my day away from the confines of the orphanage.

That was to be the first of many visits to gynaecological specialists for examinations resulting in extensive surgery to my reproductive organs and tract, over the coming years.

A couple of weeks after the first examination, I was told that I had some visitors. I couldn't think who they might be. I was thrilled that someone would think so much of me that they would come as a visitor. It was Kit and Tony. They had come to see how I was after my sudden departure from their home. I told them that I was settling into the orphanage very well, but that the court case had upset me a lot.

Kit asked, in all innocence, 'What court case?'

They obviously did not know where I had been taken to on that morning, the previous March. I told them a shortened version of the day and Kit hugged me tightly. She then gave me amazing news.

'We have arranged with the sisters that you can come to us for a week's holiday, later in the summer. It will be in August.'

I was overjoyed at the thought of going to somebody who wanted me, for a holiday.

Before they left they gave me a present of a crinoline doll, with beautiful pearls on her dress. Afterwards I hid the doll in my bedside locker, which was the only thing I could call my own in the orphanage. The next morning I checked to see if the doll was still there, but it was gone. I was never to see the doll again. I was heartbroken, but I did not cry about it. Instead I counted the days until August when Kit and Tony would come to collect me.

August finally came and I did have my holiday with Kit and Tony. They treated me as if I was their own. They took me for picnics, to a funfair and to the beach.

When the week was over I did not mind going back to the orphanage, although I did cry as I said goodbye at the convent gate. They had promised me that they would come and see me as visitors and that I could come for my summer holidays again the following year. They kept their promise and visited me about twice each year during my time at the Mount.

While my life had changed slightly for the better with Kit and Tony now part of it, the regime at the orphanage remained strict. When Kit and Tony visited me the following Easter, they gave me a large chocolate Easter egg. I remember that it was made by Suchard. I was not allowed to eat the egg. The sister said that I could only unwrap the packaging. I took it out of its box and I unwrapped the silver paper from around the egg. I was not allowed to touch the chocolate. Then the nun took the packaging and the egg, and disappeared with them. I never tasted my Easter egg but I was able to smell it. It smelled delicious.

Life at the orphanage went on as before. I had been there a year and nothing had changed. Work was just as difficult as ever, but I never complained. There was no sexual threat and I felt safe. I could cope with anything after that.

I used to clean the priest's parlour and serve his breakfast. He had a fruit cocktail and then was served a fried breakfast, followed with bread and butter. He usually had a grapefruit as well, with a special spoon. If we got the chance we'd lick the priest's plate to get a taste of his fried breakfast.

The laundry belonging to the nuns was done in a separate area. It was treated as something special. Either the novice nuns did it or the younger professed nuns. The nuns that had to do the washing and the ironing were not of the same high status as the other nuns. The orphans were not even deemed suitable to wash the nuns' clothes.

But there was one job that the orphans were seen as suitable for. When the nuns' habits were washed and dried they were sent down to the orphanage. We had to inspect the habits, for stains on the black cloth which had remained after the washing process. These were generally food and drink stains on the bodice of the garment. They obviously occurred during meal times when a nun might actually spill their soup or their food. The nuns were constantly celebrating a feast day and there was always a lot more washing.

To remove these stains we had to constantly dab them with a cloth soaked with liquid ammonia, until they disappeared. We had to hold the cloths at arm's length. The ammonia was the reason that we 'orphans' were allowed to touch the nuns' habits. It was used undiluted, from a large Winchester bottle. It gave off very strong vapours if you inhaled them directly, they would take your breath away. The vapours were highly toxic, but we were never told about any safety procedures. Many young girls' lungs were probably irreparably damaged by exposure to the ammonia fumes.

One evening, after another girl and myself had finished removing stains from the habits, we folded them up and returned them to the nuns' laundry area. When we got there, we left the habits with a young nun. She had just taken a delivery of fruit and was putting it away in a cupboard. As she became distracted by the now, stain-free habits, we were able to steal an apple each, when her back was turned. Both of us began the walk back to the orphanage, through a network of corridors, secretly eating our apples. We had only taken a few bites out of our apples, when we met the Deputy Mother Superior of the entire convent.

'What are you girls eating?' she snapped. 'Where did you get those? Give me those apples at once, and follow me.'

Before we could produce an answer, she snatched the apples from us and marched us into the office of the Mother Superior of the whole convent.

'These girls stole apples from the pantry, Mother Superior,' she said.

We both opened our mouths to deny the theft.

'Silence,' yelled Mother Superior in our direction. 'Take them away, and deal with them,' she ordered her second-in-command.

The sister caught each of us by the ear and led us out of

the office. We tried to protest our innocence but were once again told to be quiet, by a stern command of, 'Silence, you evil pair of thieves'.

She took us to a marble staircase, between the ground and first floor. The staircase went halfway up between the floors to a wide landing and then turned. At the landing, on the wall, there was a large crucifix. She told us to kneel down in front of the crucifix and join our hands in prayer.

'Both of you will remain here until the morning. You will not move, you will not speak to each other and you will pray to Our Blessed Lady for forgiveness.'

We knelt down and dared not look at each other. We remained in that position for many hours. As kneeling on the solid marble began to feel like agony and my legs started to cramp, I just tried to ignore the pain. When all the lights were turned out, we realised that all the nuns had gone to bed. Only when this happened did we dare to speak to each other, in a barely audible whisper. Eventually we sat down under the crucifix. All night we debated the injustice of the harsh sentence, but every time we heard a sound, we jumped back into the kneeling position.

Eventually morning arrived and the first nun appeared down the stairs, 'What are you two girls doing here? Get back to the orphanage, at once.'

We both looked at one another and before I could get moving, the nun pushed me. As I was not expecting it, I unbalanced and fell headlong down the marble steps. My face hit the steps with an almighty thud and immediately my nose started to spurt blood. I tried to stop the flow with my fingers. The flow was so strong that it was impossible. It began to drip all over the floor. The other girl was gone.

The nun began screaming at me hysterically to get some cloth from the kitchen and clean up the bloody mess. She half dragged me to the kitchen where she squeezed my nostrils to stem the flow. It took a long time to slow down.

She left me leaning over the sink holding my own nose. She said that she would wipe up the blood on the floor.

When she came back to me the bleeding had stopped. She wiped and cleaned my face and calmly told me not to tell anyone what had happened. She said that if I did, she would report me to Mother Superior and have me transferred to the 'Good Shepherds'. This was an industrial school with a fearsome reputation. No one wanted to be sent to the Good Shepherds' torture chamber.

It was that old familiar threat, not to tell anyone what had happened to me. I had been keeping silent about bad things happening to me all my life, so one more would not be difficult.

In the following days, my nose swelled up to an enormous size. Some of the girls and maybe even one nun did ask me what happened to my nose. I said that I had fallen down the stairs, but I never mentioned that a nun pushed me.

I learned a valuable lesson that day.

Don't take something that belongs to someone else.

FIVE

Tough Love

My time at the orphanage was drawing to a close. From the time Sister Bernadette had told me about my parents, my emotional balance was disturbed, particularly during my last year there. After her visit I had been ecstatic. I had told everyone in the orphanage that I had found my long lost parents. I told everyone that I was going to meet my parents. I told anyone who would listen that my parents were going to take me away from the orphanage. But as week after week passed by and nothing happened, I began to modify my expectations.

I stopped talking to other people about my parents. I began to only think about them in private.

The strange part of the revelation was that I found the story about my father acceptable. I believed that he was a very important solicitor, with a large family, who would be scandalised, and that maybe the whole fabric of society might be damaged if this important man was to be embarrassed in any way, because of the public exposure of my illegitimate existence. So I concentrated on my mother.

I became consumed by my mother.

I became consumed by her actions.

I became consumed by the decisions she made.

I became consumed by the consequences of her decisions.

I became consumed by the fact that she had never tried to find me.

I became consumed by the fact that she had consigned me to the scrap-heap of life.

I became consumed by the fact that she had condemned me, as a young child, her daughter, to a life of sexual degradation, at the whims of uncontrolled paedophiles.

I became consumed by my mother, absolutely!

How could any mother do those things to her young daughter? How could my mother do any of those horrible things to me?

The more I thought about it, the more it affected me. My behaviour changed. I became difficult and uncooperative about my work duties. I couldn't stop myself looking sad. Over the previous 18 months, I had earned the nickname 'Smiler', as my demeanour was always bright and happy and I always had a smile on my face, but it was not always a happy smile. I reasoned that if I smiled at everyone, I would not get into trouble with anyone. It didn't really work and most of the smiling faces that I wore were yet another attempt at personal survival.

I persisted in asking the nuns when I could meet my mother. I never gave up asking to meet her. After about a year, Sister Bernadette had a message delivered to me, to tell me that she had arranged for my mother to visit me. She was to arrive at the orphanage on a Sunday afternoon, three weeks later. I was over the moon with excitement. I was unable to sleep at night. Every thought that ran through my mind concerned my mother.

What would she look like?

Would she like me?

Would I be acceptable to her?

I was 14 and a half years of age and this would have been the first time that I would have met my mother, the only time since the day that she gave me away, at five months of age.

All the preparations were in place. But it was not to be. I came down with the mumps and so the visit was cancelled.

I was so ill on the day that I couldn't even get out of bed. I remember I was just left in the dormitory all day. I was heartbroken. I was so disappointed that I had been unable to meet my mother for the first time. But I was optimistic that another visit could be rearranged quickly – it was not to be.

* * * *

When we reached the age of 15, the nuns used to find us jobs outside the orphanage. It was a sort of training for becoming a housemaid. We would go and work for families during the day and we would return to the orphanage at night. We were not paid any wages for this work as it was considered training. We would stay for a period of three months with one family and then we would be swapped around to another house. It was slave labour and to this day I feel that the nuns owe me my pay. I had about five such jobs, one in a pub and others in some posh houses before I left the orphanage for good.

At the age of 16 it was time for me to leave the orphanage and face the big, wide world on a permanent basis. In other words, I was now ready to have a paying job and learn to make my own way in the world. In reality, my credentials for earning a living were very poor. I had no formal education to speak of. I was barely literate. My strengths revolved around the fact that I had experience of cleaning toilets and floors, peeling vegetables and changing babies' dirty nappies. Yes, I was qualified to work as a housemaid.

I was released into the care of a Mrs Wall from Dublin in the beginning. She was a Limerick woman who had moved to Dublin and I was to be her housemaid. The job only lasted three weeks and I was returned to the orphanage at the Mount because there was a job available to me, as a housemaid in a large farming house on the outskirts of Limerick City, if I successfully passed an interview. I was given the address of the house, with rather vague directions telling me how to get there. I was to present myself for interview at two o'clock in the afternoon of the following day. I had worked outside the high walls of the orphanage for the previous two years so I had some knowledge of how to navigate my way around the city. I had no money for a taxi, or even a bus. I had to walk. I asked a large number of people for directions and eventually found the address. The lady of the house met me at the door. She asked me to come in and take a seat. An old friend of hers was visiting her and she told me he was going to interview me, as well as herself. She reassured me that the interview was nothing elaborate. She said that they were just going to ask me a few simple questions. Her friend turned out to be a priest, Father Bernard O'Dea. He was a Benedictine priest from a local school nearby.

Mrs Cooke asked me easy questions, like my name, my age, how long I was at the orphanage and what kind of work I did there. I answered all her questions as best I could. She seemed pleased enough with my answers. Then Father Bernard asked about my education. What class was I in at school? I told him that I had hardly ever been to school. He asked me if I could read and write. In a very low voice, I said that I could. He asked me to write my name on a piece of paper, which he handed to me, along with a pen. I wrote what I considered to be my name, Celine Clifford. I had always practised writing my name. I was not sure why I practised writing it so much. Maybe it was because I liked it, but later in life I felt that it reassured me that I actually was a person, in my own right.

Then he asked me to write the sentence 'the dog barked long and loudly'. I was able to spell 'the' and 'dog' but I was not able to spell the other words. I attempted the entire sentence, but I am sure the writing was illegible. He looked at it, and said, 'Thank you, Celine.'

He then nodded at Mrs Cooke.

She said, 'Let me show you the house and I'll tell you what your duties would be as we go along.'

When the tour was over, she announced that the pay was two pounds and ten shillings a week 'all found', with a half day off per week. She asked me, 'Do you think that you would be able for it?'

'Yes,' I answered shakily. The nuns had warned me that if I was offered the job, I was to accept it, there and then.

'Are the terms acceptable to you?' asked Father Bernard.

I nodded that they were.

'Well then,' said Mrs Cooke, 'I am prepared to offer you the position, do you accept? Or, do you need time to think about it?'

'No, no,' I blurted, 'I would be delighted to accept the position, Mrs Cooke.'

'When can you start?' she asked.

'On Monday morning next, if that suits you,' I recited.

'Well, that is settled then,' said Mrs Cooke. 'Bring your belongings around on Sunday evening. You can move in then, and start on Monday morning.'

As I got up to leave, Father Bernard stood up, came over to me, shook my hand and said, 'I am delighted to have met you, Celine. I am sure we will meet quite often, as I visit Mrs Cooke regularly.'

'Thank you, Father,' I responded.

I was not to know at that moment in time what a valuable and important role Father Bernard O'Dea would play in my life, for many years to come.

I started working for Mrs Cooke on the following Monday as planned. The work was not too hard. Mrs Cooke was middle-aged and was somewhat unwell at the time. She couldn't do any kind of manual work around the house. She tired easily and her doctor had recommended that she rest as much as she could.

Her husband was dead. She lived with her two children who I used to get ready for school. When I had finished my daily duties, most of the remainder of my time was spent listening to her. She wanted, or needed, someone to talk to. I filled that role. It was busy yet enjoyable, just listening to her ramble on about old times. I grew to be a good listener. Father Bernard came to visit about once a week, except when he was away on his travels. He seemed to travel to many exotic parts of the world.

For my first real job, I could not have had a better start. Mrs Cooke was extremely kind to me, and I looked forward to Father Bernard's weekly visits, as they both included me in their conversations. This alone made me feel acceptable. I would have liked an increase in my weekly wage, but this was not forthcoming. I was afraid to ask for it, so my disposable income remained low.

While still working for Mrs Cooke, I wrote to Sister Bernadette, with Father Bernard's help, requesting a meeting with my mother. Instead of posting the letter myself, Father Bernard said that he would post it on his way home. Thinking about it now, I think that he contacted Sister Bernadette directly, either by telephone or in person. I think that his intervention was responsible for what happened next.

In July 1965 I received a letter from Sister Bernadette informing me that she had arranged for me to visit the convent at the Mount, where I would meet my mother. The letter said that she would contact me to arrange a date that would be mutually suitable to both my mother and I. My world was turned upside-down once again, as I thought about meeting my mother for the first time.

I was not contacted to see what date might be suitable for me to meet my mother, but I received another letter from

Sister Bernadette one week later. She told me to present myself at the Mount Convent at three o'clock, on Tuesday afternoon of the following week. The letter politely informed me that my mother would be present, accompanied by her sister.

My every waking thought for the next two weeks was concentrated on the meeting. I fantasised about every aspect of the meeting.

We would fall into each other's arms.

We would hug each other for a long time.

She would call me her long-lost daughter.

She would say that at long last we have been reunited.

She would tell me that I was coming home with her that very day.

She would tell me how much she missed me.

She would tell me that she had been searching for me for years.

She would cry her heart out and plead with me to forgive her.

She would promise me that she would make up for lost time with me.

She would explain to me, 'Why?'

It was five minutes to three o'clock on that fateful Tuesday. The scene was set. The players were in place. At age 17, I was ready to meet my mother for the first time. It was a beautiful sunny summer afternoon.

I rang the doorbell at the side of the big heavy wooden front door of the convent. I had agonised over my clothes for days. Eventually I chose a turquoise blue suit. Underneath it was a floral blouse. A pair of blue shoes complemented the clothes, to complete the outfit. I thought it was in good taste, and felt comfortable in it. My hair was long, blonde and curly.

I wanted everything to be perfect. I wanted to be acceptable in every way.

A young nun that I did not recognise opened the door. At her shoulder was Sister Bernadette, who greeted me. She directed me into the wood panelled parlour. I recognised the sweet smell of the lavender floor polish. Sister Bernadette directed me to sit on a seat, by the wall opposite the door. 'Your mother has not arrived yet, but will be here in a few minutes,' she reassured me.

Within two minutes the front doorbell rang again. My pulse began to race. I could hear the young nun walk across the hall floor. I began to feel really nervous. As the front door opened, I heard two or more women's voices. The palms of my hands were sweating. Sister Bernadette must have recognised the voices because she left the room to greet the visitors. My floral blouse was wringing wet.

The door opened, and Sister Bernadette ushered two women into the room. The first lady was tall and blonde. She wore a navy dress and jacket. Her face was quite expressionless and her head was tilted back slightly, to give her an air of haughtiness. I thought that she was such a posh, elegant lady. I knew immediately that this was my mother. The lady with her wore a yellow dress and a brown cardigan. She looked dowdy by comparison with her sister. Sister Bernadette ushered the two ladies to the opposite side of the large room, directly across from me.

I stood up, in preparation for the long walk across the room to hug my mother. 'Celine, I would like you to meet your mother,' said Sister Bernadette, and without pausing continued, 'Doreen, I would like you to meet your daughter, Celine.' At this, I broke down in tears and hung my head.

None of us moved.

I wanted to move but I was rooted to the spot. I had trained myself over the years not to initiate physical contact. But to my shock, my mother did not move towards me.

She just said, in a distant cold voice, 'Hello, Celine.'

Though I desperately wanted to, I was unable to mutter even a single syllable. The silence in the room was palpable. Sister Bernadette initiated conversation with my mother's sister. Instead of coming across the room to me which I desperately wanted her to do, my mother turned towards them and joined their conversation. I was still sobbing uncontrollably, but my mother ignored me completely.

My mother, her sister and the nun were having a conversation about people in my family. I heard names mentioned but I did not know who they were talking about. I thought the names of the children were lovely.

There was another lull in the conversation. My aunt gave a brown paper bag to my mother. My mother then walked across the room towards me. I thought, at last she is going to hug me.

I found it hard to stop crying. My breathing was very irregular and I could not speak a word.

My eyes were trying to say what I felt. 'If she could hear what I was saying through my eyes, she would respond as any mother in this situation would,' I thought.

If my mother had thrown her arms around me and said, 'I love you,' I would have forgiven her everything, there and then. I would have forgiven her for the 17 years of sexual abuse, pain, torture, starvation and deprivation that I had suffered through.

She stopped in front of me, more than an arm's length away from me. As she began to speak, I think I realised subconsciously that the physical distance between us represented an emotional chasm.

'I think that you should change your name by deed poll, to a completely different name, so that nobody will find out who you are. I do not want anybody to realise that I am related to you,' my mother said to me. 'I think that it would be better, for all concerned, if you could go and work in

America. Nobody would know who you are there. I will never admit that you are my daughter. Here are some presents for you. These are rosary beads and white scapulars. Both of those came from a grand-aunt of yours. She is a nun in America. Oh, I nearly forgot, here is some Roses' hand cream from your Aunt Rosaleen,' whom she pointed to across the room, as if in introduction. In her own friendly, yet distant, way, Aunt Rosaleen waved daintily at me.

'We will be going now, and I wish you well in the future,' my mother said to me, in final farewell.

She turned away from me.

'Come, Rosaleen,' she commanded. 'Thank you so much, Sister Bernadette,' she said to the nun, as all three disappeared out of the parlour.

I heard no more conversation.

She was gone! And she had not shed even one tear. She had not even touched me. Sister Bernadette came back into the room. I later found out that my grandmother had gone to school in Laurel Hill, Limerick, with Sister Bernadette.

'Will you be all right?' she enquired, as she held the parlour door open for me.

It was obvious that it was time for me to leave. The heavy outside door was already open. She led my slouched shoulders and my heavy heart through it, out into the bright sunlight.

'Well, goodbye, Celine. If you need me for anything that you think is important, please write to me. You have my address,' said Sister Bernadette.

With my mother's speech ringing in my ears, I walked back to Mrs Cooke's house. At least I must have walked back to the house. I do not remember. I was so traumatised, that the remainder of that afternoon, even now, is a complete blank.

I was up bright and early for my work, the following morning.

SIX

Daring to Dream

For the next six months I remained with Mrs Cooke, working as a housemaid. She had a bad heart and she became progressively weaker. She was unable to do even the slightest physical exercise, without having to rest for a long period afterwards. As her condition worsened, she was unable to climb the stairs so she decided to live downstairs.

She had her bed moved down to the large sitting room. Her doctor and Father Bernard O'Dea seemed to be the only visitors that she received. To her doctor, she was a patient who required his medical services, and their relationship was business-like. But Father Bernard was a special friend. She was well able to socialise with him. She called him Bernard and he called her Peggy. They seemed to have a close friendly relationship.

My duties as a housemaid became less and less formal. Most of my time revolved around Mrs Cooke's daily needs. I had to cook her light meals, when she felt hungry. I had to prop her up in bed when she slumped down off her pillows. I had to help her go to the bathroom, when she needed it. I had to give her a bed bath, as she was unable to wash herself. But most of the time I was required to sit and talk to her, or to sit and listen to her.

Mrs Cooke and I got on very well together. While her

body was lethargic and unable to sustain itself physically, her mind was bright and as active as ever. She used to have *The Irish Independent* newspaper delivered every morning and read it from cover to cover, over the course of the day.

One day she called me over to the bed.

'Celine,' she said. 'Would you be so kind as to read the newspaper to me aloud today, as my arms do not have the strength to hold the paper aloft?'

'I will try my best,' I stuttered. 'I cannot read very well.'

'Of course you can, everyone can read these days,' she insisted.

I took the newspaper, and looked at the front page.

'What would you like me to read for you?' I asked sheepishly, as I tried to find some familiar words, as well as the shortest possible ones.

'Start on the front page, read any article you like,' she said in anticipation.

After about five minutes of my reading to her, she said crossly, 'Stop child. You really cannot read. I cannot believe it. How can you expect to get on in life if you cannot read?' she asked me, incredulously. 'We will have to remedy this, my girl.'

Father Bernard called that particular afternoon to see Mrs Cooke. As soon as he was settled, sitting at Mrs Cooke's bedside, with a cup of tea, and a piece of porter cake, Mrs Cooke raised the topic of my illiteracy.

'This lovely young girl is only able to communicate verbally, Bernard. She is unable to read or write,' she scolded. 'You being a man of letters, Bernard, will you help her? I need somebody to read my newspaper to me in the mornings.'

'I would be delighted to assist,' he said.

'I want you to promise me that you will ensure that she will be able to read and write perfectly, even if I am not here to supervise her progress. Will you promise me that?' she exhorted.

'When you put it to me so strongly, it does not look like I have much of a choice,' he replied with a smile. 'I would be delighted to help and if I make you a promise, I will adhere to it.'

'Would you like me to help you, Celine?' he asked me.

'Yes, I would like that very much, Father Bernard,' I replied earnestly, and I meant it.

'Well,' he said, 'you can start today. You can write me a letter telling me all about yourself. We will proceed from there. A letter will give me some idea of how much you already know. Here is my address.'

My first attempt must have been somewhat less than satisfactory, as it took me the best part of two weeks to write two pages. I must have used ten envelopes just trying to write his address correctly. But I loved it. I was determined to be able to read and write perfectly.

After he received my first epistle, he brought my letter back to me on his next visit to Mrs Cooke. He had corrected all my misspellings. There were so many, but all his comments were positive and encouraging. I wrote him a letter as often as I could, sometimes two or three per week, telling him different aspects of my life but keeping many things about my past hidden.

He never complained. He continued to correct my misspellings and always commented positively. He encouraged me to read more, and gradually both my reading and my writing began to improve noticeably.

I began to visit Father Bernard at his home, which was only a short walk away at Glenstal Abbey, on my half-day off each week. We used to have tea and biscuits at the Abbey, and he would talk to me about life in general. On one of my visits to him, I told him that I wanted to be a nurse. I expected him to laugh and say that it would be impossible without examinations. But he did not ridicule me. Instead, he said that he would write me a reference, and he gave me some advice on what to expect, if I set out on my journey towards a career in nursing.

In between times, while I was learning to read and write, and dreaming about a career as a registered nurse, I used to go to dances with some of my friends from the orphanage. Many of them were also working as housemaids in various wealthy houses around the city of Limerick. We used to meet, usually at a dance in the Jetland Ballroom, on a Sunday night. We had great times, laughing and giggling about the sometimes funny characteristics of our respective employers.

These shared experiences were also great when it came to knowing how to deal with the unwanted advances of the husbands of employers. Alcohol was usually the reason behind their indiscretions. The talks were also useful for sharing shortcuts and making life easier for us poor skivvies. We were generally regarded as the lowest form of life by our employers, and were exploited in any and every way possible.

At one of these Sunday night dances I met a fellow called Michael.

He asked me to dance, and I said yes. The dance ended and he asked me to stay for a fast dance. I accepted once again. The band played a medley of rock and roll Elvis-type songs. He whisked me up and down the floor. I was exhausted but impressed. He asked me to 'stay with him' for the remainder of the night, which I did. He was a superb dancer and he wore his hair in the Elvis style. I really thought that he was lovely.

After the dance he took me home in his black Morris Minor car. He asked if he could meet me again, on the following Sunday night. He said that I was one of the best dancers that he had ever seen. He said that he would collect me before the dance, next time. I just nodded my head. I was too pleased to speak.

On the following Sunday evening he called for me at Mrs Cooke's house. This time he had a motorbike as transport.

He told me how to hold on to him, as we were speeding along. I was scared silly trying to get my balance. As we went around corners, the motorbike would lean over, and I used to think that I would surely fall off and be killed. I eventually got used to the technique of 'lean into the bend, will ya,' and really enjoyed the thrill of speed.

Michael used to ride that motorbike very fast. I think he wanted to try to scare me. The high speeds did frighten me at first, but then the thrill of the speed also excited me. I used to urge him on, ever faster, once I got used to it. He did not seem to get as much pleasure, once he realised that I was not as scared as he would have liked. He told me that I had a bit of a tomboy streak in me.

After a Sunday night dance, we were sitting in the Morris Minor just down the road from Mrs Cooke's house, kissing. We always kissed in the car after a dance, before I went home. That is all we ever did, just kissed.

'Will you marry me, Celine?' he asked, while retreating from my lips, after a long, lingering kiss.

'Yes, Michael, I will,' I said, without pausing for thought.

'Great, I really want us to get married,' he added.

'Does this mean that we are now engaged?' I asked gingerly.

'Yes, it surely does,' he assured me.

'I'll see you next Sunday so,' he said, as he leaned across me to open the car door, so I could get out of the car.

For the next two weeks I told all my friends that I had become engaged.

'You're up the pole, aren't ya?' some of my friends taunted me.

Being well familiar with the language used, I assured them that it was not the case.

'Well, you're a fuckin' eejit so,' they said in reply.

But I was officially engaged, as far as anyone was concerned, and that was final. A few of my friends did think that I should tell Sister Bernadette, as I was still technically her 'case'.

'It is none of her business,' I replied.

But a doubt was created in my mind and it niggled me for days.

After a few days the guilt got the better of me, so I wrote her a letter, informing her of my momentous decision to get married. I described Michael as best I could. It was a short letter, as I did not know too much about him. She wrote back to me by return. She reminded me that she was the contact between my mother and grandmother, and my 'auntie nuns', as she referred to them. She invited myself and my fiancé, Michael, to lunch.

That lunch was to be on May 27, 1967, in the convent, at Mount Trenchard, Foynes, County Limerick, where she was then based. I felt uncomfortable about the entire set-up. We drove there in the Morris Minor, and were treated to a pleasant but uncomfortable convent lunch. Afterwards, Sister Bernadette suggested that I should wait in the chapel, whilst she took Michael for a walk in the convent grounds. She said that she wanted to tell him about my family and background. I now felt extremely uncomfortable.

That day was to be the end of our engagement.

They came back from their walk after about an hour. They collected me at the chapel and after the usual pleasantries with Sister Bernadette, we left the convent. He drove about two miles outside the town and pulled the car into the side of the road. He had not looked me in the eye since we met in the chapel. He told me that he would have to break off our engagement.

'Why?' I asked. I already knew the reason.

He said that he could not handle what Sister Bernadette had told him. He said that he came from a huge family of thirteen brothers and sisters. He said that he could not tell this large clan that he was engaged to a girl who was

illegitimate. Being illegitimate was my terrible shame back
then, and here was my greatest fear laid bare for all to see.
He also said that when he married he wanted children.
Sister Bernadette had told him that I would be unable to
have children. She also told him the reason why. He also
told me that he had an uncle – a priest, and an aunt – a nun.

I knew that our engagement was now doomed.

I could feel the pain of rejection once again. It was
beginning to engulf my very being. Why was I being rejected
for something that I was not responsible for? If I was good
enough in every way, why was I being rejected because of my
paternity?

He drove me home.

I never saw him again after that day.

I told Father Bernard all about my troubles in the love
and marriage stakes, as they unfolded between Michael and
myself, with the aid and assistance of the spectre of Sister
Bernadette.

'I think it is time for you to begin your career in nursing,
Celine,' Father Bernard announced one day, as I was serving
afternoon tea.

I blushed heavily, as I was putting the tray down on the
bedside table between them. I had never mentioned to Mrs
Cooke, at any time, that I harboured any ambitions to be a
nurse. In fact, I had never mentioned to anyone, except
Father Bernard, that I yearned for a career in nursing. I had
felt that it was so far out of my reach, and that I was not
acceptable enough socially, to even contemplate nursing as
a career. My self-esteem was so low, that I considered myself
lucky to be employed as a housemaid.

I realised as Father Bernard had made the announce-
ment so loudly, especially for the benefit of Mrs Cooke's
hearing, that there was no going back. He had effectively
given Mrs Cooke notice of my intention to leave her
employment. She was not surprised by the fact that I wanted

to be a nurse. She said that she and Father Bernard had discussed the matter. She said that they had plotted and planned between themselves, as to how they would be able to assist me best. I was still in full blush, and extremely embarrassed that somebody else knew about my lofty ambitions, but I was secretly thrilled and excited as well.

Father Bernard said that they had investigated the possibility of my becoming a trainee nurse in an Irish hospital. He immediately dismissed the possibility. It was a non-runner. He never explained why. I just accepted the fact that it was not to be.

So another avenue had to be found. He said that he had arranged for me to work as a children's nurse. My pulse raced. I could hardly contain my excitement. He explained that it would be a good experience for me on my way to becoming a hospital nurse.

Mrs Cooke asked, 'Would you be interested, Celine?'

'Of course I would,' I replied. 'When would I start? But what about my job here, will you be all right, Mrs Cooke?' I asked with genuine concern.

'Don't worry about Mrs Cooke,' interjected Father Bernard. 'You just go away and become the best nurse that ever was.'

'Even if the clergy do not care what happens to me,' Mrs Cooke said, in mock begrudgery, as she stared at Father Bernard. 'Thank you for your concern, Celine, but you must look out for what is best for yourself. Everything has been arranged,' she continued, 'I will take one month's notice from you today, and next month you will begin work as a children's nurse for our good friend Desmond Woods, in Belfast.'

I mumbled a thank you to each of them and probably genuflected to both of them. I was so grateful to them, as well as being excited. As I floated out of the room, I am sure that my feet did not touch the ground. When I got to the kitchen, I danced around, continually chanting, 'I'm going to be a nurse, I'm going to be a nurse.'

A yell 'Celine' from Mrs Cooke, from the front room, brought me back to reality.

As I walked over to the bed, Father Bernard handed a ticket to me.

Mrs Cooke said, 'Celine, here is an invitation for the William Street Traders' Exhibition at the Jetland Ballroom, tomorrow. A friend of mine, who has a stand there, gave it to me. I was to give it to Father Bernard but as he is unable to go, you may as well have it. You might enjoy yourself. There will be loads to see there.'

'Thank you, I would love to go to the exhibition,' I enthused, as I anticipated a day out, with loads of the latest products to see.

I finished all my duties and chores as fast as I could the next day. One final check that Mrs Cooke was all set up and comfortable for the afternoon, and I was away to the exhibition.

I knew my way around Limerick City quite well at this stage, and could navigate my way to the newly opened Jetland Ballroom, with my eyes closed, as I had been to so many dances there on Sunday nights. I hopped off the bus close to the ballroom and walked up to the entrance.

A man at the door said to me, 'Sorry, young wan, what do you want here?'

'I have been invited,' I said cockily, and promptly showed him my invitation.

'Oh, in that case, you must be very important,' he said, as he bowed and opened the door for me to enter.

The ballroom had a totally different atmosphere on a sunny Wednesday afternoon, than it did with 2500 young people crammed together in it, at a Sunday night dance. It did not seem to be the same place at all. There were very few young people at the exhibition. For one small moment, however, I felt important and carefree, as I walked up and down, perusing the display of goods for sale, on the rows of stands, lined up together, from one end of the hall to the other.

My enjoyment was short-lived.

I was not there for five minutes, when I found myself standing not ten paces away from someone that I recognised. I saw a tall, elegant lady standing, slightly bent over, while examining a piece of decorative cut glass, at one of the stands. I recognised her immediately from our previous meeting at the convent. It was my mother.

I was frozen to the spot. I did not know what to do. Any little feeling of cockiness or confidence that I'd had about me, deserted me.

Should I turn on my heel and slink away without being seen? Should I sprint away through the crowd, out the front door, and away down the Ennis Road, in either direction, just to get away from her? But I did neither.

A tightening in my chest and an overwhelming desire for contact with my mother kept me rooted to the spot. My feelings towards my mother came at me in waves.

I wanted to touch her.

I wanted to talk to her.

I wanted to be hugged by her.

I wanted to tell her that I loved her.

I wanted her to tell me that she loved me.

All these emotions flowed over me.

She had not noticed me yet. This meeting was opportunistic.

There was no planning this time.

There was no time to fantasise about what might happen.

I walked over to her and I put my hand on her gloved forearm, as if to distract her. She was pinned between the wooden counter and me. She could not escape. Before I could say anything, she turned around to meet the person whose touch indicated that someone wished to speak with her. She was smiling. As soon as she saw me, her arm snapped back and her smile became a pair of pursed lips. There was not a grain of humanity evident in their taut, anaemic denial.

'Are you Doreen Clifford?' I asked quickly, as she prepared to depart.

She folded her arms as best she could. She drew herself up to her full height. Her chin jutted out as she looked directly away from me, up at the high ceiling of the ballroom.

'No, never was!' she hissed and pushed me away from her. I stumbled back a step or two. I was shocked beyond belief. I ran to the ladies' toilet and crashed in through the door. The familiar ladies' toilet that I had visited so many times, during Sunday night dances, was now empty. I entered a cubicle, locked the door and cried. From my orphanage experiences, I had learned that if I had sunk so low that crying was necessary, it was also important that I should be able to compose myself, equally quickly. I put my experience to work, and tidied myself up. I left the ladies' toilet, confused yet composed.

I sat in the main hall on one of the many seats and stared through the passing people, my mind entirely blank, incapable of any rational thought. After a short time had passed, I decided to go to the bar to get a glass of lemonade. There were about twenty people in the bar area. Some of them were sitting down at tables, but most were standing in small groups. Most of the drinkers were men, but about five were women. Two women drinking together at a table included the woman who was responsible for my trip to the ladies' toilet.

I went to the bar and ordered a glass of lemonade. I took my glass and positioned myself where I could see the two women at their table. I looked at my mother, but she never allowed her eyes to meet mine. Yet she brazened it out. I think that she was confident that she had persuaded me, her own daughter, that she was not my mother. How could a mother do such a thing to her daughter? How could she think that she had been successful in persuading me that she was not my own mother?

I was in no doubt that it was my mother, but as she denied it, I still needed absolute proof.

As I was watching the two ladies, my mother's companion approached the bar to order a drink. I walked over to where she stood at the bar, ordering the drinks.

'Is your friend's name, Doreen Clifford?' I asked politely.

'No,' she responded, with slow curiosity. 'No, no it's not.'

'Oh,' I said, 'thanks anyway,' as if I had made a mistaken identification.

'Are you related?' she enquired vaguely, but slightly intrigued. 'There is a resemblance.'

'Ah no, I just thought that she might be a cousin,' I replied.

I looked over at my half-finished glass of lemonade, and decided to leave the bar. As I headed for the bar door, I passed within two feet of the lady whom I was positive was my mother. As I neared her table, I stared at her. Our eyes met. This time she did not break her gaze away from me as I passed. I smiled at her, as I thought that I detected a smile forming on her lips. As I got closer, her eyes stared at mine, but it was not a friendly smile on her lips. It was a sneer of triumph.

She had won.

When I left the bar, I raced the remaining distance to the front door. I broke down in uncontrolled crying when I got outside the ballroom. Once again I spent an afternoon walking, all the way across the city, back to Mrs Cooke's house, sobbing. I was in a state of uncontrolled grief because of my mother's rejection. What had an 18-year-old girl, done to deserve this sort of treatment? I was at a loss to know.

It was to be another 16 years before I would meet her again.

Four weeks after this encounter, I finally left Limerick.

SEVEN

New Horizons

When Father Bernard had told me that my position as children's nurse was to be in Belfast, I had to get my first lesson in geography. I had no idea where Belfast was. I had vaguely heard of it, but had no idea where it was situated. Father Bernard came to the rescue with his atlas. He was a well-travelled man and was constantly away on foreign travel. Even then he had visited each of the five continents. By the time I was due to leave for Belfast, I knew well where it was.

I had nothing but bad memories of Limerick. I had no family ties and I was looking forward to leaving it well behind me.

When the day for my departure for Belfast did arrive, there was no great fanfare. Everything I possessed fitted into two cardboard shoeboxes. Apart from the clothes that I was wearing, I had two other changes of clothes. I was wearing one pair of shoes and I had one other pair. I rolled everything that I had up tightly and crammed it into either of the two shoeboxes. Each box was tied individually with string, and then, both boxes were tied together.

Father Bernard helped me to sort out my money. I had six pounds and 14 shillings as savings. Father Bernard said that he would pay for my train ticket to Kingsbridge Station in

Dublin. I would have to pay for a cab to take me from
Kingsbridge Station to Amiens Street Station, where I
would have to purchase a ticket to Belfast. The cab fare and
the ticket to Belfast had to come out of my own six pounds
and 14 shillings.

I learned a valuable lesson from all this financial
planning. It made me realise that I would have to be
financially independent, if I wanted to do anything or go any
place or even to survive on my own. I realised with a shock
that if I did not have my own money, I would have had to
remain in Limerick, for ever. But, he told me, in order for me
to pay for my cab from Grand Central Station in Belfast to
the Malone Road, I would need a different currency. Because
of this currency difference, Father Bernard presented me with
four pound notes and two ten shilling notes in sterling,
specially ordered from the Ulster Bank.

With the equivalent of 11 pounds and 14 shillings in my
purse, I set off for Belfast at seven o'clock one summer's
morning. I hugged Mrs Cooke goodbye, as soon as Father
Bernard came to collect me. He took me to Limerick train
station and bought me my ticket to Dublin. Before he waved
goodbye, he said, 'Our friendship is only beginning, and I
want you to write to me as often as you wish.'

I sat in the carriage and slowly chug-chugged my way to
Dublin on a steam train. As the smoke from the engine,
smelling of coal, wafted in the open windows every time the
train descended down even the slightest incline, or rounded
a bend, I did not mind. I kept thinking, 'At last, I am free, I
am starting a new life.'

I arrived at Kingsbridge Station in Dublin and got a cab
to take me to Amiens Street, where I bought my ticket to
Belfast. I got my train to Grand Central Station in Belfast.
From the station a cab took me to Herberton Park, Malone
Road, where I was to be employed as children's nurse to the
three children of Desmond Woods and his wife, Anne.

My transfer from Limerick to Belfast had gone smoothly.

I was so lucky with my new employers, Desmond and Anne Woods. They were very kind to me. We had a very good working relationship. I had my duties to attend to and I did my work to the best of my ability. I really enjoyed looking after their children. It made me realise something very important – I loved kids. It made me realise that I really wanted to have kids of my own.

Time passed quickly. I experienced all sorts of new freedoms. I began to learn what it meant to have a social life. I went out for meals in a Chinese restaurant. I was able to bring friends back to the house and cook them dinner for the first time.

I also had my first proper birthday celebration. The first birthday card that I ever received in my life was for my 21st birthday. It may seem a long time to wait, to receive a birthday card, but it had just never happened to me. Early on, I had realised that birthday cards were sent by people to convey good wishes to their friends, to mark or remember that special day when they became part of the human race. I was not surprised that I had never got one.

By this stage I was 20 and still working in Belfast. I was living in Herberton Park, off the Malone Road. On the evenings when I did not have to work, I got involved with a charitable organisation called the Legion of Mary. When I had first arrived in Belfast, I did not know anyone. Through the Legion of Mary I met quite a few people, many of whom remain close friends to this day.

The year was 1968 and was a carefree time in my life. That year it seemed like all my friends in the Legion were having birthdays during the summer. I had been to three or four different 21st birthday parties and enjoyed each one, every time.

As that untroubled summer drew to a close, and I realised that there were no more parties imminent, I thought that it would be a great idea if I had a birthday as well. But I did not want just any old birthday. I wanted a 21st birthday. I thought that if I was 21 years of age I would be more acceptable to everyone. My birthday was due, so I put the word out that I was going to have a 21st party in November. But there was a problem. I was only 20 years of age. A wait of over twelve months seemed interminable. I just could not wait another year, so I decided to risk it. I pretended that it was my 21st birthday, in November 1968. I wanted to get lots of birthday cards, and have a birthday party of my very own. Up until that year, it was as if my special day had never existed. I was just the maid at the parties of other people's children, where I had to cook, or more often than not, clean up after it was over. At the parties of Mrs Cooke's children I even bought presents out of my wages of two pounds and ten shillings per week.

My friend Eileen had what she called a 'great wee flat', just off Shaftesbury Square. When most of the furniture was removed to the bedroom, there would be lots of room for dancing. The flat was above a home bakery shop, called 'Whites'. That was to be the venue.

That was the first problem solved.

My boss, Anne Woods, said that she would pay for all the food. She ordered loads of vol-au-vents and other fancy confectionery, from the bakery on the Ormeau Road, which was quite famous at the time.

Music was needed, but this was not a problem as someone was always eager to bring along their black plastic Dansette portable record player, and all the girls were expected to loan a representative section of their record collection suitable for both slow and fast dancing.

Of course, I could not invite any family members, as I was an only child whose parents were dead. That had been my story for two years and would be for quite a lot of years to come. I was sticking to it, rigidly.

I had noticed that 21st birthday parties, in particular, had a certain importance to the adult family members. I also noticed that the person who had reached the magic age of 21 became a very acceptable member of the larger society of his extended family and friends. They got lots of birthday cards and gifts, but it was the birthday cards that meant the most to me.

On the morning of my special day, as I came downstairs to prepare breakfast, Anne Woods and her children were waiting by the table. They greeted me, singing a very harmonious version of 'Happy birthday to you, Happy birthday to you, Happy birthday, dearrrrrrrrr Celine, Happy birthday to youuuuuuuu!'

Then Anne Woods handed me an envelope. I knew that it would contain a birthday card for me. I opened the card and a pound note fluttered to the ground, but it was the words that I noticed. 'To Celine, Best wishes on your 21st birthday, from Desmond, Anne and the children.'

I was overcome by a wave of emotion. As I cried, a feeling of great joy engulfed me.

This was a feeling that I had never experienced before. As I stood there crying, Anne Woods and her children sat at the table smiling. I think that they may have been a little shocked by my response, but I was too out of control to notice. This was for me the very first time that I had ever received a birthday card or present for my birthday.

For the rest of the day, I floated on air. I grew more excited as the evening approached. I was free at six o'clock. By then, I was already dressed in my light blue slim-line satin dress, fully made up and warmly covered in my heavy dark overcoat, to keep out the smut-laden, freezing Belfast fog.

As I ran all the way to Eileen's flat, I could hear the low droning sound of the foghorns coming from the harbour. Eileen and I worked like beavers to get the place ready.

Monica then arrived with her record player and her 18-year-old brother Eamonn, who was instructed to play some records, to create some atmosphere. As the first sounds of Eamonn's treasured copy of *Sergeant Pepper's Lonely Hearts Club Band* LP began to filter around the flat, all work stopped. Three girls rounded on him, all yelling at the same time, 'Take that record off the turntable, yeh little twit yeh, nobody will be able to dance to that rubbish. Put on some decent rock and roll.'

The preparations were complete.

Eight o'clock arrived.

There were no guests.

I began to feel nervous.

I began to realise the risk I had taken. What if nobody at all came to my party?

At twenty past eight, everyone seemed to appear at once. While there was no alcohol, there was lots of music and dancing and everyone was chatting to each other. The music was non-stop and got louder as time passed. The atmosphere was terrific. For the first time in my life, I was the centre of attention. I was thrilled.

The party came to an end just after eleven o'clock. After everyone had left, and with just Eileen and myself remaining in the flat, we spent a few gossip-filled hours discussing the events of the evening, from beginning to end. Eileen got everybody that came to the party to sign a small autograph book, which I still retain to this day. Some of the entries are funny rhymes, others are a bit more poignant.

Oranges grow in Florida,
Peaches grow there too,
But it takes a place like Balmoral Road,
To have a twit like you.
From Michael.

To Celine,
It matters not, how straight the gait,
How charged with punishment, the scroll,
I am the captain of my fate,
I am the master of my soul.
Wishing you a bright and happy future, Mary Lester.

Celine,
Have many friends, and treat them well,
But never to them your secret tell,
For when your friends become your foes,
Around the world, your secret goes.
Best wishes for the future, T. Grosset.

I still have all the cards I received that day. I will always keep them, to remind me of those special friends who celebrated, what for me was MY FIRST BIRTHDAY, even though they thought that it was my 21st birthday. I feel sad that I had to pretend, but it was my belief then that I was accepted only, as they knew me. To tell them the sad saga of my existence, before they knew me, would have put up even more barriers than those that already existed.

I spent two years in Belfast altogether. I was as happy there as I ever was at any time or place, in my life. But the instinct in me to pursue a career in nursing was very strong. I had applied to do nursing in some of the hospitals in Belfast, but I never got past the written entrance examination stage. I was always turned down because I had failed the written examination.

While my written English left quite a lot to be desired, I was not to be dissuaded from my goal of working as a nurse. I felt frustrated by these written entrance examinations and I had heard that some hospitals did not require them. I mentioned this to just about everybody I met as this time.

One evening I met a girl who told me that her sister was a nurse in a hospital in London. I asked her if she thought that her sister might help me to train as a nurse there. She promised me that she would get her sister to meet me the next time that she came home to Belfast.

She was true to her word, and her sister called to see me about six weeks later. She was as nice to me as I could have hoped for. She told me who to apply to, what references I needed and what examinations I would need. My heart almost stopped for an instant.

'Examinations?' I shrieked.

'Yes, just a medical,' she added casually.

'No written exams to be done at the start?' I enquired further.

'No, not at the beginning,' she told me.

That is all I wanted to hear.

I was definitely interested. Interested wasn't the word, I was ecstatic beyond belief. I duly got the application forms and filled them in.

Anne Woods, my employer, and Father Bernard wrote two glowing references for me. I went to Anne Woods' doctor for a medical examination. The medical examination was very general. There were no specifics. My prospective employers did not ask for a gynaecological examination, so consequently they did not receive one. My gynaecological records left quite a lot to be desired.

I sent my application to the Central Middlesex Hospital in North London. From the time I sent the envelope, I had the paint worn off the door, just grabbing at the post each day, to see if I had been accepted.

Two weeks later I received a reply. I gingerly opened the envelope.

This was a big risk for me. If they refused me, I know I would have been inconsolable.

The answer was, 'Yes'.

I was shocked.

I couldn't believe that they had accepted me, almost unconditionally. They hadn't asked if I had parents or any other nasty questions about my past.

I wrote a letter of acceptance immediately and posted it off.

I was on my way. I could not believe it.

I resolved, there and then, to be the best nurse that the Central Middlesex Hospital had ever produced. I was so grateful to them for accepting me. I think everyone was pleased for me. I received a reply by return, stating that I was to present myself at the nurses' home attached to the hospital, two weeks from the date of the letter.

There was no great fanfare for my leaving. I gave Anne Woods two weeks' notice, which I worked through. I had a few more clothes than I had when I came to Belfast, but very little more money. I planned out my journey to London with Desmond Woods' help, because once again I had no idea how to get to London. Desmond said that he would pay my fare to London by way of a bonus for doing such a good job while working for him. He also said that he would take me to the ferry.

So, on August 4, 1969, I boarded the ferry at Larne, just north of Belfast, bound for Stranraer in Scotland. I would take a train from there to Crewe in England, where I would change trains for London.

A period of my life had closed.

I could leave behind all the people that I had told lies to. I was able to clean the slate and that suited me just fine.

I have never been back to Belfast since that day in 1969, although I have remained in touch with some of my friends of that time, over the years.

EIGHT

A Time for Fun

I arrived at the nurses' home attached to the Central Middlesex Hospital on a Sunday afternoon. I was to start my preliminary training school lectures the very next day.

The person in charge of the home was called the home sister. She was expecting me and immediately put me at my ease, while being polite and business-like at the same time. She showed me to my room, told me to unpack and relax a little. She said that she would then return and show me around what was to be my home for at least the next one to two years. I was thrilled. I was not afraid. In fact, I was looking forward to the challenge.

She later gave me a tour of the building, which included the sitting room, the dining room and the kitchens. She gave me a brief run-through of the rules. The most important rule was that I had to be in my room by 12 o'clock at night. No overnight visitors and no men friends were to be entertained on the premises. Those rules suited me perfectly. She assured me that I would learn by experience.

The residence was home to all sorts of nurses, from the type of trainee nurse that I represented, all the way up the ranks to the matrons at the top. I was to learn that a hierarchy existed, but I was used to living at the very bottom of a hierarchy, so that would not cause me any problems. For example, the dining room had a ritualistic code of conduct, whereby the junior nurses were sectioned off from the sisters and matrons. I recognised this class distinction from my previous institutional experience and resolved to avoid getting caught up in its politics. During my training, if I had a bad morning on the ward making mistakes, I made sure not to make eye contact with that particular sister while she was in the dining room after work.

I was also to later learn that I, myself, did not want to remain at the bottom of the pyramid. That day, I realised that I had some ambition in me. I shocked myself but I was also pleased. I wanted some respect for myself.

I started my preliminary training schedule at the Central Middlesex School of Nursing. My salary was 14 pounds per month and my accommodation and my meals were all taken care of at the nurses' home.

I would have to do some of my training on the ward and some of it doing block periods of study, which were lectures away from the ward. There were to be written and practical examinations at the end of the first year. I found that the world of medicine had a language all of its own. For a young, almost illiterate, girl some of the words were real tongue twisters. I kept repeating them to myself until I got them right. Spelling them was an altogether more difficult task. I persisted. I would get the better of this new terminology at all costs. It took a lot of hard mental work. I loved every minute of it. Even after one month, I knew that this was the career for me.

From the very first day that I went 'on the ward' I felt that it suited me very well. I felt needed by the patients. I remember my first ward placement, when I was about 20, was a male cardiac ward. We had to wash a male patient and the other nurse was explaining his anatomy to me. I had seen all these things long ago but I had to pretend I didn't know and that it was all new. I think that I could empathise with the pain and discomfort that they were feeling because of my past and I was able to respond sympathetically. Subconsciously, I needed to be needed. I liked the feeling of being needed. It gave me a sense of purpose. As I continued my training, I realised that looking after my foster-mother and Mrs Cooke had been good preparation. In some ways I had been a nurse since the age of 12.

Now I was in a situation where I could help everyone who was sick, on a daily basis, but now it was my choice. I was definitely in the right business.

While I enjoyed working as a nurse, I found that, in some ways, I enjoyed the social life attached to the nurses' home even more. The communal sitting room was where everybody congregated when they had nothing else to do. The first time that I ventured there on my own, I was made so welcome by all the other nurses that I had no inhibitions about going there after that.

'Living in' at the nurses' home meant that three meals per day were included in my conditions of employment. I learned quickly that this was essential in order to free up the spare cash I needed to go dancing at night, as often as possible.

In the first few weeks at the home I met a girl called Lucy who was one year ahead of me in her training. Lucy remains one of my closest friends to this day. She took her training very seriously but once she was off-duty, all she thought about was going dancing. We got on well from the very start, so when she suggested that we go dancing, I did not need to be asked twice. It soon got to the stage that we went dancing six or seven nights a week. If it happened that we were both off-duty on a Sunday, we would go to an afternoon dance, which was held at The Buffalo in Camden Town, as well.

With Lucy and I as a core, we always got a small group of girls to go with us. I made friends quickly. Nobody asked too many questions about my past. If they did, they got the same old stock answers that I had readily supplied before. The story of my parents being killed in a car crash usually was enough for them to hear. In general, I found that no one was particularly interested.

With all this dancing, living was expensive and cash was tight. We became experts at getting free lifts home from the dances, from any part of the city. Generally, if a group of nurses went out together, it was an unwritten rule that everyone would look out for each other and make sure that we all had a lift home. There was also a pact made at the beginning of the night that everyone in the group would keep an eye out for a fellow 'with a smell of petrol on him'. He was the man designated to give the entire group of us a lift home in his car, no matter which girl he got away with for the night.

Eventually fellows at a dance would realise that if he 'got away' with a nurse, the implicit contract was that if you took one home, you had to take the lot.

It also worked the other way. On the first dance a fellow would ask you what you worked at. Sometimes when you told him that you were a nurse, he would throw his arms up in horror and walk away from you on the dance floor saying, 'Awww noooo, I'm not giving half the nurses in London a lift home.'

All this dancing and staying out late at night had to be done within certain rules. One of the greatest constraints to our dancing enjoyment was the fact that the nurses' home had a curfew of 12 pm. This curfew was enforced by a mature home sister, who took pleasure in making sure we followed it. We had to become increasingly innovative to maintain our late-night dancing schedule without getting caught.

We used to call this home sister, 'Creeping Jesus', as you could never hear her walking about. She was in charge of locking all the doors and entrances. She also had to check the fire escapes and windows for security. We used to wait until she had done her rounds and then leave for the dance. Before we left we would make sure that at least one fire escape could be opened from the outside, by jamming a piece of cardboard in it. It must have been some sight to see seven or eight young nurses climbing up to the fourth floor on the external fire escape, each one carrying their shoes in their hands, so as not to make a racket on the metal stairs. As we did not drink any form of alcohol in those days, we always remembered the designated opened door.

There was one nurse who used to fall foul of our system but because of her seniority we were unable to interfere. This particular assistant matron used to regularly ask us on a Friday night which fire escape door would be left open for the latecomers. Then later, with the eyes popping out of our heads, we would watch her returning home, well inebriated and much the worse for alcoholic wear. Invariably she would stagger up the fire escape, forget which door she was meant to use, and create so much noise trying every door, that the home sister would wake up with the racket. She used to get a telling-off each time but was so oblivious to the message, it fell on deaf ears. She never did get much respect on the wards afterwards. We always held the knowledge of her drunken escapades as ammunition against her, if she ever tried to overstep the line at work.

Although we played hard, we always felt that we had our priorities right. Come Sunday, we never missed mass. We never dreamed of staying in bed on a Sunday morning. If we were working on a late duty, we would go early in the morning. If we were on split duties, we would rush to make the 12 o'clock mass and go back to bed afterwards, depending on how the legs were feeling and what was planned for later that night.

I never had any trouble sleeping but then the girl, whose room was next to mine, decided to learn to play the tin whistle. She used to practise her scales as a method of unwinding after coming off a night duty at 8 am. The sound of her playing was torturous. Waking up in the morning to her rendition of 'The Soldier's Song' guaranteed my early arrival on the ward for work. Apart from that, I never had time to feel sorry for myself and that suited me perfectly.

One topic of conversation among us trainee nurses, that always held my attention, was astrology. I was fascinated by it. As my past life had always been dismal, I eagerly wanted to know what the future held for me. I would have investigated any method of being able to predict the future.

Most of the markets around London had at least one fortune teller. They would read your palm, read the cards or search in their crystal ball to predict your future. The visits usually cost a few pounds, but unfortunately for me they did not seem to have any accuracy attached to them.

I had a patient on the ward around this time that could read tea leaves. I drank a lot of tea during her stay in hospital and got her to read every cup that I drank. I also told my friends about her talents. That lady got so much attention from the nurses. As soon as she woke up in the morning, I would have a line of four or five nurses ready and waiting to have their tea leaves read.

This went on until I heard 'on the grapevine' of a fortune teller who lived in a suburb of Kilburn. It was said that she was in a class above her market colleagues. Rumour had it that she was expensive but very accurate with her predictions. My friend Lucy said she would come with me, so we set off one Saturday afternoon. When we eventually found the house, a large black woman of Caribbean origin welcomed us. We were invited into a room decorated with lots of chains and multi-coloured ribbons. Diaphanous scarves were hanging everywhere and haunting music was playing in the background. She told me that I had to cross her palm with 30 shillings of silver. She took 30 shillings from each of us.

As soon as she had stashed the cash away safely on her ample person, she held both of my hands lightly and began to chant a mantra. After about three minutes of humming, she stopped and told me that she knew that I had endured a hard life. She said that my future life would be much easier, but that my health would give me trouble in the future. I was beginning to think she knew what she was talking about, but then she said that I would have two sons. Then she said, 'In two days' time you will meet the love of your life.' I didn't believe her. I was sure I'd wasted my money.

That was it – The End! The consultation was over and we were ushered out the door. We were flabbergasted. I felt cheated that I had not got value for money. I was angry all the way home and vowed never to visit another fortune teller.

Two days later, I met 'the love of my life'. His name was George.

A bunch of us young nurses regularly went to the Monday night dance at the Gresham Ballroom, on Holloway Road. One of the fellows who asked me to dance that night was a particularly good dancer. He looked very smart and was good looking. He asked if I would keep dancing with him for the rest of the evening. He had lovely manners and was polite, so I agreed. I found out that George was about 30 years old and from Wexford. He was a bus driver and was living with his cousin in Willesden. He was Catholic but his father was a Protestant. In a strange coincidence we later discovered that his first cousin, Dolores, who had been a boarder at the school attached to the orphanage, had actually been the one who wrote my letter to Sister Bernadette when I asked to meet my mother. We were having some soft drinks together at the end of the evening, when he asked if he could see me again. He seemed gentle and attentive, so I eagerly said yes.

This first meeting resulted in a series of magical dates. For me, they were the start of what was to become the closest thing to love that I was ever to experience. We went everywhere together, dances, theatre, walking in parks and musical concerts. They all became part of a relationship with George that was completely new to me. Even the simple act of walking in a park was new to me. I had never been in a park before. On one date I nearly got us arrested. I picked a bunch of flowers in a beautiful small park near Harley Street. The park warden chased after us and warned me, 'You can't pick the flowers here, Miss. I'll let you off this time but don't do it again.' George was mortified.

We went to the seaside one Sunday and to the Royal Albert Hall one night. When everyone stood up for the standing ovation, I blessed myself by mistake. I was so embarrassed.

We held hands and kissed lightly on the lips as he took me home at night. George never made any sexual advances towards me, but as time went on and my feelings for him grew, I think I would have agreed, if he had said anything. After about six months I tried to tell him that I loved him but while I did feel something for George, I was unsure what those feelings were. I had no tangible experience of the word 'love', so while I said the words I wasn't entirely sure what they meant.

One thing I was sure of was that I did not feel loved by George. I did not feel that I deserved to be loved by him or anybody else. Also, as a form of self-protection, I could not allow myself to be loved by anyone. The risk would be too great. I could not allow anyone to get that close to me. If I committed to someone so completely and they then rejected me, I would be destroyed. It was not an option. I could not allow anyone to love me.

As it turned out, I did not get the opportunity. About a year into our relationship, George received news that he had inherited a large farm in Ireland, from a close relative who died. He said that he would be expected to go home to Ireland and work his inheritance as a business. I'll never know for sure, but he may have been close to asking me to marry him and to go back to Ireland with him as his wife.

If he was going to ask me, I pre-empted his request. I told him that I was illegitimate. While he may have been a carefree bus driver in London, George was from staunch conservative Anglo-Irish Protestant stock. When I told him I could immediately see the disappointment in his eyes. He muttered something about how his parents would never approve of me. I knew then that I had lost him. He returned to Ireland to claim his inheritance. I was devastated when he went back. We wrote three or four letters each week to each other. He promised to return to London to be with me. I believed him and I would not go out dancing at night with the others. They had pestered me to go dancing every other night but I declined each time, saying that I was George's girlfriend. I was staying true to him until he returned.

As time went on, the letters became fewer and less frequent. It took me about three months to realise that George, 'the love of my life', was not coming back.

I became sick with all the stress and matron helped me to organise a holiday in Ireland. I was to stay with Kit and Tony. I went to see George and met his parents. I'll always remember that George's mother kissed me when we first met. It was a lovely feeling. She even used to make me presents afterwards, little pieces of crochet. I still have some of them. But it was obvious to me that George felt uncomfortable and I only stayed one night. He gave me a jewellery box at the train station when he was seeing me off, saying that he'd write, but I never heard from him again. He had let me down.

Once again, I was not fit to be accepted by anyone.

NINE

Uninvited Guests

I did my best to move on and to try to forget about George. It was made a bit easier by how busy I was. When I wasn't working and socialising, I was studying. I studied hard and eventually I got the better of the difficult medical terminology. I did well in all my exams and was over the moon when I qualified as a nurse, in February 1972. It was only a few weeks later when I met my husband-to-be, in March 1972. Harry Roberts was a member of my branch of the Legion of Mary and of the Pioneer Total Abstinence Association. Both of these organisations are run in close association with the Catholic Church. I was aware of him as an associate member, but until March 1972, I had never been interested in going out with him, or being linked with him in a romantic way. Then everything changed.

I was at the hospital one Sunday. I was working on-call duty, in accident and emergency theatre, on the night shift. Being on-call meant that if there was no surgery actually taking place in the theatre, I was free to amuse myself. I could pass the time in whatever way I chose, as long as I was immediately available to attend an emergency surgery. Accident and emergency is usually a quiet enough spot on a Sunday evening.

There was an assembly hall attached to the hospital. This

hall was used for all sort of occasions connected with the hospital: conferences, department meetings and any larger gathering of hospital personnel. When it was not in use by the medical staff, it was available for use by the local community. The local branch of the Pioneer Total Abstinence Association was one of the organisations that used the hall, for its meetings and social get-togethers.

On this particular Sunday evening, the Association was having one of its socials, namely a dance for its members. As I was on-call and more or less confined to the hospital I found my way to the Pioneer's dance.

As the dance was in full swing, I went in to have a look rather than participate. I was just passing the time really. One of the first people that came over to greet me was the ever-gregarious Harry Roberts. Harry was in ebullient form. He had just returned from a pilgrimage to Lourdes, in France, as a helper with the Legion of Mary. He had enjoyed his trip immensely and was bursting at the seams to tell his friends and anyone who would listen, all the details of his busman's holiday. Somewhere, during his story, which ranged from intricate details of people's disabilities, to the actual witnessing of miracles by himself, he asked me to go out on a date with him. While I had never considered him in a romantic way, I thought that he might have some caring qualities, which I admired. As I was on duty that evening, I agreed to meet him later in the week.

On the following Wednesday night we arranged to go to the cinema. As far as relationships went, I still felt the same way as I did with George. I wanted a relationship with a man on the basis that we could go out dancing or to the cinema or theatre together, and that was it. There was to be no physical intimacy.

I had to struggle with my extremely different needs. On the one hand, I wanted a relationship without physical intimacy, while on the other hand I wanted to be married and have children. An Immaculate Conception as experienced by the Virgin Mary would have suited me fine, but even Harry Roberts, with all his 'pull' within the Catholic Church, could not have supplied that.

And yet my need to have children was very strong. I just loved kids. I knew that this was a problem I could not avoid for ever.

Over the years I had many problems with my internal reproductive system. I seemed to spend half my time visiting gynaecologists. At each visit, the result of the examination always had the one common conclusion – it would be unlikely that I would be able to have children. Those gynaecological conclusions, while very pessimistic, always left me with a tiny hope that I might be able to have a child. This hope was indeed very small. Most of the gynaecologists predicted that I would not be able to live any form of stable life, never mind have a baby. While I knew the damage to my reproductive tract was serious, deep down I kept nurturing that spark of hope, however miniscule.

Of course, I did not mention any of this to Harry on our first date. We went to the cinema and afterwards he took me for a cup of coffee. Of course, Harry wanted to know about me. He began to ask all the usual questions that come up when two young people meet. My personal background loomed large once again. Having suffered through the pain of George's recent rejection, I decided that I was not going to let it be an issue again. I was not going to waste my time with somebody, if I was then going to be unacceptable, when they found out the truth about my background and parenthood. Towards the end of our first date I decided to declare my parental status. I came straight out and told him, 'I am illegitimate.'

I waited for the usual response of concealed shock but none came. Looking back, I should have realised the disadvantage at which I had placed myself. But I didn't. I gave all my power away in one small sentence. I let him know my weakness without knowing anything about him. I was to greatly regret parting with my secret so casually. But I did not realise it at the time.

If only we all had the benefit of hindsight. If only I had had the benefit of some maternal advice or support. I was on my own. I had to make my own decisions, whatever their consequences. At the same time I could not disclose my secret to everybody; otherwise I would not be wanted. It was the nightmare scenario that I wished to avoid at all costs.

Harry did not seem to mind. As he walked me home, he asked me to marry him. Yes, on the first date, he said, 'Will you marry me?' He was always joking, so I laughed it off, but afterwards I thought that it was a cheeky thing to do on a first date, particularly since I had just told him my biggest secret. I was glad though that, even knowing about my illegitimacy, he genuinely seemed keen to see me again and be with me.

Harry worked as a security man in a city-centre bank. As we both worked shift hours, we met at all different times in the days that followed. We met two or three times a week initially. We usually went dancing or to the cinema. Neither of us drank alcohol. I was very pleased to be taken out dancing, especially by somebody to whom I felt totally acceptable. Before that I had not felt acceptable at all to anybody; Harry seemed like a knight in shining armour to me.

We began to spend more and more of our free time together. I sometimes cooked for him at the flat that I now shared with Lucy and some other nurses. Five of us had moved out of the nurses' home a few months earlier, as we had begun to earn a little bit more money when we qualified. We also used to work back-to-back shifts to make extra money. It was worth it to get away from living under curfew!

We may have kissed on the lips occasionally but no sexual intimacy ever took place between us. I felt unable to contemplate any sexual behaviour and Harry seemed content to have that type of relationship with me. I was quite happy to continue together on this basis and in July 1972 we became engaged to be married. None of my friends ever criticised Harry but none of them ever commented on Harry in a positive way either. Harry was just Harry. He did not offend anybody. He never antagonised anyone. Neither did he ever engage anybody in any kind of serious debate. Everything was relatively simple in Harry's life. He had simple personal rules, which he adhered to. He knew his place in the way of things and in the world, and he was not going to rock the boat.

Harry came from Graiguenamanagh, County Kilkenny in Ireland. His parents had a small farm and a large family. Harry was the youngest of a family of 12 children, five boys, six girls and Harry. The farm was not large enough to sustain and educate 12 children, so at 15 Harry had left school. He was sent to work in his cousin's pub in Dublin. When we met, I didn't know or care what formal education Harry had behind him. His aspirations and prospects as regards a career were not even an issue. Here was somebody to whom, I, an illegitimate bastard child, was acceptable. That was all I needed to know.

We decided to get married early in the following year.

Our relationship continued on through the summer of 1972 and into the following winter, much the same as it had begun. We went dancing quite a lot at the Irish Club, where they had many dance bands or show bands. The show bands were very popular in Ireland at the time and were very popular with the Irish crowd who went to the Galtymore Dance Hall in Kilburn, North London. The only time we touched physically was when we were dancing. The fact that we were engaged to be married changed nothing. This suited me perfectly. I do not know how I would have reacted to sexual advances from Harry at this time. I imagine that I would have rejected them. I would have used the excuse that any sexual behaviour, outside marriage, was unacceptable to me. Harry had been brought up in a strict Catholic regime, within a strict Catholic family and his moral values were those dictated by the Catholic Church. The hierarchy of the Church tolerated no deviance from the rules and Harry followed these dictates to the letter. His obedience to the laws of the Catholic Church and its God was absolute. The Catholic faith dictated that pre-marital sex was sinful and not to be engaged in. It was not allowed.

But people did engage in pre-marital sex. I was proof of that. I wondered how did he see me in this context? I didn't ask him but I believed that he did not hold me in very high regard. It was the teaching of the Catholic Church in those days that illegitimate children had to pay for the sins of their parents, with their own suffering. The nuns at the orphanage told me that, frequently. I heard that message so often, that I detest hearing it, in any context, to this very day.

How did Harry view my parents?

All his life he was indoctrinated in the teachings and propaganda of the Catholic Church. It inculcated itself in Harry to such a degree that to this day he thoroughly believes himself to be a far superior human being to people who are not supporters of, or who have fallen foul of, the Catholic Church's rules and regulations. My parents were an example of sinners who had broken its laws, by indulging in sexual relations with one another, while unmarried. If he had known them at the time, he would have regarded them, as sinners of the highest order. I'm sure he would have seen them as unfit to consort with, at any level. I, as their product, would not have rated much higher. And there, the dichotomy introduces itself. I should have realised it at the time, but didn't. I continued on with the plans for the wedding, unaware.

There was no love between us. The word love was never mentioned. The same feeling that I had for George did not develop in this relationship. The feeling of wanting to be with someone special, all the time, did not exist. I just knew that I wanted to be married and to have children. All my friends were getting married, so I assumed that it was the normal, natural and proper thing to do. Harry must have assumed the same thing, as he never once told me that he loved me during our engagement.

During the Christmas holidays of 1972, I was working most of the time. I would work so that other nurses with young families, who would prefer to be at home with them over Christmas, did not have to miss out. I was not bitter about working the unsociable Christmas shift-hours. London was a cosmopolitan city, as opposed to the incestuous, Catholic-dominated atmosphere of Ireland, at that time. On the wards there were many nurses of different religious backgrounds, to whom working over Christmas was just another day. As I had no family to visit, it was better for me to have the distraction of work. The girls in the flat had all gone home to visit their families, so I had the entire place to myself.

I worked the 8 am to 5 pm shift on Christmas Day and went back to the flat after work. Harry had Christmas dinner with his brother Paddy and his wife, and was due to come and see me at the flat later in the evening. I hadn't been invited but I was on-call anyway with a nurses' agency. As he arrived I had just finished cooking my own Christmas dinner. It consisted of two sausages. That was all that was edible in the flat at the time. It sounds very meagre fare for Christmas, but I was not one bit bothered.

Harry arrived and we listened to some music. After an hour or two had passed, an extraordinary thing happened. He compromised himself and his strict adhesion to Catholic moral standards. He made advances towards me. I was unprepared for such an approach and also shocked. It was totally out of character for Harry.

'What are you trying to do?' I asked.

'I want to have intercourse with you,' he replied.

I quickly made it known to him that his advances were being rejected. Having sex with me was definitely out of the question.

'It won't matter, I'll marry you anyway,' he persisted.

'No way,' I replied. 'It cannot happen.'

'All right so,' he huffed.

With that, he sucked in his breath, stuck out his chest, turned and marched across the room, slammed the front door with an almighty crash as he left. We managed to patch things up after this, but sex or 'intercourse' in Catholic Church terminology, as used by Harry, was never mentioned again between us while we were engaged.

Over the years, I had written to Father Bernard regularly, but not as often as previously. I had gone to see him in July in Glenstal when I got engaged and told him that I was getting married to Harry and that the ceremony was to take place in the spring of 1973. Father Bernard said that he was so pleased for me and insisted that he would perform the ceremony, wherever it might be.

When we had announced our engagement in July 1972, we had arranged to be married in St John's Cathedral in Kilkenny City in Ireland on February 24, 1973.

A wedding breakfast and reception for 50 guests was also booked at the time. I had wanted to have a small quiet ceremony in London without fuss. But when Harry's parents heard that their youngest son was to be married, they insisted that it had to be at home in Ireland. While they insisted on the geographical location, they did not insist that they would pay for any of the expenses. I had to fund everything.

In the lead-up to our nuptials, the number of uninvited

players in my life increased. I had no control over who they might be. I had no guidance from anyone about how to handle the unexpected intrusion into my life of so many new, unknown people.

First of all, was the arrival in my life of Harry's parents. They turned out to be a couple in their mid-sixties. They made a poor but honest living on the home farm, which was now being run on a daily basis by one of Harry's brothers. They were a conservative, uneducated, but pleasant couple, who lived their lives according to the strict moral teachings of the Catholic Church. They were not unusual in the rural Ireland of the early 1970s.

As I was now going to be a permanent fixture in Harry's life and, more importantly, as I would be his legal wife, problems arose. The first problem had been Harry actually telling his parents that he was going to get married. As most of the remainder of his 11 brothers and sisters were already married, I hadn't thought that Harry getting married would come as a great shock to his parents. I assumed that they would accept it as fact and give him their blessing. In fact, at the time they didn't seem very pleased, but we got over that. His father wrote me a letter a few months later to welcome me into the family.

The second problem was, of course, that he was not getting married to just anyone! He was marrying an 'illegitimate girl'. Harry was under pressure.

"T'would kill Mam and Dad if I told them that I was getting married to a bastard,' he announced to me one evening.

My heart sank. Here it was again. My past had come back to haunt me once more.

'Tell them that my parents are dead,' I offered immediately, without doubt or hesitation. I had used this explanation so often previously that it tripped off my tongue as easily as if I had available as proof in my handbag a validated copy of their death certificates, and a letter from the Pope to say that he himself had officiated at their burial.

'That would be for the best,' Harry accepted gratefully. 'We won't say anything to the brothers and sisters either, 'cos they wouldn't approve if they knew the situation,' he added, taking a mile, having been given an inch.

When I met both his parents for the first time, Harry introduced me to them and, barely pausing for breath, he added, 'This is Celine that I am getting married to. Her parents are dead!'

It was his first denial of me.

I did not remark on it, but to hear myself introduced in such a manner, hurt me. I ignored the hurt and carried on with the pretence. After all, I had been the one to suggest it in the first instance. I felt so insignificant and of such a low social standing, that I would have agreed to any excuse about my parenthood. I wanted to be acceptable to his parents, and if my illegitimate status was so bad it might cause their premature demise, my parents were going to be dead first. It worked. Everyone just assumed that if my parents were dead, they must have been legally married to each other before they died. Once again we had 'an Irish solution to an Irish problem'. And so it was that the entire Roberts family thought that my legally married parents were dead. I was therefore entitled to become Harry's wife. While I understood about his parents, I could not really figure out why he could not tell some of his brothers and sisters the truth about me. I also wondered why I was so acceptable to him and not the others. The bottom line was that he did not have the courage to tell anyone that mattered to him that I was illegitimate. It was for his own protection. He felt that he would have been lowering himself, in their eyes, if he had to declare my illegitimacy.

I have often thought over the years: 'Who is he, to consider himself so important in the grand scheme of things, to deny me? Who are his family, that they are so important that I had to pretend that I was something I was not, just so their dignity would not be tainted by my existence?' At the time though this did not bother me, as my goal was to get married and have children.

I was going to achieve that ambition, whatever it took.

Whatever we had to say to his family, to maintain the status quo, I would agree to it. The scandal, created among the neighbours in Graignamanagh, County Kilkenny, when it became known that the youngest son of Harry and Cathy Roberts was to marry an illegitimate girl, would have been too much to contemplate.

The day of the wedding finally arrived, February 24, 1973.

On the night before the wedding I stayed with one of Harry's sisters, Alice. As Harry did not drink alcohol, he did not have a stag night. He stayed at his parents' home, a few miles away. It was all planned between Harry and I, to be a very low-key wedding, an event to be got through, with a minimum of fuss.

On the morning of the wedding I was up at dawn. I could hardly sleep, as excitement, such as I had never allowed myself to experience previously, took over. First of all, the dresses! Under no condition was I wearing anything that was less than perfect. With my history of second-hand clothing from charitable organisations, there was no way that I was getting married in anything less than brand-new.

For months I had devoured women's magazines, looking for suitable ideas for my wedding dress. *Bride Magazine* provided the answer. Their 'Wedding Dress of the year 1973' was the one for me. Nothing less would do. The dress was white, with lace on the cuffs and a low-cut neck. It was for sale from Berketex for £265 in London and I duly purchased it for my most special day, without the slightest consideration of the cost.

I had my own bridesmaids for the day. Breege Dolan, who was also a nurse and had trained with me, was my chief bridesmaid. Anastasia O'Mahoney, Harry's niece, was the second one. I also had a page boy, Harry's nephew. The bridesmaid dresses had been subject to the same level of pre-purchase search as my own. They turned out to be turquoise and white with a matching hat. All our shoes were white and plain enough, but they were as expensive as I could find. I did not want to be reminded of the time when I could not afford shoes at all. Their flowers were white carnations, with entwined ivy.

All organisation and preparation for the wedding was done by myself, or with the help of my friends. I had no family to help me. Part of my 'manufactured' family began to arrive at the house later that day. It consisted mainly of my previous employer Mrs Cooke's extended family. Mrs Cooke's health had deteriorated dramatically following surgery and she had died about two years after I had left her employment. I had gotten on very well with the entire family and had kept in touch with her relatives. They were very genuine, good people. If I could have looked upon any of my employers as being family, the Cookes were as close as it came. When they heard that I was getting married, they were thrilled and genuinely delighted for me.

Old Mrs Dillon, who was Joan Cooke's mother, had asked me what I wanted as a wedding present. Without hesitation, and half in jest, I had replied, 'A family.'

'Without any parents,' I had added cautiously.

'I will be your grandmother,' she said with a grin. 'John, my son-in-law, will be your uncle,' she added, obviously enjoying the proposed charade. 'And Carmel, John's wife, will be your aunt. What else do you need in the way of manpower? A chauffeur? A butler perhaps? I am really going to enjoy this wedding.'

John 'my uncle', who was to 'give me away' arrived early

on the day, looking much the worse for alcoholic wear, from the night before in his favourite pub. He headed straight for the kitchen and became another liability for Alice. She had to cope with my hung-over 'uncle' and his ceaseless requests for more whiskey and copious amounts of tea, which he insisted he needed to drink to carry him through his 'niece's' wedding day. Every time he mentioned 'his niece', he stared in my direction, catching my attention with a very exaggerated wink of his left eye, simultaneously accompanied by a short nod of the head. Every time he winked at me, all I could do was collapse with laughter.

My chief bridesmaid, Breege, could not be roused out of the bed. She had arrived from London, late the previous evening, also a bit the worse for alcoholic wear. She had travelled over with about five of my friends, who were all nurses in London hospitals. I think that there was quite a lot of alcohol drank on the journey from London to Kilkenny. Not all Irish nurses in London at that time were teetotallers! Six off-duty nurses on their way to a wedding in Ireland were quite a formidable force to contend with. But they promised that they would be on their best behaviour on the day of the wedding.

Alice and I dragged my hung-over bridesmaid out of the bed. Hot strong sweet tea, with a shot of Jameson whiskey added for fortification, did the trick. She was stuffed into her very expensive bridesmaid dress, which she had only tried on in London once before. The dress fitted perfectly. Breege had not put on an ounce of weight. She was pretty well ready. Anastasia, the other bridesmaid, had been waiting patiently the whole time and was ready. We had packed the page boy off with his father, so he was ready at the church.

My 'uncle' John was ready.

Alice was ready to leave.

I was the only one who was not ready. My hair was being done by a local stylist, and was taking ages.

Breege had joined John at the kitchen table, as he had produced a bottle of Bushmills whiskey. He was looking for willing assistants to help him drink the bottle dry. She was keen to accommodate him.

The place was in bedlam. It was now ten o'clock and I had to be in the church by eleven.

I eventually separated John and my chief bridesmaid from the, by now, half-empty bottle of whiskey. Outside, I bundled John, along with myself, into a waiting white Ford Zodiac. I had booked it as a wedding limousine to take us to the church and afterwards to the hotel. The February air was still and chilled, as we followed Alice's husband's tiny, post-war baby-Austin, with the bridesmaids inside. After three long miles, along the narrow road, twisting down the hill to the church, we arrived in convoy.

It was five past eleven. I was getting married, and I did not want to be too late, just in case Harry changed his mind.

There was no great excitement at the church. Michael, Harry's brother, the best man, with his lean and angular good looks and self-assured cocky attitude, was already waiting at the door of the church. He smiled when he saw us arriving on schedule. He gave us a two-handed thumbs-up signal and disappeared into the gloom of the church entrance. He came out again almost immediately, brandishing an unfinished cigarette, to explain his hasty reappearance. It made a large arc through the air as he flicked it from between his fingers, to where it landed on the ground, close beside me. 'Stub that out, will ya, before ya come in,' he ordered with a grin, before he turned and disappeared once more into the darkness.

I ignored both the cigarette and the accompanying order as I took hold of my 'uncle' John's proffered arm. We stopped in the entrance hall of the church. I took a deep breath, while John coughed up his lungs, the result of too many early-morning cigarettes. As our eyes met, in an eloquent look, the two of us moved off.

Breege held open the inner door, as we passed through. When she opened the door, the church organist began to play the leading strains of 'Here comes the bride'.

One step in, 'Oh sweet Jesus, where is my bouquet?' I shrieked.

'Oh Christ, it is in the holy water font,' said Breege, as she rushed to get it. I had left it there, as I smoothed out the imaginary wrinkles on my dress, before my triumphal march up the aisle.

'Jaysus, it's wringin' wet,' said Breege, as she manically shook the living daylights out of the once-pretty bunch of roses, intertwined with scented white hyacinth tips.

'They will do as they are,' I groaned, as I aggressively snatched them from her.

John shrugged his broad shoulders and inclined his head towards the altar as if to ask, 'Are we ready now?'

Off we went again, on our second attempt at progress towards the contrasting brightly lit, high altar.

I noticed that the number of people on each side were somewhat unbalanced. On 'my side', on the left, were about six or seven of my colleagues from nursing, my 'aunt' Carmel and my 'granny', old Mrs Dillon. But on the right-hand side we were outnumbered by about five or six to one. We were running at 70 or more – so much for a small wedding! Harry's relatives had appeared out of every nook and cranny, for Harry's big day out. There was nothing that I could do about it now.

Father Bernard's beaming, welcoming smile, beckoned. When we reached the gates of the railings that enclosed the altar area, John took hold of my hand and placed it in Harry's hand. Harry had appeared, as if out of nowhere.

As John left me and moved away, time and space seemed to stop for me for an instant. A cold, clearly defined thought flashed through my mind. Its guilt-laden reality said to me, 'That man who has just 'given me away' should have been my father!' This was immediately followed by, 'I wonder what he looks like?' It was such a small instant in time but it really shook me. In 25 years of my life, I had never asked myself that question. On the few occasions that my father's identity had arisen, for example, when in conversation with my minder, Sister Bernadette, it was always made into a non-issue. 'Your father is now married with a family of his own, and if he were to find out about you, it would wreck the whole family,' is what I was always told. Consequently, I never even thought about him.

I could not contemplate being the cause of the disintegration of his entire family, especially of his two sisters who were nuns. I had been told about them a million times at the industrial school and that, as Mercy nuns in Cork, if they were embroiled in a scandal involving my father, the results would be cataclysmic for both them and possibly, the entire Catholic Church in Ireland. Subconsciously, I had decided that I was not going to take on those responsibilities. I had enough to deal with at that stage, just trying to survive every day. But then at the very moment that I was going to take my prospective husband's hand in mine, at my wedding, I wanted to know what my father looked like! I could not believe it. I was just about to get married and all I had was a blank picture of my father in my mind and I wanted to know what he looked like.

I did not realise it then, but it was to be a life-changing moment for me.

After that tiny immeasurable pause, I was brought back to reality, by the reassuring touch of Father Bernard's hand. He grasped my wrist and whispered, 'Celine, I am so happy for you today.'

He then turned to Harry and said, 'Harry, I know that you will make a wonderful husband for Celine. I have known her for a long time. She is a special friend of mine.'

There may have been an implicit threat to Harry in Father Bernard's comments, but I think he could see that I looked like I was happy in my choice, and he was willing to respect that. Harry detected no obvious or even subtle threat, as they subsequently became very good friends.

The remainder of the ceremony went really well. Everyone gave the correct responses when asked. Michael, the best man, produced the gold wedding ring from his inner jacket pocket on cue. Father Bernard pronounced us man and wife for better or worse, for richer or poorer, until death us do part.

As we were officially married, I felt an emptiness. Whatever magic I had expected to feel just wasn't there. I just hung on to the fact that I had to get married.

We then accompanied Father Bernard and our best man and chief bridesmaid, into the sacristy, a little room just off from the main altar area, where we both signed the State Register of Marriage. Michael and Breege, who for a short space of time were transformed from best man and bridesmaid, into witnesses for the state, duly witnessed our signatures. Once the paperwork for the governing bureaucracy was completed, we returned to our positions at the altar rails. We kissed and walked back down the aisle, arm-in-arm, smiling and bowing to the attendant Roberts' family to our left, while grinning at the exaggerated fawning of the fake 'Clifford' family on our right-hand side. I still couldn't quite believe that this was really happening to me.

Out into the bright February sunlight and a photographer awaited us. When we emerged, it was high jinks from everybody as we were showered with rice and confetti. In front of the church we were pushed to and fro by the photographer and ordered to smile on demand, as he clicked his camera shutter and wound on the roll of film to the next frame. In between shots, we chatted to everyone who wanted to extend their best wishes to us for our future married life together. It was all an exciting whirl to me.

Then, 'The bride and groom with their respective parents,' ordered the photographer. 'Granny' and 'uncle' John obliged immediately on cue. They stepped forward and arranged themselves at Harry's side, without a prompt. Harry never batted an eyelid. He participated in the parental charade, as if he, himself, had been at my parents' wedding. The photographer completed the various permutations and combinations of all the possible groups that might have been offended, if they had not been included in a photograph.

Then Harry and I sat in the back of the Ford, which was all decked out in various coloured ribbons, and away we went. We were at the head of a posse of cars, all blowing their horns and generally making quite a din, in Kilkenny City just after midday on a Wednesday. When I got out of the car at the hotel, I was mortified to find that our car had three or four old rusty tin cans, accompanied by three or four old worn-out leather boots, tied to the rear bumper. I always thought that the tradition of old boots and cans was beneath me. I must have had some little bit of pride in me, however small and difficult to locate at times.

That ended the church portion of the wedding of Celine Clifford and Harry Roberts, whom were now known as Mr and Mrs Roberts.

I was delighted – I now had a different name. Illegitimate Celine 'O'Brien' Clifford was gone for ever.

The wedding party arrived at the hotel for the reception. Most people went straight to the bar for a drink. In mid-afternoon everyone was called to the dining room. There was still quite a lot of ceremony to be got through. As soon as everyone was seated, the wedding breakfast was served.

Everyone had made an early start that morning and were glad to have an opportunity to eat something warm.

As people ate, Michael was preparing his speech, and sorting out the various telegrams that had arrived from the members of the family that either could not attend, or were not invited. Those who were invited but could not attend generally lived in some far-flung region of the world, like the USA or Australia. Michael leaned over to Harry and I in the middle of his preparations. 'Jaysus,' he said, 'all the telegrams are from the Roberts' side of the family.'

Overheard by 'uncle' John, and as if by magic, he produced a sheaf of telegram forms. 'Here are the Clifford telegrams, I collected them at the desk earlier,' he coughed, as he handed over an appreciably thick sheaf of papers.

'Oh, oh great, great, I just wondered where they were. I knew that there had to be some from the other side. Thanks, thanks a lot,' said Michael.

As the sound level of people talking together rose, Michael took this as a signal to recommence his duties as best man. He stood up and tapped a glass with a spoon to gain everyone's attention. This was the beginning of his speech, the part of his job that he liked least.

'Reverend Father, ladies and gentlemen, I am not used to public speaking, so I decided to start off with a joke. My mother told me not to tell this joke because there is some bad language in it and she would be embarrassed. So here goes, prepare to be embarrassed, mother.'

Everyone chuckled.

'Because there are so many Irish people here today who work in England, this joke is especially for you. Two Irishmen, Paddy and Micky decided to go and work in England, because there was no work to be had in Ireland, and the streets of London were paved with gold. After a few weeks in London, they could find no work. They spent their time wandering the streets. One day, while looking in an upmarket shoe-shop window, Paddy said, "Jaysus, Micky, look! Crocodile shoes £375! Imagine paying that much for a pair of shoes! The English must be awful eejits, altogether. We would make a fortune if we could sell crocodile shoes. Crocodiles live in Africa, let's go to Africa." "Naw, you go ahead Paddy, I'll stay in London and take my chances," said Micky. "Right" said Paddy "I'll go on my own and make my fortune. I'll be back in twelve months time. I'll be rollin' in money!" Three years passed and Paddy had not returned, so Micky decided to go to Africa and find Paddy. When he reached Africa, he started to ask people if they knew where Paddy the Irishman lived. "Aw yeah, he lives about 30 miles upriver, in the jungle. Just follow the bad smell and you'll find him," he was told. About 25 miles upriver, Micky began to see thousands and thousands of rotting crocodile carcasses piled at least ten feet high on the riverbank. The stench of the dead crocodiles was unbearable. Five miles on he found Paddy. He was out, standing in the middle of the river, sleeves rolled up, with his eyes staring fixedly at the flowing water. Micky waded out to him and asked, "How are ya Paddy? How're ya doin? Did you make your fortune yet?" "Ah no," said Paddy, "I'm fed up, if the next fuckin' crocodile comin' down the river is not wearing shoes, I'm goin' home!"'

The indigenous Irish laughed at the joke, but the London Irish were not able to laugh at themselves in those days and so their laughter was polite. But Michael visibly relaxed. When he was finished, he asked Father Bernard to 'say a few words' as it were, and sat down.

Father Bernard stood up and delivered the usual inoffensive speech, delivered at such occasions by the priest who conducts the wedding service. It was as if he hardly knew me. He wished Mr and Mrs Roberts the best of luck for a long and happy marriage, and then sat down. Michael then proceeded to read out all the telegrams from people who wanted to wish the happily married couple the very best of luck on their wedding day.

When the attending Roberts family recognised a telegram from a member of their family, a loud cheer went up, as if to say, 'That's our side and we're proud of them, even if they are not here today.'

When the Roberts family did not recognise the sender of a telegram, 'uncle' John raised his arm and roared in support. He became cheerleader. As my friends had not got a clue, they followed John's lead in vocal support. As soon as John lifted his arm, it became a signal to my gang to cheer and applaud loudly, as if they were musicians following the leader of an orchestra.

I had many best wishes from relatives like Auntie Penelope in New Zealand, Great Aunt Maud in Gibraltar, Cousin Theodore, twice removed, from Rhodesia and Cousin Jeremy who lived in Malta. I did not recognise any of the names. It seemed that I had many relatives who lived abroad and could not be contacted in a hurry. There were more Clifford telegrams than Roberts telegrams.

I reached over and asked John, where he had got the telegrams. 'Your bridesmaid, Breege, along with my good self and the help of a certain amount of whiskey, wrote them out at the kitchen table this morning. I got the empty forms from a friend of mine who works in the post office,' said John, with a note of undying support in his voice. All I could do was laugh.

I know, to this day, that 'uncle' John would, if it were humanly possible, support me in anything that I wanted to do. I will never forget his kindness to me. I even overheard my 'granny' explaining to Harold Roberts, whom she was seated beside, that the Clifford family had wanderlust in its members and that she thought that I was no exception. I do not know, to this day, how she explained away the sad death of both my parents to Harry's parents. Her explanation was obviously acceptable to them. I did overhear her say to them at one stage that I never spoke about their deaths, as I became extremely upset and was unable to cope with the tragedy.

I was always able to tell people that my parents were dead when I wanted to hide my past. As time went by and the number of times that I told my tale of woe increased, the nature of their untimely demise changed to suit my particular mood or circumstance, at the time. My parents had died in a car crash, or train or aeroplane accidents. Robbers, the police or crazed gunmen had shot them, in error of course. They had drowned! They had died in a fire!

Their deaths had also occurred in many different locations over the years and the circumstances were always tragic. I became good at playing the victim and accepted any sympathy that would have been available to me at the time. However, I did not want too much sympathy.

I always had to balance the amount of sympathy available, with the amount of further investigation into my past it might lead to. Generally I said that they were dead, and that I did not want to speak about the accident, as it was too painful for me. My walls of defence would not tolerate too much pressure. If I really did not want any conversation about their fate, I delivered, 'they committed suicide together' and that usually stopped the conversation as dead as my parents.

After the meal and the speeches were over, it was time for some music and dancing.

Michael concluded his best man duties with the traditional Irish compliment of, 'And I'd like to thank the hotel for a lovely, lovely meal.' All the drinkers adjourned back to the bar, while the hotel staff cleared the tables to the sides of the room. The band that we had booked appeared and set up their instruments in one corner. As they tuned up their instruments, people began to return to the room.

While all this moving was going on, Harry and I, as the new Mr and Mrs Roberts, became the subject of many congratulations and pats on the backs. Time was flying by and everybody wanted to talk to us.

Then the band asked for the bride and groom to lead off the dancing for the afternoon. I was hoping for a romantic song for my special day, but they played a country and western song and we danced to 'Pretty little girl from Omagh, in the county of Tyrone.'

We had the floor to ourselves for a short time, and then everyone joined in. I asked the singer later if they could have played a more relevant song for the first dance. 'Shure, we always start with that song, Mam, it gets us warmed up,' was the explanation I received.

Hours of dancing and singing went by.

At some time, Father Bernard, excused himself and left fairly early. Dancing at weddings was not really his forte. Before he left, he caught my wrist and said that if I ever needed him, I was to find him, because he would be there to help me.

Harry then suggested that it was time to change out of my dress, as we had to leave. I got Breege to help me. We had a room at the hotel where all the paraphernalia attached to the bride and her wedding was stored. Off came the wedding dress, into the 'going away outfit' and I was ready. The girls packed up all the bits and pieces that we were finished with, or did not require. Everything had to come with us, as we were finished in Kilkenny. We were heading to Dublin for our honeymoon.

As all my friends were going back to London the following day, they were coming to Dublin as well. They packed everything into the car before I made my final appearance at the wedding reception with Harry. As soon as we appeared at the door of the ballroom everyone rushed over to us. They thought we were leaving without throwing the bouquet.

I walked to the centre of the room, checked that all the girls were collected together, turned my back to them, and launched the bouquet into the air, over my head in their direction and ran for the door. My memory of that room is of about 15 women, squabbling and fighting over my bouquet.

The two of us ran down the corridor of the hotel, pursued by the vigilant members of the wedding party, and those that were waiting for us to leave. We were drowned in confetti as we went outside. We all got into the cars and away to Dublin with the gang of us.

We were booked to stay at the North Star Hotel in Amiens Street. Before we went to the hotel, we went for a meal at the Rainbow Café in O'Connell Street. It was early, about 8 pm. Then we all headed for the North Star to check in. We checked in and signed the register as Mr and Mrs Roberts. Harry and I, and the girls, went to our respective rooms.

Harry suggested that we go to bed and I agreed.

I got undressed in the bathroom and put on a nightdress that I had bought specially. Harry was already in bed when I emerged. I lifted the bedcovers and slipped into bed beside him. It was the first time that I was ever in bed with Harry.

I had thought that the act of physical love within a marriage might be something I could enjoy, but I was wrong. My naivety, perhaps, was to some degree my own fault. Once the sexual abuse stopped and I was committed to the industrial school in Limerick, I completely turned off my mind, regarding any sexual thoughts. I put a mental seal on my body, preventing any sexual pleasure. All through my teenage years, my past had made me lose my sexuality. I spurned any sexual conversation. I avoided occasions where I might become sexually active.

I realised that the physical side of our marriage was going to be difficult for me, and I resigned myself to my sexual fate, there and then.

'Would you like to go dancing now?' Harry then asked, as if it was the most normal thing in the world to do, on one's wedding night.

I got out of bed, had a bath and got dressed in my going away outfit once again. We went to the girls' rooms and asked them if they would like to come to a dance with us. They enthusiastically agreed and so we all went to a dance in the Irene Ballroom, on my wedding night. We danced all night and when the dance was over we all walked back to the hotel together.

On the way back, I overheard Breege say to one of the others, about Harry and me and our marriage, 'She won't last long with him. Imagine a fella who wants to go to a dance on his wedding night.'

Although we parted as friends the following day, I have never spoken to or seen Breege since our wedding day. Her remark has remained with me down through the years.

When we got back to our hotel, we agreed to meet the girls in the dining room for breakfast the next morning. Harry and I went to our room. I went to the bathroom, undressed and got into my nightdress. I came out to find that Harry was already asleep.

I got into bed, drew the covers over me and silently cried myself to sleep. I cried not for myself, or Harry, or my marriage, or any of the things that had happened that day. I cried myself to sleep on my wedding night, beside my sleeping husband, wanting only one thing – I wanted to know what my father looked like.

TEN

A Miracle

The following day, we all returned to London. The honeymoon was over.

Harry had lived in a small flat in Stockwell before we were married, so we had decided to rent that together. We moved in as soon as we got back.

I found it extremely difficult to cope with the sexual demands of our relationship, and sadly, over the 33 years of our marriage, this aspect did not improve. I learned to cope better, by being able to switch off any feeling in the lower half of my body. The mind is an extremely powerful tool. I am always amazed by its capability to recognise danger and its ability to control the physical functions, in order to protect the body.

I began to feel that I had little in common with Harry, in any area of life. Our wedding had taken place in February 1973. Five months later, in July, I discovered that I was pregnant. I had started to experience morning sickness every day. I began to feel that my body was different from normal. The weather was warm and sunny, and I normally felt good and fit during the bright summer months. Being a nurse, I took a urine sample from myself, and sent it to the laboratory for an unofficial test. There were no do-it-yourself pregnancy tests in those days. I told the laboratory technician that it was my own and that I wanted him to give me the results unofficially.

After all the examinations by gynaecologists, I was not optimistic about my prospects of conception, never mind carrying a healthy baby to full term, but I knew there was a chance and being a Catholic, Harry would not use contraception. Condoms were freely available for sale in the United Kingdom but in Catholic-dominated Ireland it was illegal to sell condoms, so the culture of using contraception was unknown. The fact that Harry was not using contraception was never an issue between us.

Once again, I had told a white lie. I told Harry that because of an accident I had as a child, it was unlikely that I would be able to have children. I told him this news long before we got married. He seemed to accept it without any bother. I did not think about his easy acceptance of this fact at the time, except to make a subconscious note that it seemed a tiny bit strange to me. All other fellows that I had been involved with, or had known, had wanted to have children at some stage in their married life.

The contraceptive pill for women had been available for many years, but 99 per cent of me believed that I did not need it, due to my damaged internal reproductive tract. The remaining one per cent of me hoped that I would become pregnant. While I had such a case history working against my becoming pregnant, I did not want to aid and abet it by taking the pill. If one of Harry's sperm was determined enough, and wanted to make its long and troublesome way up as far as my Fallopian tube, it was going to get all the help and encouragement that I could provide.

I told the technician in the laboratory that I was expecting a negative result. I told him that if it were positive I would go to my GP and have it confirmed, officially.

Two days later the laboratory staff phoned me, while I was working on the ward, and asked me to go down to the laboratory for the results. When I got there, he told me that while the results were unofficial, they were accurate. He said that the result was positive, and that, I was indeed, well and truly pregnant.

I was ecstatic.

I was over the moon with happiness.

I was full of uncontrolled joy.

I kissed him on the lips, with thanks, for giving me the joyful news.

'I thought that you did not want the result to be positive,' he replied with a frown.

'Ah well, I might as well make the best of it,' was all the explanation I could produce, while I was obviously consumed with happiness. I can still remember him walking away from me, shaking his head from side to side, muttering to himself incredulously, 'Women, women!'

I went to my GP the next morning. First thing that morning I had taken another urine sample, in a sterile plastic container. I gave it to my doctor and asked him to have a pregnancy test done for me, as I suspected that I might be pregnant. I could barely conceal my happy expectation. He said to call his office in a few days for the result.

I could not sleep for two nights, while awaiting the official confirmation of my pregnancy. Sure enough, two days later the test yielded a positive result. I had the precious gift of life inside me. I could not believe it!

It was my most distant dream, come true. I promised God that, whatever happened, I would do everything in my power to bring that spark to life, to fulfil its place within this world, the world that it was entitled to be born into. I promised God that I would love and cherish it.

I would never give it away to anyone.

I would never cause it to suffer, in any way.

I would never abuse it physically.

I would never allow anyone else to abuse it physically.

I would never allow any of the horrible things that happened to me as a child, to happen to my child.

I was going to be the mother to my child that I never had myself.

I told Harry the news that evening, when he came in from work.

'I am pregnant, we are going to have a baby,' I shrieked, as I jumped up and down, before him. In my happiness I threw my arms around him, in a giant hug. He was disappointed.

'Could you not have waited?' was his reply. I felt that he was implying that I was to blame for becoming pregnant or possibly not using contraception, but I hoped that, given time, Harry would accept the idea of me being pregnant with his baby.

I wasn't able to tell him why being pregnant meant so much to me.

At 10.25 pm on March 26, 1974, my first child, Anthony Joseph, was born. He weighed nine pounds and it was a very difficult delivery. I ended up having an emergency Caesarean operation. All those gynaecologists who had examined me previously were not entirely wrong in their diagnoses. The only thing that I remember, after the injection to put me to sleep, was waking up to find a priest that I had never seen before, leaning over me in the bed, praying furiously. I thought that I was dying, because I could not see my baby in the room. I got into a state of panic. I caused such a commotion, while yelling and screaming for my baby, that the nurses said that they would wheel my bed down to see him in the nursery.

I realised immediately that I had a baby boy. They pointed to a tiny pink face wrapped in a white cloth. When one of the nurses lifted him up close to me, I thought that he was the most beautiful baby that I had ever seen.

I had become a mother. I was so proud. I could not stop crying with emotion every time someone congratulated me. I was permanently in tears during my stay in the maternity ward. All his tests were normal. He was a healthy baby and I couldn't wait for the three of us to be a family together.

After recovering from the initial trauma of having a baby, the hospital had me back, after four months, to follow up on and investigate the problems that had arisen during the birth. The result of this consultation was that they advised me that any future children would have to be delivered by Caesarean section. Natural birth would be impossible.

Before the consultant could utter another word, I jumped up from the chair in which I was sitting. 'Future children?' I shrieked. 'Does that mean that I can have more children? I would love to have more children. How many more children do you think I could have?'

'Mrs Roberts, Mrs Roberts,' he addressed me gravely. 'I would urge you strongly, NOT, I repeat NOT, to have any more children. If you have any more children, it would be at great risk to your own life or the baby that you might be carrying.'

I thanked him very much for his advice and left his office. While the consequences of having another baby were serious, I found myself in a different gynaecological dilemma, which was, should I have another baby or not? The situation, as far I was concerned, was that 'could' had become 'should'. The risk was the same, as before, 99 per cent should not, one per cent should. As previously, the one per cent dictated the pace.

I desperately wanted to have another baby. The urge to become a mother for a second time was even stronger than the first. Our sexual behaviour continued on as it had started, without the use of contraceptives.

* * * *

Around this time, we returned to live in Ireland. Anthony was four months old then and Harry decided that he wanted to return home. I had this fantasy that we could build a house there, as a home for Anthony, on his parents' farm and it would be a nice place for him to grow up. It sounded like Harry had had a safe and happy childhood there. I wanted that for my own child so I agreed to go. I had left work to have Anthony so I didn't need to give any notice. We went to live in Kilkenny at Harry's family home, with his parents. That was our only option, because my parents were dead.

Living with Harry's parents did not work out so well. While there were no wars between us, Harry's mother and I did have a few skirmishes. It was the usual classic 'two women in the same kitchen' type rows. I was the younger woman who had never been used to parental advice or authority. I saw his mother's verbal offerings as unwarranted interference and I was unprepared to accept them as anything else.

It wasn't long before we moved out of his parents' house, and rented a house in Waterford City. I went to work as a nurse in the local hospital and Harry got a job as a barman in a city pub. As we were both working, we had to get someone to look after Anthony. We employed a local woman to look after him, mostly while I was at work. Every time that I left him in her care, my heart was beating twice as fast as normal. I wanted to be with him. I was thinking about him constantly. I felt that the woman was not particularly good at looking after him. I had reservations about her caring abilities. I was torn emotionally. I felt I was abandoning him to the same sort of life that I had experienced, through no fault of his own. History was repeating itself.

In Waterford, I had no support, family or friends. While Harry's family were not too far away in Kilkenny, his parents would offer no support. But I felt that we could not expect any help from his brothers and sisters either. They were busy living their own lives. Whatever support Harry might be able to garner for us, from family or friends, my contribution lay somewhere between nil and negligible. So after spending eight months in Ireland, I decided that living in Ireland under such circumstances was decidedly less than romantic and at best, it was an unmitigated disaster. I began to put pressure on Harry to move to somewhere that my baby and I would feel secure. We returned to London in April 1975.

* * * *

At first, when we returned to London, we stayed with friends in Harrow. Then we rented a small flat in Clapham. I felt that I had support from a large group of my own friends very quickly after settling back in London. I had made my own friends over the years, and most of them were involved in nursing. I went back to work, on night duty, at St John's and Elizabeth's Hospital. I wanted to be with my son during the day. I did not want anyone else to look after him except Harry, who looked after him while I was on night duty. It was very hard-going because the only sleep that I got was when the baby went down for a nap during the day. Finally I started working in a position with full-time night duty, on June 16, 1976 in St Thomas's Hospital.

Nursing is a vocation, and as such it either becomes an integral part of, or takes over, your life. It is also a 24 hour, seven days per week job. It is a lifestyle, and consequently, is not a career for everybody. So inevitably, people tend to make quite a lot of friends who are also nurses. It is easier to make friends within the nursing profession, as you already know the type of character that another nurse is likely to have.

The job of nursing is worked on a shift basis. So you are always meeting some of the same people, some of the time.

It is not like a nine-to-five office job. Nurses and their friends do not live in one another's ear all the time, but when you are in need of help or support, nurses are friends to be treasured.

I needed a friend when I began work on full-time night duty, because as I was coming off duty in the morning, and when Harry was beginning his day's work, there was an overlap. So Anthony had to be left with somebody on Harry's way to work, so that I could collect him on my way home. In the end Harry used to leave Anthony with a friend of mine who lived near the hospital. I collected him at about 9 am and stayed up with Anthony during the day. I'd go to sleep when Harry came home in the evenings. After we had dinner, I usually went to sleep from 6 to 7.30 pm. I then bathed Anthony, got him ready for bed and then Harry and he would drop me to work at 8.15 pm. I was soon exhausted. I can remember that I sometimes had to tell Anthony to keep quiet just so that I could have a few minutes' rest. But I still thought it was the best way to ensure that Anthony was safe.

We had settled into our new routine when, in December 1976, after having my bath one day, I discovered a small lump under my left breast. It is one of those moments that every woman dreads. My hand stopped moving. I felt no lump. But I knew that I had felt something. I tried to make my hand go backwards to where it had been. With difficulty, my hand movement reversed.

It was there. I could feel the lump. I moved forward again – there was no lump. Backward again – there was definitely a lump there.

I did not want a lump to be there because I knew what it meant. In my career as a nurse I had seen women at every stage of breast cancer. None of the stages of breast cancer are easy to deal with. But I was tough. I did not want to fall down in a heap, on the floor. I would not collapse mentally. I would fight it. I had seen women fight it. I had seen women fight it successfully. My first thought was, 'I have a young son, and I want to see him grow up, and I want to see his son grow up. I will fight the Big C, and I will win.'

The next day I went to visit my GP. I was in fighting mood. I explained to him what I had found under my breast. He examined me and suggested that I should go and see a Professor Ellis at the Westminister Hospital.

'I will write you a note and you can bring it with you,' he said.

'How soon should I go to see him?' I asked him, my voice was at least two octaves lower than when I had entered his office.

'Immediately. I'll get you an appointment today if I can,' he said, as he picked up his phone. After a short conversation he told me, 'Professor Ellis can fit you in at 4 pm this afternoon, make sure you are there.'

Professor Ellis's examination was over quickly. 'There is no doubt, you must have immediate surgery, my dear,' he announced loudly.

I had become a mouse.

'When?' I asked. I could hardly hear myself.

'In two days' time, on Friday morning. I will arrange for you to be admitted on Thursday,' he replied.

I was dismissed.

I was drained of all energy. I tried to stand up to leave. My two legs got a message from my brain, which asked them to stand up. The muscles were unable to take messages. There was no power in the muscles. I somehow muttered a low sound that resembled 'Thank you', to the Professor. I do not know how I managed to walk out of the building and hail a cab to go home.

My mind was a blur of thoughts. Over a period of just 48 hours, the strong, tough, courageous woman that was going to fight breast cancer, and win, was now reduced to a woman, with all the strength of a jelly. I was so upset.

I checked into Westminister Hospital as appointed. Harry came to visit me in the hospital and brought Anthony with him, which lifted my spirits. The doctors, nurses and medical students, were a great support to me, as it was near Christmas. They used to take me to their pantomimes, in the doctors' mess. It sort of helped me to recover from the shock.

Luckily, I did not need to have a full mastectomy.

I got out of hospital on December 19, just in time for Anthony's second Christmas. We spent that Christmas with some friends and for New Year's Eve, we had a party in our flat. By this stage we had moved to Trinity Crescent, Tooting. It was a great party with lots of singing and dancing, but my heart was not in it, I was weak and tired all the time.

I got pregnant for the second time, immediately after the breast operation. I was so happy because it would be company for Anthony. This baby was due on August 19, 1977.

I was on night-duty in May, and started to have some pain in my stomach. The next day I was admitted to St Thomas's Hospital. After the doctors had done a scan, they said that the baby was fine, and left me to listen to her heartbeat. It seemed all right from the scan. We found out that it would be a girl and I decided to call her Mary Ellen.

I was taken back to the ward at 6 pm. At 2 am I started to haemorrhage quite badly. They rushed me to theatre but could not save her.

I was very depressed after losing this baby. I had a new GP at this time and his advice was that the best way of getting over it was to try for another baby. I decided that, while he had my medical notes, he should have been as familiar with my history as my previous doctor. I did not need to be told twice. I did not refer him to my previous history, which was in my notes. I still had that one per cent chance of pregnancy, shining like a beacon before me. I wanted to have another baby. I felt the chances were becoming greater as time went on. I knew I was capable of conception. I just had to be more careful about how I cared for the foetus, during its nine-month stay with me.

Just as things were looking up, life dealt me another blow. In October of that year, 1977, I found another lump on my breast. I went back to Professor Ellis for a consultation. He found not just one lump, but two. There was a lump on the other breast as well. He said that more surgery was necessary. I told him that my periods were late and that there was a possibility that I could be pregnant. He got a gynaecologist to examine me, who said that I was not pregnant. Also a urine test proved negative. So, with all the negative pregnancy tests, surgery went ahead.

I was very sick after this operation. I also had a lot of abdominal pain. The gynaecologist decided to do a laparoscopy to check the ovaries and uterus for cancer.

They found none.

I knew that I was pregnant. I wanted another pregnancy test. This time it was positive.

By this time I had been in direct contact with radiation. I had also been through two general anaesthetics, in the space of a two-week period. The senior registrar and some of the other doctors in charge of my case became very concerned. They strongly advised me to have a termination. I could not agree with this.

I felt under a lot of pressure. I did not know what to do.

They called Harry into the office on a Saturday morning. They told him that if I went ahead with the pregnancy, I would be risking my own life and that of the baby. They said that the baby would be very likely to be handicapped, because of the radiation from X-rays. They got a priest to come and talk to me. He said that if I had a termination under these circumstances, it would not be a sin.

I felt that everyone was against me.

Harry's friends felt that I owed it to him and Anthony to

have the termination. My friends were leaving it up to me. I said that I could not destroy a life under any circumstances. In desperation, I phoned Father Bernard, late one evening, and told him of my predicament. He was a great support, and told me that whatever my final decision was, he would stand by me. That was what I needed to hear.

First thing the next morning, I discharged myself from Westminister Hospital. I went home and prayed. I prayed that whatever handicap, physical or mental, that my child might be burdened with, that God would give me the necessary strength to cope with it. In any event, God had other plans.

One night, about 12 weeks into the pregnancy, I started to haemorrhage. Once more, I was admitted to St George's Hospital, Tooting, as an emergency.

They could not save the baby.

1977 was another sad year in my history.

ELEVEN

A Place to Call Home

The new year of 1978 dawned. I decided to try and put 1977 behind me. I had lost two babies but I really wanted another one. Anthony was now three years of age. He was enrolled at a local nursery school and seemed happy there.

The New Year optimism had me thinking that I might become pregnant again. I wanted a brother or sister for Anthony, so that he could learn to share. I did not want him to grow up as an only child. I had an obsession with the fact that only children can be selfish. They don't want to share. It is entirely understandable to me now why they should do this, but at the time I did not like the trait.

My wish list for 1978 also included our own house. I wanted to buy a house for us, but I realised that to buy our own house I had to have a lot of money. Saving was never one of my strong points. Saving money was a subconscious acknowledgement of the fact that I might need or have use for it in the future. The reality for me was that I did not expect to have a future. The monotonous repetition of the fact that I was no good and that no one wanted me, meant that I had no hope for any kind of a positive future.

Having a child changed this. He gave me a sense of hope for his future, a hope I had never had for myself. Anthony's existence made me feel a sense of responsibility. I wanted my child to have everything that I did not have. He had a mother and a father. That was a good start.

The next thing that he needed was a house. He needed somewhere that he could call 'home'. A house of his own would provide him with far more than just the basic human needs of shelter and warmth.

It would be somewhere he would feel safe and could come to, in times of danger.

It would be somewhere he would be accepted unconditionally and be loved by his father and mother.

It would be his family home.

The first problem was money. We didn't have nearly enough! The building society told me that if I could raise 20 per cent of the purchase price, they would loan us the remaining 80 per cent as a mortgage. In order to save money for a deposit on a house, I started to work extra shifts at the hospital. Doing extra shifts at work also helped me to forget the trauma of the lost babies. Between working such long hours and looking at suitable properties to live in, I recovered from my loss to some extent.

In October 1978, after spending most of the year saving, we bought our first family home. We got a loan of £2000 from a friend of Harry. They were both members of the Pioneer Total Abstinence Association and she held him in high regard. We got a loan of £600 from Austin, Harry's brother-in-law. I myself had £2500 in savings for a rainy day. I decided that the rainy day had arrived.

I was so proud. The house we bought cost us £15,000. We arranged a mortgage of £9000. We moved in and I busied myself with buying furniture. Harry carried out any small repairs and painted the entire house from top to bottom. Things seemed to be going all right for a while. But then I found another lump in my right breast.

I felt cheated once again.

I went to St George's Hospital in Tooting, where they at

once referred me to a consultant called Mr Gazet. He recommended a partial mastectomy. He carried it out himself two days later. I found him to be extremely supportive. Mr Gazet continues to check me on a regular basis to this day.

Once that was over with, we fully settled into the house. I concentrated on making a home for the three of us. I felt so whole, so satisfied at being a mother. I continued to work nights at the hospital and look after Anthony during the day. My work continued to be my form of running away from any emotional problems that I might have. While at work, I was completely absorbed in what I was doing. I could not be distracted.

Or so I thought.

The distraction materialised in the form of a beautiful baby boy of about six months of age, called James. He arrived on my ward at work suffering from a life-threatening enteritis. As he recovered, over a period of about two weeks, he became the focus of the entire nursing staff. Every nurse loved him and gave him their every attention. He responded to that attention by recovering into a thriving, active, laughing baby boy.

When his mum came to visit him, you could see the bond between them. He loved her with a ferocity that can only be generated and nurtured by a parent for its child. She used to hold him up in her arms, a few inches from her face and pucker up her lips, as if to kiss him. When she did that, he used to throw his arms in the air, beam his widest smile for her and launch himself forward with such enthusiasm, as if saying, 'If there is a kiss on offer, I am definitely coming in for it.'

I witnessed their bond from an emotional distance, until one day I was coming on duty and I walked into a commotion at the nurses' station. Veronica, the mother of baby James, was at the centre of it.

James was now well and healthy. He was due to be discharged that day. When it came to discharge him into his mother's care, it was found that she had no home to take him to. The hospital would not discharge a six-month-old baby to a homeless mother. He would have to be put into care. It all unfolded in front of me. Veronica was a nineteen-year-old single mum. She had given birth to James in Ireland and had run away to London. She was staying at a hostel that would not allow babies. She had no money. But she did not want to be parted from her son. She was putting up a loud fight for him, but it wasn't enough. The hospital was adamant, she had no home address to go to, consequently they would not discharge James to her care. As the duty sister lifted the phone to call social services and put an end to the argument, I piped up, 'She does have an address; she can stay with me at my house.'

The entire crowd turned to look in my direction.

'Are you sure?'

'You don't even know her.'

'This would be above and beyond the call of duty.'

Even Veronica was gaping at me, with her mouth open. It was true that I did not know her at all, but I had seen her interact with her son. I saw how she was so concerned when he was near death with the enteritis. I saw how much he loved her and how he wanted to be with her, when he had recovered. I thought, 'I cannot allow this boy to grow up without his mother!' I knew the possible hardships and difficulties that could lie ahead for him and I did not want anything to happen to him. I was determined that they would not be separated.

The duty sister wrote my address on the discharge form and a crisis was averted.

I called Harry and told him that Veronica and baby James were coming to live with us. I didn't ask him, I told him. He was always very generous in that regard. He said that it was not a problem. He never objected. He never complained how long anyone stayed at our house.

Mother and baby came to live at our house. It was a lovely time. They stayed for six months while Veronica got back on her feet. She got herself a job and a flat where she could raise baby James without being separated from him.

James is now a healthy adult man in his twenties who still loves his mum and sees her often. To this day, Veronica remains one of my close friends. While I have never told her all the facts about my past, except in general terms or in vague detail, I think she subsequently suspected that my empathy in her time of crisis was not entirely unfounded.

She bounces into my life about two or three times each year. I treasure her company dearly. She is not intrusive. She never asks me any difficult questions. She is always light-hearted and outgoing. She makes me laugh. I think myself that she is really keeping an eye on me, just to see that I am okay.

After work I used to be so engrossed in caring for my beautiful son that my mind never had any inclination to wander. Any time left over was used up with sleep, to regenerate my tired body. As things settled down again, I did manage to find a small bit of time to renew my friendship with Kit and Tony in Buttevant. Over the years, since I left the orphanage, I had lost touch with them. I was not a great letter writer. The only person that I used to correspond with regularly was Father Bernard. I wrote mainly in response to his letters, probably out of guilt, as he would continually remind me that I had not answered earlier letters.

Once communications had been restored between Kit and me, it was as if we had never lost contact. I invited herself and Tony to visit us in London. They came for a week, in the summer of 1979. It was as if they were my own family. We all became really close during that week.

I was so relieved when 1979 came and went, without any bad emotional trauma. If it had remained so, I would probably have convinced myself that I was happy with what I had. In truth, I would have only been fooling myself.

TWELVE

Pushing the Odds

I was pregnant again, for a fourth time.

I was due in hospital on the evening of Sunday September 14, 1980.

Harry drove me there. Kit and Tony, who were staying with us while I was in hospital, came along as well and stayed while I was admitted.

As soon as the battery of admission tests began, I asked who the anaesthetist would be. As a nurse, I was very particular about whom I wanted on my case and who I did not want on my case. I wanted no mistakes. I had a healthy baby in my uterus, and I wanted him to land in this world in the same healthy condition. The short journey from uterus to life outside can be fraught with error. I wanted all possible mistakes eliminated, not just minimised.

I also asked if Professor Trussell, my gynaecologist, was going to deliver the baby himself. The midwifery staff were unable to tell me there and then, who would be the overall consultant for my delivery. I was somewhat nervous under the circumstances and because of my history, I became extremely agitated at the lack of clarity regarding my case.

Kit tried to reassure me with, 'Don't worry Craythur, shure won't you have it all over with shortly.'

This just made me feel more aggressive.

At this stage Harry took control. He must have recognised my aggression from some previous encounter and realised that I was best left alone to deal with it. He swept Kit and Tony out through the door of the ward, so fast that they never had a chance to say goodbye. Harry said that he would be back later.

An anaesthetist appeared. After speaking with him, I calmed down. He offered me a range of options for my anaesthetic. We agreed that it would not be a general anaesthetic, unless complications arose. A spinal epidural was agreed on, mutually. As I lay there in bed, I prayed to God that everything would work out well for the following day.

As I was about to fall off to sleep, a head with two glaring eyes popped through the door. The eyes moved from side to side, checking out the immediate area, as if they belonged to someone in a detective movie. Then the rest of Harry's body came crashing through the double doors of the ward, with the sound of Kit's admonishing voice following closely behind, 'Would ya get in there, and don't be actin' the eejit.'

They brought Anthony in as well. We talked for a little while. I kissed Anthony goodnight and then they all left.

When they were gone, I once again felt all alone in the world. I burst into floods of tears.

On a practical level, I was happy that the technicalities involved in the delivery were sorted out. On an emotional level, I cried all the time. Even though they had all been in to visit me, I felt that I was on my own again, left to cope by myself. I wanted my mother to be with me! At difficult times in my life, my mother was never there for me. I always imagined that my mother could make things right. I wanted somebody strong to ask the questions that I felt fearful or intimidated about asking.

As with Anthony's birth, my next baby's time of arrival into the world was also predetermined. With the lower half of my body numbing up, I was wheeled into theatre at 9.30 am, on the dot. A baby son was delivered alive and healthy by Caesarean section by 9.35 am. Somewhere in the five-minute interim as I was awake, I heard one of the theatre staff, a colleague that I knew well, say jokingly, 'Celine wants a daughter, so if it is a boy, stuff him back in.'

I even muttered back to her, 'That is not true. I do not care as long as the baby is alive and well.'

I was aware of them lifting something out of my uterus and in one fell swoop they landed a baby boy on my chest. As I was looking at him, the nurse in me took over, 'He looks as blue as a bluebird, he must be cyanosed. He needs oxygen.'

As a result of the nurse's joking comment, I felt a really strong urge to protect my baby, whatever its sex. They then separated our umbilical cord. I do not recall any sense of pain, either physical or emotional, on separation. I do remember a sense of relief and spiritual gratitude that my baby had arrived safely.

The staff then took him away to be checked out by the paediatrician. With that, the surgeon announced to the staff, 'That's it.'

Then a porter wheeled me back to my room. I felt that it had all taken just a matter of minutes. My baby was brought back to me in my room after about 30 minutes. A nurse said, 'You have a normal healthy baby boy and he weighs 7lb. 3oz.'

I was elated. I was so happy to have a normal healthy son. I thought he was so beautiful. He had a head of dark hair. I thought that he looked like a 'real little individual', with Harry's colouring. I checked him out myself. I began to count his toes. I checked the number of fingers. I checked all digits to make sure he had the correct number. The numerical audit revealed that all were present and correct. I hugged and kissed him and welcomed him to my world. I promised him that I would always take care of him and love him.

I named my new son Ronan Gerard. While I received lots of congratulations and cards when Anthony was born, I was virtually deluged with gifts and cards when Ronan was born.

Kit brought Anthony in to the hospital to see his new baby brother and me. Anthony was wearing a red T-shirt that I had bought him weeks earlier. It had the words 'I want I want' emblazoned across his chest. I remember saying to him as soon as I saw it, 'You've got, you've got.' Harry came with them to see Ronan for the first time. He looked at him and smiled. I was a bit disappointed by his reaction. He seemed totally nonplussed by the fact that he was the father of a second son.

Ronan and I remained at the hospital for seven days. Those seven days are a blur of so many friends and other people's relatives coming to visit me. The time in hospital also included the usual instruction of 'how to bath a baby' which I went along with for the sake of peace and quiet.

All my time was spent bonding with Ronan. Of course I cried at the 'drop of a hat', once again. I found it so emotional. His little cradle was right by my bed. I attached two or three religious artefacts to his cradle, which I believed would protect my son. I was scared stiff that any harm might befall him so I felt that I needed all the help I could get, whether human or spiritual. I had waited so long for him. I felt that I really was blessed to be given another child. If any harm came to him, I could never forgive myself.

Finally, the day came when we were discharged from St George's. Before we left, the paediatrician gave Ronan a final check-over. 'He will be a brain surgeon or a pianist, because he has such long and delicate fingers,' were his parting words.

As we were standing by the lift, on our way out, Ronan joined his hands, as if in prayer, and I remember thinking, 'He will be a priest.'

Harry drove us home. When we arrived, many of our neighbours were there to see my new son. I was pleased to be home. Kit took over and did everything for me in the house. She really mothered me for the next few weeks and over that time the household routine returned to normal. It was a great change but I still couldn't help wishing that I had my own mother there. When Kit saw that things were running fine, she and Tony returned home to Ireland.

I went back to work six weeks after Ronan was born. Before I started back, I advertised for a childminder to come to our house for three days a week. I chose a mature lady called Margaret, who was in her sixties, from a group of four interviewees, as the most suitable. She used to come from 10 am to 3 pm because I was working night duties. When she arrived at 10 am, I would have Ronan bathed and ready for her. Then I would go to bed until 2 pm.

Even though another person was looking after him, I felt I was with him, because we were in the same house. If he was crying, I would wake up. I would go down to him and investigate the reason.

When Margaret left at 3 pm, I used to take Ronan with me to collect Anthony from school. We all came home from school together, and I prepared dinner for the four of us. We ate dinner when Harry arrived home from work. I would bath both sons and prepare them for bed. Then all four of us were loaded into Harry's old Ford Escort and the whole family drove me to work at the hospital for 8.15 pm. I would work the night duty until 7.45 am. I took a bus home in the mornings. I usually arrived home about 8.30 am. As soon as I arrived in, Harry would leave for work. I would then wrap Ronan up in his pram and we would take Anthony to school. We used to say our morning prayers on the way to school. As soon as I had safely dispatched Anthony at the school, Ronan and I turned on our heels and returned home, to be on time for Margaret. I headed for bed for a well-earned, if short sleep, and the daily cycle began once more. I worked the night shift four nights, on Wednesday, Thursday, Friday and Saturday each week, on a full-time basis, for ten years, without a pause. Sometimes it was very hard but I still loved nursing, as it gave me a sense of purpose and the friendships I had made there meant a lot to me.

On November 14, 1980, we held a christening for Ronan. He was baptised into the Catholic faith, at a 6 pm mass at St Bartholomew's Church in Norbury, south-west London. I employed a folk-singing choir for music and hymns. Anthony's class at his school were preparing for First Communion. They were encouraged to attend any religious ceremonies, as part of their preparations. So Anthony arranged for them all to come to Ronan's christening. They had a ball. They thought it was one big party. After the service, we held a christening party at our home in Glencairn Road. At least 80 people were squashed into our house for the celebrations. There was a bar set up in the breakfast room. It was fully stocked with bottles of all kinds of spirits. While pregnant, I used to amuse myself by buying all sorts of strange and different kinds of bottles of spirits. I knew we would need them for a christening party. But instead of looking for a person's favourite tipple, I would base my alcoholic purchase on the pretty colours of the liqueurs. Also, every time my friends went abroad, I would give them money to bring me back some duty-free alcohol, for my baby's christening party. My friends had really been good to me and I had 'oceans of booze' for the party.

Anthony had two goldfish called Starsky and Hutch, who lived in a glass bowl, on the mantelpiece, in the breakfast room. When the bar was being set up for the party,

Anthony saw that Starsky and Hutch had been moved about from one room to another. As the furniture and carpets were moved he felt that the fish were becoming agitated. He insisted that they be left precisely where they had always lived. He got his way. They were installed in their usual home, on the mantelpiece.

It turned out to be a great party, which I enjoyed immensely, as Ronan was the centre of attention. Quite a few people became drunk, due to the plentiful supply of booze. At some stage, the music volume was increased and dancing started. The party did not end until 3 am. After the last person had left, everyone went to bed.

Next morning I was awoken early to hear the screams of an angry Anthony. He was baying for blood. 'My goldfish, Mum, they are both dead.' I jumped out of the bed and ran downstairs, only to find Starsky and Hutch floating belly-up in their bowl. We never did find out exactly what killed the goldfish, but, during Anthony's subsequent investigations, somebody told him that his uncle, Paddy Roberts, had given them a 'drop of brandy' to see if the fish would get drunk. I do not know if Anthony directly accused his uncle of the murder of his pets, but for years after the goldfish incident, Anthony was very wary of Paddy Roberts' behaviour at our house, and he always watched him carefully from a distance.

For many years after that party, I had a collection of bottles of alcohol of many different colours, which I could not throw out or find anybody who could bring themselves to drink them!

THIRTEEN

Maternal Woes

A new year, 1981, and I had pains in my tummy. They performed an ultra-sound scan on me. The scan indicated a possible cancerous growth. I was taken to theatre directly from the scanning department, for explorative surgery. When the surgeon operated, he found the cause of my pain to be an ovarian cyst. He removed the cyst. He also removed my appendix. This all happened under a general anaesthetic. I felt ashamed. I was on night duty when it happened and my boss was ringing home from 2 am to 7 am, when Harry finally woke up to go to work. He came in to see me later that day. It was a help but I was in bad form. I was sick of having operations.

The surgeon told me that he had removed my appendix as a precaution. He said that he did not want me to be unnecessarily anaesthetised any more, and that he was concerned at having to reopen the old scar tissue too often. He jokingly suggested that because my stomach had been opened so often, I should probably have a zip inserted!

Later that year I found that I couldn't maintain my balance while standing. Many checks were carried out on me. They discovered that I had damage to the bone structure of my inner ear. This damaged bone structure was infected and this is what triggered my lack of balance. They treated the infection with antibiotics. I was allowed home from hospital, with an arrangement to return for the surgical removal of the damaged and decayed bone in my ear. Three weeks later, I returned to St Thomas's Hospital for my ear surgery. The correct name for my ear operation is called a tympanic graft.

The system at home was being held together with the help of many of my friends. This operation turned out to be a painful, uncomfortable and totally unpleasant experience from start to finish. It brought back painful memories from my childhood, particularly when the surgeon asked, 'Did your parents never take you to a doctor for treatment to your ears as a child?'

I untruthfully answered, 'Yes, of course they did.'

He wasn't convinced and asked, 'How could any doctor have missed something as serious as this?'

I jokingly replied as best I could, 'He was an old doctor in the country.'

But deep within myself I was angry that this entire surgery was unnecessary and could have been avoided. It was due to neglect.

I was discharged after two weeks. This time I was told to return for reconstruction surgery on my ear, about six months later. This further surgery was to replace the now missing bone with synthetic plastic bone. Their aim was to restore some hearing to my damaged right ear. Hearing loss was 100 per cent in this ear after the surgery.

I was at home, but I was feeling shattered both mentally and physically. I went to my GP feeling extremely low and depressed. My head was reeling. I could not understand why I was having so much trouble with my body. Was I still being punished for being bad or any one of the other negative attributes showered on me, by other superior people over the years? I had many memories coming back to me, haunting me, from my childhood. I remembered once going into the school and my ear was full of pus. The nun simply turned my head sideways and let it pour out on to the desk. She didn't do anything else. I even had to clean it up.

I used to try to laugh the operations off to all my friends. 'How do you cope with all the operations and pain?' some people would ask. 'I am just an old crock,' I would reply, and make light of it, as best I could. But, within myself, I could not laugh it off. I really wanted to die. Every time that I visited my GP, I had some medical tale of woe to relate to him. At this time my GP put me on a course of antidepressants. Valium was the fashionable choice. I was 33 years old. I should have been in my prime.

When I came home after the ear operation, I was too weak to climb the stairs. I had a single bed set up in the dining room for myself. I had lost a lot of weight at this time. I weighed just under six and a half stone. I was really weak, both mentally and physically.

Two days after I arrived home, two friends of Harry's, a nun and her mother, came to stay for a week. I could not believe it! I had to get up from my bed and cook dinner for them every evening and breakfast for them every morning. They used to sit and talk with Harry, reminiscing about the 'good old times' on the farm in Ireland. They never once offered to wash the dishes or help me with the children. They felt sorry for Harry who had this sick wife, who was unable to cope with life.

I could not wait to see the back of them. I put up with this treatment because I thought that one had to respect or at least defer to nuns, especially, because to me, all these people were educated and superior to me. They were also part of a family. They were everything that I was not. If the nun had a mother in tow, that had to be acceptable as well.

The only family that was ever really mine, and that I could really say were my family, were my two sons. Nobody could ever claim that Anthony and Ronan were not my family. That was very important to me.

Even the Valium did not work. Nothing took away the ever-developing psychological pain in my head.

I returned to my work on night duty after two weeks of 'recuperation' at home. In hindsight, I think a lot of my trips to my GP were questionable. Questionable in the sense that it made it easier for me to avoid having sex. Each incarceration in hospital gave me space to avoid having sex with my husband. I found that the sexual side of my marriage continued to be painful and unpleasant. I felt the only good thing about sex was that I had two beautiful children from it.

Sex for sex's sake was repugnant to me, but it was very important to Harry. He wanted to have sex every night. To him, sex seemed to represent love. To me, it was something I wanted over with, as quickly as possible, as I received no enjoyment or pleasure from it. I often heard my friends and colleagues at work talking about being 'turned on' by sex. I had no idea what they were talking about. I had never experienced an orgasm. I was so 'turned off' by sex, that I read books or watched television while it was taking place.

I said some horrible things to him and wished he was dead. It must have been hard for him but he didn't react. Even though I said those things to Harry, I always believed that it was my fault that I could not enjoy sex. I believed that he had a right to use my body sexually and also that he was not responsible for the fact that I could not feel anything sexually, as a result of what had happened to me during my childhood. I had never openly discussed the sexual abuse with Harry. I had asked Father Bernard, before I got married whether or not I should tell him. He said that it would serve no useful purpose to tell Harry all the gory details. I do not know what criterion he based his advice on but I chose to take it. If I'd told him; I don't think we would have ever got married. Illegitimacy was enough to handle.

One evening, Kit rang from Ireland, to ask how I was doing. As usual, in her phone calls she pleaded, 'Come on home for an auld holiday, shure 'twill do you good. The Cork air is in good form at the moment.' I told Harry that we were going to Kit's home in Ireland for a ten-day holiday. 'Right,' said Harry, 'No problem.'

It suited Harry because every time we went to Ireland by ferry, we would include a visit to Harry's parents in Kilkenny. They lived close to the ferry port on the Irish side, and we always spent a few days with them.

Two weeks later we loaded Harry's Ford, with everything necessary to keep two adults and two children clothed, and with enough gifts for all the people we would visit, during a ten-day stay in Ireland. Off we headed to catch the ferry to Ireland, at Fishguard, in Wales. We landed at Rosslare, County Wexford, on the south-east coast of Ireland a few hours later. Harry was born and reared only 25 miles from Rosslare, so the first place that we always visited was his parents' home.

Harry's parents were not demonstrative or tactile people. The most I would get on meeting them was a handshake, and a weak, unfriendly handshake at that. They did not grasp your hand, and shake it enthusiastically in welcome. I always felt like shivering in revulsion at their handshake. When they shook hands with me, I felt immediately that they did not like me. I like a handshake to be grasping and warm and welcoming.

The first time that I met his mother, I kissed her in greeting. I immediately felt really stupid, as I realised that it was not something which they normally did. I also realised that Harry never kissed his mother either.

While Harry's mother was not tactile or demonstrative to me, I felt she was kind to my sons, or maybe it was because they were Harry's sons. We usually stayed two or three days there, before we moved off somewhere else. Harry's two married sisters and one married brother, along with an aunt of his, lived in the same area as his parents. We would frequently visit one, or all of them, during our stay in Kilkenny.

By midweek we had all piled into the car again, and headed for Kit's house in Buttevant, County Cork. A visit to Kit and Tony was in total contrast to Harry's parents. We all hugged and kissed each other on meeting. Once we arrived, I had to do nothing for the children. Kit took over completely. She looked after my sons so well that she spoiled them rotten. They wanted for nothing. Either Kit or Tony, or both of them, packed the kids up, fussed them, took them places and had special foods ready for them. There was normally a big meal ready for us all when we arrived. There was always loads of food. Tony would say in his Cork accent, 'Ah go on and eat it, sure it might not fatten you at all.'

A holiday with Kit and Tony was usually spent visiting their neighbours and going on shopping trips to the town of Mallow or Cork City. There would also be a day trip to Blarney or Killarney. On this particular trip I was driven in a different emotional direction. While I was still feeling very frail and unwell, I contacted Sister Bernadette, my religious minder, and maternal go-between. I wanted to see my mother.

My son Anthony was now almost seven years old and he had a brother. I decided that I wanted my sons to know their maternal grandparents – both of them.

I had this fantasy that if my parents saw my children they would want to accept them. I thought about this concept first in terms of my mother only, as she was the only parent that I had access to, however limited. But then I thought that my father should also be part of the equation. He was out there somewhere. I had no idea where he was but he became part of the fantasy. I thought that if he saw my sons, then he also would want to accept me.

So I decided that both of my parents would meet my sons. I decided that I would arrange it somehow, however difficult it would be to set up, or whatever length of time it took. I decided that if my parents saw my sons, they would love them. They would cherish them, and somehow I stretched the fantasy so that they would ultimately love me. It was a crazy idea to have, but it was what I believed.

I spoke to Sister Bernadette on the phone and requested a meeting with my mother. She said that she would do her best to arrange it. She asked me to call her again, two days later. I duly called her back and she said she had arranged for me to meet with my mother, at two in the afternoon the following day, in the lobby of Cruise's Hotel, in Limerick City.

I was apprehensive after the call. I was thinking, 'Another meeting with my mother, is this a good idea, as the previous meetings did not go so well?' I began to plan, in my head what I would say to her. I especially had some demands on behalf of my two sons. Number one on the list was that I wanted my sons to meet BOTH their maternal grandparents. They had already met Harry's parents, so I wanted both of my parents to complete the grandparent set. I wanted reassurance that if anything happened to me, one or both of them would look after my sons. I believed that if they could see my two lovely little boys they would want them and be willing to take care of them, if I was not able to. Even though Kit and Tony were the ones my children loved, I still hoped that my parents would become real grandparents to their grandsons. I really wanted to test them out.

I told Kit what I had arranged and, while she never tried to stop me going, I felt her disapproval. She said, 'If she did not want you when you were born, it is hardly likely that she will want you now.' I knew that Kit had experienced her own maternal rejection, and while we never had any in-depth discussions about her past, her comments weighed heavily on my mind.

However, over the years I had become quite stubborn, not assertive, just stubborn. If I wanted something, I would go after it. How I achieved it did not matter, be it underhand or above board, whatever had to be done, had to be done. There were no rules in my life. Whatever it took to survive was fair game. This was to be no different. I kept the appointment. The following day at two o'clock, Harry, Anthony, Ronan and I all piled out of the car and into the foyer of Cruise's Hotel. Sister Bernadette glided up to us from nowhere, like a spider hiding in the corner of its web. She kissed all four of us in greeting. I gave her a present of a black cardigan. She probably said thanks, but I was scanning the area looking for my mother. She asked us to sit down in a secluded corner, adding that my mother would be along any minute.

I ordered tea, sandwiches and soft drinks for us all.

Sure enough, after a few minutes had passed, my elegant, blonde-haired mother approached us. She was dressed in a tweed coat, with brown leather gloves, brown leather handbag and brown leather, high-heeled shoes.

She kissed Sister Bernadette first.

Then she kissed me very lightly – barely a touch really – on the cheek. I felt she was looking at me with silent disapproval, because I had brought her here in the first place. I ignored this and proceeded to introduce Harry. I said, 'This is my husband, Harry,' to which she replied formally, 'I am pleased to meet you.'

I followed on with, 'These are my sons, Anthony Joseph and Ronan Gerard.'

She acknowledged Anthony's presence by asking him if he was going to school and whether he liked it. Anthony chirpily replied, in an English accent, that he liked school. He also volunteered that he was a member of the cub scouts.

Suddenly I lifted Ronan and more or less threw him into Mother's lap. Ronan settled down and made himself at home, before my mother could do anything. Harry was, by now, standing some distance away from us. He gave a loud shout and there was a bright flash. I had asked him to take a photograph, if he could manage to get us all together. I was really grateful to him for taking that photograph. It was the first photograph that I had of my mother and myself together. I had told Harry to just take it and not to ask permission first.

Even though she had looked relaxed enough with Ronan, as soon as she realised what had happened, Mother rose from her seat like a frightened rabbit and almost threw him back to me. It was as if she had been contaminated by being in the same picture as us. She stood bolt upright, as if getting ready to make a dash for the door. Sister Bernadette jumped in, like a referee at a boxing match, to restrain and calm her. She looked so shocked and was glaring so intensely at Harry that he blurted out, 'Ah, sure I don't think that old camera is working properly anyway.'

My mother made a lunge at him as if to snatch the camera. He stuffed the camera and his hands into the pockets of his long gaberdine overcoat. He turned on his heel and swaggered towards the front door. I thought he looked like James Cagney in a movie scene.

When the photograph was developed, it showed me sitting beside my mother, while she was holding Ronan on her lap. I think she looks decidedly unhappy to be caught in such a situation, with what were, after all, her daughter and her grandson. She isn't even looking up. Any other mother would be proud to be in a photograph like that.

My mother eventually calmed down and she even sat down beside me.

'Does my father know of my existence yet?' I asked her
snappily. 'I believe that if he saw me, he would accept me.'

'No, he has never been told. If it came out now, it would
break up his family,' she said firmly.

I said, 'I would not want that to happen. I would not
want to be responsible for that.' Bearing in mind how frail I
felt, I then added, 'I pray that somehow I would be able to
see him, before I die.'

At that point my mother began to talk to Sister
Bernadette about her parental home in Clarina, County
Limerick. I was being ignored, as if I was not there. She said
someone had removed an Adam's fireplace from the house
without anyone's permission. When I heard about the
Adam's fireplace, I believed that she must have grown up in
a mansion of a house and that her family must have been
extremely wealthy. It compounded my belief that I could
never be good enough to be a part of such an illustrious
family.

I was just a 'nobody', somebody with 'bad blood', just an
illegitimate bastard, just an 'ill-gotten person that nobody
wanted'. I felt that my mother was part of an aristocratic
class of people and I would never be good enough to even
'darken their door'. I had worked in enough mansions, as a
skivvy, to know the style and value of an Adam's fireplace.

My mother continued to ignore my family and me. She
was talking to the nun about the weather and her own
health. Without engaging me in any more conversation, my
mother then stood up and haughtily announced to
everyone and no one in particular, that she had to leave.
She bent down to me and kissed the air between us and
said, 'I hope you feel better, keep in touch with Sister
Bernadette.' With that, she rose to her full height, stuck her
chin in the air and without looking back at us, strode out
the front doors of the hotel, with Sister Bernadette
following, as if in attendance.

Sister Bernadette came running back to us to tell us not to follow my mother. She told me that my mother was worried about my following her, and causing trouble.

I was just too numb. It had never crossed my mind to follow her. I had been unable to ask her most of the questions that I had prepared and I had received no answers. My mother had walked out of my life once again. I wondered if I would ever see her again. This was the fourth time that she had left me. But it was the first time that she had walked out on her grandchildren.

Harry's head appeared around the door, in that comic fashion of his, looking first one way, then the other. With an impish smile he enquired 'Is "Der Führer" gone?!'

As this was the first time that Harry had met my mother, I asked him, 'What did you think of her?'

He politely answered, 'She is very nice.' And then under his breath, but loud enough for me to hear, 'Let's get out of here, before she comes back.'

Then Anthony asked, 'Who was that lady, Mum?'

'She is Auntie Kathleen,' I lied.

I'd said the first name that came into my head. We left the hotel and went to a cake shop to buy cakes. I remember going to the cake shop, but I was in such a state of mental anguish, I can't remember buying or eating the pastries at all.

The next day we returned to London.

FOURTEEN

The Hunt Begins

After we returned to London I was still not feeling myself
and we decided to go on a family holiday. I thought it might
be just what we needed. Before we were married, Harry had
wanted me to go and live in Canada. I did not want to go so
far away, as I had unfinished business on this side of the
Atlantic Ocean but I thought it might be the very place for
a holiday. Seamus, Harry's brother, and his wife Colette,
lived in Ontario, in Canada, and were always inviting us to
go there for a visit. We decided to borrow some money from
the bank to fund a four-week stay in Canada in August. We
flew with Freddie Laker Airways, one of the first low-cost
airlines, to Toronto. We got health insurance for the two
boys, but not for Harry or me. This was to turn out to be a
very stupid decision. Even without the benefit of hindsight,
I should have realised how stupid it was. Maybe it
demonstrates how badly my thought processes were
performing. I must have thought that the premium was too
expensive, or that nothing serious could happen to the
adults. With my medical history, it was a very naive decision
on my part.

Two days after arriving in Canada, at Harry's brother's
house, I developed a rash all over my body.

Harry's sister who also lived in Canada, in Calgary, came

to visit us. She came up with the theory that the rash was due to the cream in the beef Stroganoff that we ate on the plane. 'With the reputation for cutting costs that Freddie Laker has, he could have put anything in that sauce, you know,' she said.

I first went to the local pharmacy to get some anti-histamine pills. I thought that I might be able to treat it myself. They did not work.

The next day Seamus took me to their local doctor. He was unsure what the cause might be and told me to go to the local hospital. They ran some blood tests. The test results revealed that my haemoglobin was low. That meant that I was iron deficient. The rash was caused by serum poisoning because I had been taking Tamoxifen for my breast cancer for the previous two years. Toxins from the drugs were building up in my bloodstream. They told me that I would need blood transfusions and that each unit would cost £300. They put me on iron, plus folic acid tablets. They also recommended a D and C to stop uterine haemorrhage. As I had no medical insurance, the cost of all this surgery in Canada was taking on astronomical proportions. We decided to go home after two weeks.

Canada was a lovely country, but I felt so bad during my stay, I could not enjoy any of it.

Freddie Laker brought us home. He was still serving beef Stroganoff on the return trip. I declined to eat any, but Harry ate my portion as well as his own. He did not suffer any ill effects.

As soon as I got home I checked into St George's Hospital in Tooting once again, for my D and C. The rash got better as soon as I began taking the iron tablets. My D and C was clear. I soon recovered well and returned to work to repay the bank loan. It proved to be an expensive holiday! But we put it behind us. That September it was Ronan's first birthday and I decided to have a birthday party for him.

Anthony and all his friends, with their mums, came to the house one afternoon. The mums had wine and the children had the usual soft drinks and party food. I had bought party hats for the kids, in anticipation.

One of the mums was a neighbour, Pauline. She invited me to a Pippa Dee party in her house later that week. These parties were common at the time. While at the party you could purchase ladies' clothing from a reasonably priced range, brought there by a Pippa Dee representative. Whoever held the party would invite all of her friends, who could then buy some clothing, if they liked what they saw.

I turned up at the party early as I was on night duty at the hospital. I said that I could only stay for a few minutes. There were about ten people there at that time. Some of them I knew, some of them I did not know. Even though it was a small gathering, I did not interact with any of them, other than exchanging small pleasantries with those standing close to me, and my hostess, Pauline. I just really wanted to get away to work, as my time was extremely limited.

As I had a look through the clothes, my gaze was drawn to an older woman who was standing across the small room from me. I thought to myself, 'I know that woman from somewhere.'

Our eyes met and I felt that she showed some signs of recognition towards me. We gravitated towards one another.

She initiated the conversation with, 'Are you Irish?'

'Yes,' I replied.

'What part do you come from?' she enquired.

'Limerick.'

'How many children do you have?'

'I have two boys, Anthony aged seven and Ronan aged one and a half. I have also lost two babies.'

The representative who was selling the clothing then interrupted and asked the woman to pay for her purchases.

She began to fumble in her handbag and took out a cheque book and began to write a cheque. Over the years I had become good at reading what someone else was writing. I developed the technique, as I had spent many years being called in front of people and not knowing the reason why. Usually if I could read the piece of paper I might have some idea why I was being called to account.

In this case I noticed that the name printed on her cheque book was Rosaleen O'Regan. That confirmed to me my initial suspicion of who she was. While I was not familiar with the surname of O'Regan, her facial looks and her Christian name, Rosaleen, meant that she had to be my maternal aunt. She was my mother's only sister.

As Harry was dropping me to work, he was waiting outside in the car. I did not say my goodbyes to anyone; I just left the house immediately. I was in shock and I splurted out to Harry, 'You will never guess, in a month of Sundays, who is inside at Pauline's party.'

'Hold on,' he said. 'Calm down, what happened? Who is in there?'

'It is my mother's sister, Rosaleen.'

'Are you sure?' he queried.

'I am positive,' I said. 'I remember her from a meeting with my mother. It was about 20 years ago but I am positive that it is her.'

I didn't know what else to do, so Harry drove me to work. As I worked through the night, I kept remembering that day, 18 years before, in the Mount Orphanage, when Rosaleen accompanied her sister Doreen, as I met my mother for the first time. I was convinced that it was the same person. As soon as I got home from work the following morning, I phoned Pauline, to know if she had Rosaleen O'Regan's address. Pauline asked me why I wanted it.

'She is a relative that I have not seen for many years, and I would like to contact her,' I replied.

For a very short moment I was quite shocked with myself. I realised that everything that I had said was the truth. As far as my birth family were concerned, the truth and I were strangers. But for once I had spoken the truth about them.

It felt very good.

Pauline did not have the address but she said that the woman was a friend of Yvonne Loftus and she gave me Yvonne's phone number. I rang her immediately and she, in turn, gave me Rosaleen's address and phone number, without any probing or questioning.

Rosaleen's address was very close to where I lived. Walk to the bottom of our street, go under the railway bridge, walk 20 yards along a narrow alleyway and you are in the middle of her road. It was less than five minutes' walk. I was incredulous that my mother's sister was living two streets away from me.

After receiving this information, I was walking around in circles, in my sitting room. I went to bed to try to get some sleep, but it was impossible, as my head was buzzing. I just couldn't sleep.

For the next 48 hours, my mind never rested. I decided that I was going to meet her. I knew where she was living, so she could not escape. I was thinking of all sorts of scenarios, about what would happen when we met. All the old fears raised their ugly heads once again. Would she speak to me, when she realised who I was? Would she accept me unconditionally?

I felt that there was no hope of that.

I tried to anticipate the conditions under which I might be acceptable to her. Would she accept my family, Harry, Anthony and Ronan, unconditionally? Harry could decide for himself whether he wanted to be accepted by her. But I decided that I would not tolerate any conditions attached to my children's acceptability. My children were better than anybody, even my mother's family.

I decided not to call her by telephone, as she could easily hang up on me. I decided not to make it easy for her, but to turn up on her doorstep and introduce ourselves. I discussed my attack strategy with Harry. He agreed to support any battle actions that might ensue, which helped me to carry it through. Privately, I hoped that there would not be any casualties.

On the following Monday evening, Harry, Ronan and myself dropped Anthony to a cub scout session at St Bart's Church Hall. He would be there for at least two hours. We then drove to Runnymede Crescent, Streatham Vale, and presented ourselves on the doorstep.

I was as nervous as a kitten, but I did not show it. With Ronan in my arms, I rang the doorbell.

The woman from the party opened the door. She said to me, 'Hello, I recognise that smile, should I know you?'

'Yes,' I said, 'I am Doreen's daughter, Celine.'

'Come in,' she said politely. 'This must be my grand-nephew.'

I was a bit surprised she was so calm about it, but I just went along with it and said, 'Yes, his name is Ronan, and this is my husband, Harry.'

She led us into a small front room, where her son, Terence, was sitting, with his leg in plaster, watching TV.

'This is Terence, my son,' she said to me. 'This is Celine and Harry, your cousins.'

To me, she added, 'I have one other son, Clifford, and a daughter, Donna, who is married and living in Ireland.'

Terence asked me, 'Where do you live?'

'Just around the corner,' I replied.

To which he said, 'I did not know that we had cousins in the parish.'

His mother then said to him, with what I thought was

nervous laughter, 'You know us, we have cousins everywhere.'

My aunt then directed me alone upstairs, as if to show me the house. As soon as we were out of earshot I asked her, 'How is my mother?'

'She is fine,' she answered. 'I did not realise that you lived so near.'

I'm sure of all the places that my aunt did not want to find herself living was in a council house, within 500 yards of where her sister's illegitimate daughter was living. There were ten million people living in London, how could she get it so wrong? It was truly ironic.

'What will I tell my neighbours?' I said, as always anxious to please, because they knew her as a friend. I was trying to accommodate this superior being. I did not want to contaminate her, by being known to her friends as an illegitimate relative.

Then she said, 'I do not mind who knows that you are my niece.'

I was really delighted by that statement. It gave me a sort of sense of partial legitimacy and acceptance. She put the kettle on and made a cup of tea for everyone. Shortly afterwards, we left to collect Anthony from the cub scouts. We had agreed that Rosaleen would come over to me, at my house, the following afternoon at two o'clock.

The next day she arrived on her bicycle, on time. As I opened the door to her, I felt immediately from her demeanour that a change had taken place. I felt coldness, towards me.

I beckoned her to come in. As soon as the door was closed behind her, she said, 'I think that we should tell the neighbours that we are cousins' children.' In other words she no longer wanted to accept me as her niece.

It was agreed that I was to call her Rosaleen only, from then on. I felt so inferior that I would have agreed to anything, just to maintain any kind of link with my mother's family.

She left shortly afterwards and the entire meeting did not last five minutes. I felt sad and hurt by this meeting.

Her whole attitude towards me had changed from the previous night. Here I was consigned to 'status sub-human' once again. I wasn't going to give up that easily.

Ever the one to get my way, by subterfuge or subtle means, before she left I invited her, along with her son Terence and his girlfriend Niamh, to dinner on the following Sunday evening. Even if my mother and her family were once more trying to reject me, I was not going to let an opportunity like this pass me by.

They had all the information, I had none. I had no idea where all this might lead, but it might lead to somewhere better than where I was, information wise. I had no fears. Instead of forming battle plans, I was now going on a charm offensive.

She accepted the invitation and they came to dinner on the Sunday evening. No direct references were made to my parental family. I was just dying to ask a load of questions but I bit my tongue and bided my time. I had decided not to antagonise her in any way.

The relationship with my aunt was in its infancy and I would nourish it and see it grow over the long-term. She had all the information and I wanted it. If she did not give me the relevant data voluntarily, I would have to get it somehow, if not from her then from someone close to her. I would have to be patient, subtle and a little devious, if necessary. If I got lucky, then that would be a bonus.

One significant aspect reared its head over dinner that evening. I asked Terence how he had met his girlfriend, Niamh. They were both in their mid-twenties at the time. He said, 'I met her at the Regional Hospital in Limerick. She a nurse there. She was looking after my grandmother while she was ill, just before she died.'

Two things were obvious from that. Firstly, Niamh was a nurse. I would be able to strike a bond with her. Secondly, Terence was speaking about his maternal grandmother. I remember thinking at the time, 'He is speaking in very loving terms about a person who is also MY grandmother. But she is the grandmother who was primarily responsible for my life. She is the one responsible for consigning me to the scrap-heap of life as a five-month baby.'

This grandmother, whom he so fondly visited while she was dying in hospital, was the same wicked woman who would have gladly seen me dead, if she could have arranged it. There were so many low times in my life when I would have preferred it if she had been able to arrange my death, either before I was born or shortly afterwards.

I was consumed with anger, but I concealed my feelings and smiled. I continued the conversation as if I had not made any family connection and pretended that everything was 'rosy in the garden'. Angry as I was, at the specific reference to my grandmother Clifford, I was quite pleased to be entertaining what I regarded as 'my biological family'.

It became a regular occurrence for my Aunt Rosaleen, Terence and Niamh, to come to dinner at my home at least every other week. Then one evening Terence and Niamh turned up unannounced and I happened to be looking at some photographs when they arrived. I asked them in and they joined me going through the photographs. Terence saw the photograph of my mother, Ronan and me.

He said, 'I did not know that you knew Auntie Doreen.'

'Yes, I do,' I said.

'Is Auntie Doreen more closely related to you than me?' he asked.

'I think you should ask your Mum that particular question,' I replied.

The questions and answers were left hanging in mid-air. There was no further probing for the remainder of the evening. At this time his mother was in Ireland on a visit. When she returned to London he asked her, was he, Terence, Celine's cousin, or was Rosaleen, Celine's cousin. He said that he was confused as to the actual relationship. He was obviously trying to place me in his extended family. But he must have come to the conclusion that there was something strange about my 'cousin' status.

His mother replied, 'Why do you ask?'

He responded, 'Is Celine more closely related to Auntie Doreen than to you?'

She confessed the truth to him. She told him that I was indeed Doreen's firstborn, illegitimate daughter.

Niamh later told me that she cried all night when Terence told her the story. She said to me, 'They were such a cruel family.'

This was the first statement of public knowledge by that family that I actually existed. Really, apart from my mother, her mother, my mother's sister Rosaleen and my 'auntie nuns', nobody else in my biological family realised that I existed, as far as I knew. But the news of my existence travelled no farther. Terence and Niamh must have been sworn to secrecy. But I did not mind, a chink had appeared in their armour. The strategy of annoy nobody and bide my time was working.

I would find a way in the end.

* * * *

Donna, Rosaleen's daughter, and her husband, Paul Bell, who lived in Dublin, came to London to visit her mother in the summer of 1983. Paul and Donna had their two children with them. They all came to my house for dinner, with Rosaleen one Saturday evening. After dinner the kids were tired, and Donna took them home to put them to bed. Rosaleen went home with them. Paul stayed on talking to Harry and I.

I asked Paul if he knew my mother.

'Ah yeah, Doreen. Sure, of course I do, isn't she Donna's aunt?' he replied.

Next, in a most casual way, couched as a throwaway remark or question, I pondered aloud, 'I wonder do you know my father?'

As the last word left my lips, Paul said without hesitation, 'Aw yeah, Tom! Tom O'Sullivan from Janesboro. Sure, of course I do. Sure there is no doubt about it, Celine, he's your father!'

I nearly fell off the chair.

He said it with such certainty. I was devastated that he knew my parentage and was so confident in that knowledge. My mind was racing. How many other people knew? Was I the only person in this awful saga that did not know who my father was?

I was fuming inside. I thought, 'No, this can not be. It must be the alcohol talking.'

Paul had drunk quite a large amount of wine during the meal and had consumed four or five stiff brandies afterwards.

Externally, I was as cool as a cucumber. I asked, 'How am I ever going to contact him?'

He said, 'Brothers are close. He has a brother called Paddy that he is very fond of. If you contact him, he is your best bet.'

I think he realised that he had committed a terrible sin, because he then added, 'Now lads, don't tell anyone that I gave you this information. This is TOP SECRET in the Clifford family. I'd be hung, drawn and quartered, if they ever found out that I told you. I'd have to take the boat.'

I had such trouble taking all this in. I could pursue it no further. I was unable to think straight.

Shortly afterwards Paul left to go home. As I watched him walk unevenly down the road, I thought, 'It *must* be the alcohol that is talking, he could not know with such certainty.' And yet I could not get what Paul had said out of my mind.

I was going to hunt down this lead, whatever the cost. I was going to control it myself. I was not going to let anyone else do any of the work for me. I would not be deterred from this. I was away on a crusade once again!

I knew that a work colleague was at home on holiday in Ireland at that time. By a torturous and circuitous route, I got the telephone number of her parents in Ireland. I spoke to her mother and asked her to get me a copy of the Irish rural phone book with Limerick phone numbers in it. I got her to promise that she would make sure that her daughter would bring me back a copy, without fail. I must have sounded desperate, because when my colleague returned from Ireland she delivered the phone book to my house, on her way home from the airport, by taxi.

As soon as I had the book, I phoned all the names of P. O'Sullivan in the Limerick area. I asked if they had a brother called Thomas, who lived in Janesboro. Eventually a man who lived in Corbally said in answer to my question, 'Yes, I have a brother Thomas in Janesboro.'

I then said to him, 'My name is Celine Roberts. My mother is Doreen Clifford. I have been told that Thomas O'Sullivan is my father. I want to make contact with him.'

The classic 'pregnant silence' ensued. There was not much dialogue between us. He said that he would, 'see what he could do'. He sounded as if he did not believe my story. He sounded nervous and subdued. Above all, he sounded shocked.

I tried to emphasise, how important it was for me to meet my father. He replied, 'The identity of a father may never be established.'

It had never occurred to me that such a possibility existed.

I gave him my address and telephone number in London. I tried to push him into contacting me if he spoke to my father, but he did not offer to call me. He did not offer anything. I thought that he was probably disturbed by my phone call.

While the entire phone call was a legitimate request from me, I had no idea what consternation I might have caused him. He was probably just about to have his dinner, while putting his feet up after a hard day's work.

This phone call took place on the second of August. The month of September passed and Paddy O'Sullivan did not contact me. My mind was now buzzing every day.

I was getting close to meeting my father. I was so close now, that I was not about to give up easily. I would have access to my father, without going through my mother. I was going to circumvent my mother, who had always protected my father's identity from me. Why did she protect his identity so assiduously?

I never mentioned my contact with Paddy O'Sullivan to anyone, in case I was persuaded not to explore the link any further. I did not want to be dissuaded from further exploration. Paul had given me the information in confidence. While it was a drunken confidence, I appreciated it so much that he had broken what was obviously a code of silence within my mother's family, the Cliffords.

He was the first person who had given me any hope of ever meeting with my father. I did not want to betray that confidence.

I checked the post every day for a letter from Paddy O'Sullivan.

None came.

October came and I decided more direct and personal intervention was necessary. I would go to Ireland and see Paddy O'Sullivan myself.

During the mid-term school break, Harry's trusty old Ford Escort was packed up again with our belongings, and all four of us headed once more for the ferry terminal at Fishguard. We made our usual stop at Harry's parents' home in Kilkenny. We only stayed there for one night, the Friday night. It was only a brief stay, as I was on a mission.

Next day we travelled on to Kit's house at Buttevant. This was to be my 'operations' base. We arrived on Saturday and settled the kids in. On Sunday I set out my battle plan. I told Kit what I was going to do. I think in Kit's own way, while she did not approve of my battle plan, she understood.

I decided to tell my minder, Sister Bernadette, what I was about to do. On Sunday I phoned her at her base in Mount Trenchard Convent in Foynes, County Limerick. When someone answered, they asked, 'Who is looking for her?'

I answered: 'Celine Roberts wants to speak to her.'

After a pause the woman's voice said, 'She is not here.'

I asked, 'Where is she?'

The voice replied that she did not know. Then she hung up on me. I was disturbed by the nun's attitude on the phone. Later that day, I phoned the convent looking for Sister Bernadette again.

They said, 'She is sick.'

I said that I had travelled all the way from London, and wanted to visit her. They gave me the telephone number of a convent in Cobh, County Cork and hung up.

When I called the convent in Cobh, I asked to speak with Sister Bernadette. 'There is no Sister Bernadette here,' they informed me and hung up. I decided that there was something strange going on, although I did not know what.

I felt that I was being given the run-around, so I decided not to continue trying to contact her.

I never spoke to her or tried to contact her further. I was never to hear from her again – ever.

For somebody who had such a large influence over such important information in my life, it was a strange way to end our communications.

On the Monday my battle plan was to go into action. I telephoned Paddy O'Sullivan and I told him that I was in Ireland and that I wanted to meet him. I do not think that he expected to hear from me again.

I felt his resistance to meeting me at first, but he eventually agreed to meet me in the bar of the Glenworth Hotel, in Limerick, the following evening at 8 pm.

I put down the phone. I was a nervous wreck. I was bathed in sweat. But I had more plans to put in to action. I rang Father Bernard, who had remained my friend and confidant throughout the years. He was at home at Glenstal Abbey, when I phoned. I told him my plan about meeting whom I considered to be my father's brother, Paddy O'Sullivan, the next evening at the Glenworth Hotel. He said, 'My dear Celine. Do you want me to go along with you to the meeting, as support?'

'I would be very grateful for your support, if you could be there,' I replied.

We agreed to meet in the bar of the Glenworth at 7 pm, so we would have time to chat before meeting Paddy O'Sullivan.

The arrangements were in place.

The people were in place.

I asked Kit and Tony if they would look after my children for as long as necessary. They readily agreed. The military support was in place.

The following day I went and had my hair done, as I wanted to look my best. I spent ages on my make-up. I tried on all the outfits that I had brought with me. I borrowed a valuable bracelet from Kit.

Time passed slowly that day.

Eventually, Harry and I set off for our meeting with Father Bernard. After thinking every day for three months about what I would say to Paddy at our meeting, I had no prepared list of questions. They were all in my head. But I would shoot from the hip. I would take no prisoners this time. I was focused and I knew what I wanted. It was within my grasp, and I did not want it to slip away.

Harry and I reached the bar first. There were a few people drinking, but we sat at a table that would be out of earshot of the bar area. It was almost an alcove. We had a soft drink each. There would be no alcohol. I had to keep a clear head.

Father Bernard turned up next. We greeted each other with our usual hug. He sat and chatted about Anthony and Ronan and other small talk. He said that he had never realised that I had wanted to meet my father so much. He thought that I was always afraid, because of the risk of damage to my father's family. He asked me why I had now decided to 'rock that particular boat' as he could see that I was determined to see it through, whatever the consequences. He said, 'No matter how much they tried to hide you and your identity, the truth will come out.'

At about 7.50 pm, a man and a woman entered the bar. They seemed a very elegant couple. They exchanged a few words between them and approached our table directly. I stood up, as I knew that it had to be Paddy O'Sullivan. My heart was thumping.

He came to me with his hand extended. We shook hands and he said, 'You must be Celine Roberts. I am Paddy O'Sullivan and this is my wife, Mary.'

'Yes, I am. This is Harry, my husband and this is Father Bernard O'Dea, a good friend of mine. He has agreed to be here, because he has known me for a very long time.'

I asked Paddy O'Sullivan if he had any objection to Father Bernard's presence. He said, 'No, none whatsoever.'

We all sat down around the table. Harry recognised his pre-arranged cue, and asked everyone what he or she would like to drink. Paddy had a soft drink, Father Bernard had a gin and tonic, and Mary had a whiskey and water. I wasted no time and asked Paddy directly, 'Have you spoken to my father?'

To which he replied, 'No!'

I was taken aback. That could mean anything.

But before I got a chance to talk about it any further, he followed on with, 'There is no money to be had here, girl.'

Harry came back with the drinks and at this point Father Bernard interjected and said in a voice which did not betray his anger, 'If Celine was after money, she could have done a lot of things, a long time ago.'

I said, 'No, I am not here for money. I am here because I want to find my father and establish my identity. I know nothing of my background. I only know what I have been told, and that is very little.'

Paddy then said, 'There is a big family involved. There are nine children; a lot of them are married with children of their own. There are a lot of people who could get hurt.'

Father Bernard said, 'Celine has had a lot of hurt also.'

Paddy then said that he would talk to a priest, a Father Houlihan, who was a friend of Doreen's. He said that he was a hundred per cent sure that his brother Tom was totally unaware of my existence. He said that what he really wanted was for Father Houlihan to get Doreen, my mother, to tell his brother Tom about their daughter.

That sounded fine to me. It was then agreed between us that Paddy would set about arranging a meeting between my mother and the priest. He qualified it by saying that he could not promise anything. Paddy then started to ask questions about me.

'Where do you live? Do you come to Ireland often?'

I replied that I came 'home' once or twice a year.

'Where is home in Ireland?' he asked.

I said, 'Mostly we stay at Buttevant, or Castleconnell with friends or Kilkenny with Harry's parents.'

He asked if I worked. I told him that I was a nurse and had two children. While the conversation had not become friendly, the atmosphere was not as frosty as at the beginning.

He then asked, 'Where did you grow up?'

'In Kilmallock,' I replied.

'Did you know the Browns of Kilmallock? They had a shop.'

'Yes, I did.'

'They are cousins of mine.'

'Do you know the Powers?'

'Yes, I do. I worked for them when I was 14.'

'Did you know Maurice Power's business partner, Pat O'Sullivan? He is my first cousin.'

'Yes, I worked for his brother Jimmy, as a housemaid, when I was 16. It was for a short time.'

My mind was in a whirr. The conversation revealed that I had, in fact, spent much of my early days close to my father's family. I had even worked for them and I did not realise it.

The meeting with Paddy O'Sullivan and his wife came to an end. Paddy asked if I knew what Tom did for a living. I replied, 'I was told that he was a lawyer.'

'No, he is not a lawyer.'

'I do not care if he is a road sweeper, as long as he is my father,' I countered.

As they rose to go, Mary said, 'You are the spitting image of Doreen, there is no doubt that you are her daughter.'

The atmosphere had become somewhat light-hearted. Paddy offered, 'Well, your father looks a bit like myself.'

To which I responded, with a smile, 'If he looks like you, he must be okay, you are not too bad-looking yourself.'

With that, my genuine Uncle Paddy shook hands with me, gave me his business card and then they left.

I felt elated. I had an uncle. This was my first contact with my father's family.

I came away from that meeting with a feeling of a degree of acceptance, however tiny. I felt that the mere fact that they had agreed to speak to me at all, meant that I was not totally the scum of the earth.

We left the hotel and walked Father Bernard back to his car. We collected our own car and drove back to Buttevant. Talk in the car with Harry was kept to pleasantries and small chit-chat. The intricate details of my meeting were not discussed, but I went over every minute detail in my head.

I was pleased that everything had gone better than I had expected. I felt content for the first time in months.

Except for one niggling little aspect.

When Mary had said that I was the spitting image of Doreen, I felt that she spoke of Doreen as if she had known her quite well. I was surprised that my father and mother would have kept in touch.

The following Wednesday, Kit asked me if I would like to go and see the 'family mansion' in Clarina, County Limerick, where my mother had been brought up as a child. Tony and herself had discovered it on a drive one Sunday. I said that I would love to see it, and that I would like to meet Clifford, Rosaleen's other son, who was living there.

'Oh great,' said Kit. 'You will be able to have a tour of the estate grounds and the mansion. We had better leave early, as it might take quite a long time to take the entire tour of the house and grounds.'

I thought Kit sounded a bit strange when she said this, but I was too excited to think much of it. The four of us, plus Kit as navigator, headed off with Harry as driver, for the Grand Estate of the Clifford Dynasty, at Ballybrown, Clarina, County Limerick.

We arrived at Clarina and took directions from Kit for Ballybrown. As we drove through Ballybrown, Kit yelled from the back seat, 'Hauld your horses there, Harry, you've passed it.'

I said from the back, 'How could we have passed it? There has not been sight nor light of a mansion for miles.'

'Reverse up there about 50 yards, Harry,' Kit ordered.

Harry reversed the car and stopped outside a small cottage.

Kit said in a low, serious and somewhat angry voice, 'There it is now for you geril. This is what all the grandeur is about. There is your mansion for you now. Your mother's family really have something to crow about, don't they?'

I was aghast. I said, 'Kit, it is no bigger than the place that I grew up in. They condemned me to that life because I was not good enough for them. Who do they think they are?' I wanted to say so much more but I didn't want to upset my boys.

It was a grey, unpainted cottage. It had three rooms at most. I mean three rooms altogether. It looked a wreck. Memories flooded back to me. I would have walked by this house many times, as part of a group of inmates who were being brought for an afternoon walk from the Mount industrial school, just a couple of miles down the road. This triggered a flashback to the few times that Sister Bernadette said that she had met my grandmother 'in town'. She referred to my grandmother as, 'The grand lady in her fur coat.' Sister Bernadette often asked her if she would like to come and meet me, to which she would reply that she wanted 'nothing at all to do with me'. She 'wanted no shame brought on her family, by acknowledging the existence of her bastard granddaughter'. If Sister Bernadette had only seen the 'large mansion' that my grandmother, the 'grand lady', had lived in, the nun might not have held her in such high regard.

The entire estate consisted of no more than one acre, two at most. I could not equate what I saw in front of me, with what I had experienced when I met my mother and her sister, and what I had been told by Sister Bernadette. How could these people have paid £300 to imprison me in such a hellhole, while they were nothing more than ordinary cottage-folk, living in hardly better circumstances than I had been sentenced to? It didn't make any sense.

Thinking back to my mother's conversation with Sister Bernadette at our previous meeting, I realised that this tiny cottage could never in its wildest dreams have accommodated an Adam's fireplace. Who was she trying to impress?

I could not even laugh at the absurdity of it all.

Reeling from a sense of shock, I knocked on the door. A man, who turned out to be Rosaleen's son Clifford, answered the door and invited us in. Both he and his wife Barbara were friendly, welcoming and hospitable. It was a very strange feeling for me, to stand in the home of the woman who had sold her first-born grandchild.

I was completely churned up inside.

I felt physically sick.

Clifford said that I was the spitting image of his Aunt Doreen. I told Clifford that I had met my uncle, Paddy O'Sullivan, for the first time, just the night before. He was visibly taken aback and very shocked at this news. I told him that my Uncle Paddy and a Father Houlihan were going to speak to my mother, to get her to tell my father of my existence.

I felt Clifford become uneasy. After that he could not get rid of us quickly enough.

We left after a short time and headed back to Buttevant. My mood lightened on the car trip, as Kit and I had some good laughs about the lifestyle of the 'rich and famous' I had imagined going on in the Clifford lands and estates!

We returned to London at the end of a very eventful week. So much had been revealed and yet, so many questions remained unanswered.

FIFTEEN

My Father's Voice

Despite my careful strategy, events now began to take on a life of their own and to spiral out of my control.

As soon as I reached London on the following Sunday night, I telephoned Kit to say that we had arrived home safely. This was standard procedure when we travelled from Ireland. Kit told me, 'That man that you went to meet in Limerick rang here looking for you. He said to call him because it was important.'

I rang Paddy O'Sullivan in Ireland immediately. Paddy himself answered the phone. When he knew that it was me he said, 'I have good news for you. Your father has been told about you.'

'So he is my father?' I asked.

'Yes, there never was any doubt about that!'

He gave me a telephone number and told me that it was my father's. He said he thought that it would be best if I waited for my father to call me, rather than I call him. 'He has had quite a shock, but you will be hearing from him.'

Then he hung up.

I slid to the floor with the phone in my hand. I sat there and I cried for a long, long time. I eventually got up, went in to the sitting room and said to Harry, 'He is my father and he knows about me.'

Once I had this information, I became impatient.

I wanted to hear his voice.

I could not wait for him to call me.

I had to call him. I dialled his number. I had prepared no speech. I had no idea what I would say to him. A lady's voice answered the phone. I suddenly did not know whom to ask for. So I blurted out, 'This is Celine, and I am calling from London.'

Then the lady at the other end of the phone said in the sharp tone of voice that I knew well, 'I hope you are satisfied now!' and hung up on me.

I dropped the phone as if it was on fire.

It was my MOTHER'S voice!

I could not figure it out. What was she doing at that number, my father's number? The awful truth slowly dawned on me.

She must live there.

She must live with my father.

She must be MARRIED to my father.

Little by little it sank in that she must have been married to him all along. All those years while she had spoken of 'her family' and 'the family', Sister Bernadette and my mother had spoken of my father's family as if it was a separate and different unit. Now I suddenly realised that they were one and the same family. My father and my mother were husband and wife. That meant that I had brothers and sisters.

Once again, I was the victim of my mother's cruel games.

I began to unpack all our stuff from our trip. I worked like a Trojan getting Anthony's school clothes out and ready for him. I had to distract myself.

I was really low. I could not believe it. My mother had won again.

In a moment of madness, I rang my Aunt Rosaleen, just two streets away. She was not there, but her son Terence was there. I blurted out to him all that had happened. I told him that my father now knew of my existence. I told him in what I thought was a calm voice. I did not tell him that my mother had answered the phone to me. I did not yell at him in anger, 'Why did you not tell me that my mother was married to my father?'

I did not hear from my Aunt Rosaleen or her son Terence after that for a long, long time, years in fact. Our bi-weekly dinner dates ceased immediately. I thought it was their way of punishing me for trying to make contact with my father. I felt that they did not want what they saw as the family's shameful secret, out in the open. They certainly did not want it flaunted about. I can only assume that I was a 'loose cannon' as far as they were concerned. Mentally exhausted, I went to bed and cried my heart out.

When Anthony came home from school on Monday evening, he was standing beside me at the sink in the kitchen, in his school uniform, hugging me before I even knew he was back. I needed that hug.

I asked him, 'How would you like to have real grandparents?'

He said, 'But we already have real grandparents, Granny Roberts in Ballyogan, in Kilkenny.'

'That's right, darling,' I said. 'But you don't have any grandparents on Mummy's side.'

'Yes, that's right Mum, because your mum and dad are dead.'

'That is not really true, Anthony,' I said.

Imagine saying this to an eight year old. It was difficult.

'The mummy and daddy that brought me up are dead, but my real mummy and daddy are still alive. Remember the lady that we met in the hotel with the nun, who I told you was auntie Kathleen, that lady is really your granny. Also you are going to have lots of new aunties and uncles.'

Anthony became very excited and wanted to meet them. I told him not to tell anybody.

He went to school the next day and immediately told his teacher that his mummy had been adopted and had found her mummy and daddy. He also told his entire class. When I went to collect him from school in the afternoon, his teacher, Sister Pat, approached me and excitedly told me exactly what Anthony had told her and the entire class. She asked me if it were true. With an air of pride about me, I said that it was.

On that Tuesday night, I had a phone call at home, at about 9 pm.

A strong, clear, male voice, with an Irish accent said, 'Hello, can I speak to Celine?'

'Celine speaking,' I replied.

'You must be my long-lost daughter?'

I felt about seven feet tall.

I cried.

He cried.

He said, 'I love you and I can't wait to see you. I have a big gang here waiting to speak to you. You will never be on your own again. All your brothers and sisters want to meet you. They are all going to speak to you and they will each tell you their names.'

A female voice then came on the line and said, 'I am Eileen. Hello, big sister.'

She cried.

And then I cried.

Eight more voices, four male and four female, came on the line, each one identified themselves and then broke down in tears.

I cried with them each time.

After nine different voices, my father came back on the

line. 'Your mother and I want to go over to London and meet you and our grandsons. Would you be able to accommodate us?'

I replied, 'It would be my privilege.'

He then said, 'I lived and worked in London after the war.'

'Where did you live in London?'

'Regent's Park,' he said.

'Well, I live in a much more humble part of London. I live in Streatham.'

'We will travel to London on Sunday next, if we can get a flight. I work at Shannon Airport, and we will be on stand-by.'

I gave him my address. I told him that we would collect him at the airport.

He then ended the phone call with, 'Goodbye. Good luck until we meet!'

When I put the phone down, I was in absolute shock. I was shattered emotionally.

I somehow dragged myself to the sofa and lay down. My mind was in a whirl.

As excited as I was, I could not help but have questions about my parents' first trip to see me. Why did they not fly over immediately? Why wait for a 'stand-by' flight when I would have happily paid for the tickets?

And most of all, where does my mother stand in all this? She had not communicated a word to me since her last, angry, phone response.

I hoped these questions would be answered soon enough.

SIXTEEN

The Royal Visit

Preparations for their arrival began. I spring-cleaned the entire house from top to bottom. Nothing could be too good or too clean for the arrival of what I now considered to be 'my royal family'.

On Tuesday of that week, in the early afternoon, my new-found sister Eileen phoned. She said, 'I can't wait to see you. I was thinking of cashing in my insurance policy to pay for my fare.'

'Don't do that, I am sure we will meet soon,' I said.

'Daddy is delighted to have found you and he can't wait to see you, either. He was mad at Auntie Rosaleen for not telling him about you.'

I found that remark really strange. I expected my father to be really angry with my mother for not telling him about me for so many years. But that did not seem to be an issue. I did not pursue it with my new sister as I was trying to build bridges, not destroy them.

She said that she had lived in London when she was first married. She asked about my children and I reciprocated. It turned out that her daughter and my son Anthony were born in the same year. We ended by saying that we would meet soon.

Finally, she said, 'I love you, Sis.'

I said in reply, 'I love you, my new-found sister.'

I found it really strange, saying such things to someone that I had never met and had just spoken to for the first time.

I discovered later that events had spiralled out of control after I had been to visit Clifford at Clarina. The following day he had set off for Janesboro. He was going to see my mother and tell her that I had visited Clarina and had talked to Paddy O'Sullivan. On the bus he had met Charlie Healy, who I would later learn was my brother-in-law. He was married to my oldest sister, Eileen. Clifford had told Charlie about my visit and my existence. Charlie had been gobsmacked and recognised imminent trouble on the family horizon.

Charlie told Clifford not to do or say anything to anyone, until he got back to him. He had then contacted his sister-in-law, who was married to Eileen's brother, Tommy O'Sullivan Junior. They had met and discussed the situation. Marion had been shocked to hear about me. They had decided to talk to their respective partners and then to question my mother.

When Tommy Junior arrived home from work that evening, Marion had told him that he had a full older sister whom he had never met. He was incredulous, but said that if he had another sister, he wanted to meet her and know her. Charlie meanwhile took Eileen to the pub that night, bought her a few stiff drinks and told her about me.

Her first reaction was, 'That is a load of rubbish. There are nine of us in the family and I am the eldest child.' As a throwaway question, Eileen then asked Charlie, 'As a matter of interest, what is her name?'

Charlie replied, 'Celine.'

'Holy lamb of divine Jaysus, it must be true. Mammy's name is Doreen Marie CELINE,' said Eileen.

Charlie then told her that Tommy Junior and his wife Marion also knew that I existed, so the four of them had got together and hatched a plan. They had all agreed that the following Saturday evening, November 5, 1983, while my father pursued his favourite pastime of greyhound racing and its attendant gambling, they would entice my mother to visit Eileen's house. When they had her on her own, they would ask her if they had a full sister, called Celine. Charlie's part in the plan, was to collect Tom O'Sullivan from the dog track, and on the pretext of discussing some business with him, take him to his house where Doreen would be waiting.

When Saturday came, the plan had been put into action and was executed faultlessly. Tom O'Sullivan was at the dog track. Charlie had collected Doreen, my mother, and taken her to his house. When she got there and all the preliminary greetings were over, Marion and Charlie, being the in-laws, retired to the kitchen, while Tommy Junior and Eileen confronted their mother.

They told me much later that Tommy Junior said to her directly, 'Have we got a sister called Celine?'

My mother, apparently, looked at him aghast and said, 'How do you know?'

Tommy Junior said, 'It does not matter how I know, is it true?'

My mother then answered, 'Yes, it is true. You do have a sister called Celine.'

Then Eileen asked, 'Who is the father?'

My mother answered, 'Your daddy is, of course, but he has never been told of her existence.'

When Clifford had spoken to Charlie initially, he mentioned that I had seen Paddy O'Sullivan, Tom's brother, and that he was aware of my existence. When the four 'conspirators', Charlie, Eileen, Tommy Junior and Marion, had talked together, they all assumed that Paddy O'Sullivan had always known about me, from day one.

Tommy Junior had then said to his mother, 'Paddy

O'Sullivan knows about Celine, do you want him to be here, when Daddy comes over, after the dog racing?'

'Yes,' she said.

Eileen had then phoned Paddy O'Sullivan, and asked him to drive over to her house. He agreed and had arrived shortly afterwards, with his wife Mary. Charlie was then dispatched to collect his father-in-law from the dog track.

The grand finale was ready to unfold. In some ways I wish I could have been there.

Tom O'Sullivan had had a good night at the dogs and was in great form as he had won some money. After they got out of the car and were approaching the house, he had recognised cars belonging to various members of the family, and said, 'You never told me that you were having a party.'

'I don't think that there will be any party tonight, Tom,' Charlie had muttered.

They entered the house and Tom had sat down beside my mother Doreen, slightly bewildered. Everyone was in the room. As Tom looked at everybody quizzically, Paddy O'Sullivan asked his brother Tom, 'Do you remember back 35 years ago, to 18 Sarsfield Street, to when Doreen and you were young lovers?'

Cautiously, Tom said, 'Yes, I can. I make no apologies; I took advantage of a situation.'

Paddy had then said bluntly, 'What you do not know, is that out of that love a baby girl was born that you have never been told about.'

Tom wheeled around and stared at Doreen and said, 'Why didn't you tell me?'

'I was afraid,' she replied.

Paddy added, 'You will be very proud of her. She is a nurse. She is married. She has two children and she lives in London.'

Tom had been shocked. He had then said to Doreen, 'I

am extremely hurt by this. You know that I would never have left you.'

There was no more to be said at this particular time. Tom suggested that it was time to go home and Charlie had got the unenviable job of driving them back to their place.

I asked my father, many months later, how he had felt at that particular moment. He told me he wished, 'that the ground would have opened up and swallowed him.' He felt so ashamed. He said that night he recalled the house that they used to make love. He remembered asking Doreen, around that time, if she was pregnant. I later asked my mother about this, and she said that she did not know what pregnant meant, at that age.

I presume that after my parents left, everybody concerned then sat there talking about the meeting. I was never privy to these discussions, so I can only speculate as to what might have been said.

The next thing that happened was that Tom O'Sullivan, officially now my father, had called a family conference for the following Tuesday evening. He did not know that I had spoken to my mother on the previous Sunday. I was still reeling from her rebuff and the realisation that they had been married to each other all along. The family conference consisted of his wife Doreen, and his nine children, at their house. The spouses of the married family members were not invited.

He sat them all down and addressed them with, 'When your mother and I were young . . . ' At the end of the speech, he had then apparently said that he was going to phone me, and that they could all speak to me. Months later, my youngest sister Thelma told me that between the Saturday of the confrontation and the Tuesday of the family meeting, she knew that something major was afoot. She thought that one or other of her parents had been diagnosed with a serious illness. Tom, her father kept asking her, 'Do you still love me, Thelma?' She had thought he was going to die. He seemed to need the reassurance, as if a major life event was about to take place.

On the Thursday of that week, my father had then made that first monumental call to me.

Even a few days after the call, my heart was still away and racing with excitement. I could not get over the fact that I had spoken to my father.

The following days were a blur and a flurry of domestic activity.

Cakes were baked.

Meat dishes were prepared.

Tables were set.

Tables were reset.

Recipes were consulted.

All was ready.

Especially me!

Harry just let me get on with it and Anthony was excited. Ronan was too young to understand what was going on.

Sunday arrived.

It was to be the most important day of my life.

Preparations continued throughout the day. Everything was in place. I tried not to think of what was about to happen. I was going to meet my father. I was going to meet my father and my mother. I suppose, having got to this stage, I really expected him to come on his own.

I had also expected a more immediate response from him. I wanted to have him alone. Instead, the dark spectre of my mother loomed. One part of me still had not recovered from her rebuff when she answered my telephone call. The other half of me now expected my father to have solved the issue of my mother's attitude to me, over the remainder of the week.

I expected him to solve all my problems. I thought that

he would make my mother love me. I expected everything to be 'absolutely beauoooootiful' from now on. Everything would run smoothly in my life, because my father was here to solve all my problems. It was stupid of me to think like that, but my thought processes were blinkered.

In reality, I knew that my mother did not want any part of my reappearance or intrusion into 'her' family. She could never accept me as part of her family. My opinion now is that she gave me life and, at five months old, she got rid of me. She locked the doors of her heart and mind to me, and consequently, she could never accept me.

I often think back to the meeting in the convent. It was at my request. Up until that meeting she had control over my disappearance. After that day she had lost some of that control and I became a very tangible threat. I think she may have realised that I was not going to disappear and that she was going to have to cope with my existence. I think it made her hate me.

I had flowers in their bedroom. I checked and rechecked them. I got dressed for going to the airport. Then myself, Harry and the two boys went to six o'clock mass at St Bart's Church in Norbury. I could not concentrate on the service. I was really apprehensive. In the middle of the mass ceremony, I decided that the outfit that I had so carefully chosen to wear to the airport was not suitable. Harry and the two boys had to stand up and I ushered them out of their seats. They were frog-marched down the aisle, out to the car and home again, where I continued to deliberate over what to wear for my father.

I got changed again and eventually we headed for Heathrow Airport. We arrived punctually, parked the car and set off for the arrivals hall. We all lined up at the barrier. Anthony and Ronan were extremely well-behaved. They really were. They did everything they were asked. They must have known how anxious I was. There wasn't a 'bip' out of

Harry either. I think that he was gob-smacked by what was going on.

I saw my mother first. There was a man walking beside her. That was when I saw my father for the first time. When I first saw him, I knew it was him. He was wearing a beige Crombie coat, beige trousers and brown leather shoes. He was a tall well-built man, who walked towards me with a strong confident stride.

I left Harry and the boys. I reached my mother first. I barely kissed her. I reached for my father's outstretched arms and cried in his strong embrace for five minutes. We returned to Harry and the boys at the outside of the barrier. He kissed the boys and shook hands with Harry. Harry carried their luggage out to the car.

My mother wanted to go to the bathroom. I showed her where it was, but I quickly went back to my father. I could not leave him for an instant. I felt that if I let him out of my sight, he might disappear again. My mother reappeared and we walked towards the car. While Harry and my father were putting the luggage in the boot of the car, my mother said to me, 'Your father does not know about our meeting at Cruise's Hotel. And I would rather that he did not know.'

I said to her, 'Because of my birth, I have had to lie all my life and I refuse to lie anymore.' My reply really set up another barrier between my mother and me. Perhaps it got things off to a bad start between us, but I was not prepared to go along with what my mother wanted anymore. This was the first time that I had refused to do what my mother wanted. I had gone along with everything she had ever said, up to this moment. After the horrific shock of finding out how much she had lied to me, I had decided that I was not going to do so anymore.

We then drove back to our small but spotless home. I had fed the boys and had dinner all prepared before I left for the airport. I cooked the meal and Harry put the boys to bed. Then Harry, my mother, my father and I sat around the table and ate the meal that I had cooked.

I was in seventh heaven. But I was nervous. I was nervous about how I could live up to their expectations.

Having seen my parents, I thought that they looked so elegant and distinguished. They were expensively dressed. I had dreamt that they were aristocratic and wealthy. I thought they fitted the fantasy perfectly.

The atmosphere throughout dinner was strange. I was having a meal with my mother and my father in my home, yet I did not know them. They were strangers to me. They would say things to each other in an intimate kind of way, as any married couple would, but I felt excluded during those familiar little exchanges between them.

The conversation between us was all small talk and was stiff. My father mentioned that he would not know his way around London anymore. I tried to ask a lot about his family, who were actually my own brothers and sisters. It was my father who did most of the talking, and who filled me in on who they were, what they were doing, and whom they were married to.

As the meal ended, Harry began clearing the dishes from the table to the kitchen, for washing. I think he was glad to have something to do. My mother offered to help Harry to do the wash-up. She said to me, 'You two stay and talk. You have been without him long enough.'

I was surprised and was glad to go into the sitting room with him. I sat on the sofa beside him, holding his hand. At one point he said, 'You know, your mother always wanted to be a nurse.'

One of the things that surprised me at the time was that when I asked about my brothers and sisters, I expected to be told that they all had extremely high-flying business or academic careers. This turned out not to be the case. They seemed to have pursued successful but normal careers. As far as I was concerned, they had their parents, their education and a family upbringing. I thought that if you had those opportunities in life, you could be successful in any career. I could not understand how people who had everything that I did not have, could not be exceptionally successful financially.

I thought that if you had parents, the world was your oyster.

The more that I learnt about my siblings' careers, the easier I began to feel about myself. I began to think, 'I am successful. I have achieved as much academically and careerwise as any of them. I am somebody, and I did it on my own. I did it without anyone else's help.' This was for me the beginning of a growing feeling of self-worth.

I began to feel that maybe, 'I am not the scum of the earth. I am somebody to be respected after all.' I began to see myself in a whole new light and it felt good.

I saw parents as protecting their children from all the bad things in the world. I asked my father, 'If you had known that I existed, would you have wanted me?'

He did not give me a satisfying answer. He said, 'Yes.' But he qualified it by saying, 'If you had been put in another place, where my sisters were nuns, you would have been looked after.' That reply gave me the nagging feeling that he did not want me either, really. I felt that he too did not want the shame of an illegitimate child. He thought that it would have been all right if I had been sent somewhere where I would have been safe, but hidden.

I went back to talking about my brothers and sisters, my new family, all nine of them. When I had started to look for my father, I had no interest in his other children, as I had presumed that I would only be their half-sister, but now I wanted to know all about them and I could not wait to see them.

Harry and my mother had completed a very long and extended dishwashing session and broke up the conversation on the sofa by their reappearance in the sitting room. It was decided by general consensus that we should all go to bed for the night and talk more in the morning. I hugged my mother briefly, and I hugged and kissed my father for at least another five minutes. Everybody then went to bed.

I could not sleep. My mind was in race mode.

My father had turned out to be everything that I had wanted him to be. Although there was one surprise – he was not a solicitor. He actually worked as a waiter. He was strong and he was smart. He was so handsome. I felt somehow, for the first time in my life, that there was a man I could trust, who could protect me. He was someone that I could be so proud of and, most importantly, someone I could finally call Dad.

My mind raced on into the night.

On November 13, 1983, I had met my father for the very first time in my life. I was 35 years of age!

The next morning I got up and cooked enough breakfast for an army.

My father said that he was going out to the shops to get a newspaper. I thought that he might have been more interested in talking to me, but then he came back and handed me a birthday card which had printed on the outside, 'To dear daughter'. On the inside he had written, 'To Celine, lots of love, Mum and Dad.'

Of course, it was my birthday. I had forgotten in all the excitement. It was November 14, exactly 35 years to the day since I was born.

It was the first birthday card that I had received from my parents. I was really thrilled to get the card, but I was slightly disappointed. The pre-printed words had been written for a daughter who had always known her parents, and did not reflect our relationship at all. Moreover, I had not expected

anything from them, but given the card, it seemed strange
not to bring some little gift, however small, to mark the
occasion of the first birthday we had ever spent together.

I had hoped for some memento of their visit or some
gift, however small, for my children. At the airport, my
father had had a parcel under his arm as he arrived. As we
had got to the car, he said, 'There's a present for ye both.
Thanks be to God I can leave it down, 'cos it has my right
arm broken.'

It had turned out to be an uncooked Limerick ham.

I wanted something to remind me of of that special day,
which was, apart from the births of my children, the most
significant day of my life. Somehow an uncooked Limerick
ham did not quite seem to fit the bill! I had thrown the
ham with uncharacteristic force into the freezer, to keep for
Christmas. It was not enough to be a lasting memory of my
most important day.

May and June, my good neighbours, came across for a
few minutes, to meet my parents. Ronan was at nursery and
Anthony was at school. My mother just sat there and did
not say very much, but my father and I spent a lot of time
talking.

After my neighbours left, initially nothing very personal
was spoken about. We just engaged each other in general
chit-chat. He wanted to know where I went to when I
visited Ireland and whom I stayed with. I told him that I
used to go to the Limerick races with Carmel Dillon. He
said that he was always at the Limerick races, and that if he
had seen me he would have recognised me, due to the
physical similarity to my mother.

Then he asked me where I had grown up. I told him that
I was brought up in Kilmallock.

'Where in Kilmallock?'

'Ballyculhane.'

He said that he knew the place. He asked, 'Did something happen there?'

'It did.'

He said, 'I knew that place and I knew the reputation of that house.' He turned to my mother and asked her, 'Did you know that your daughter had been raped there as a child?'

I couldn't believe that he had asked the question in such a very matter-of-fact way. I was astonished that he knew of my foster-parents' house. I was even more shocked that he knew of 'our' house's reputation.

My mother answered his question in a haughty manner, 'Some people should never be allowed to bring up children.'

I thought that was rich, coming from her, but she meant it. She obviously saw herself as a fully acceptable member of the child-rearing community.

I said, 'What happened during my childhood, has affected my entire life.' I haltingly began to explain about the sexual problems in my marriage. I don't think my father knew what to say because he went on to ask about the same relatives in Kilmallock that Paddy O'Sullivan had inquired about when we first met. Since meeting my parents, I was having quite a few flashbacks. Occurrences that had made no sense at the time were now finally becoming clear. My father asked me if I knew O'Sullivan's pub. I said that I had actually worked there for a short period. The mention of Jimmy O'Sullivan immediately triggered a flashback. Before I had ever met my mother, I had always begged Sister Bernadette to ask my mother to write a letter to me. While I was working for Jimmy O'Sullivan and his wife Nonie, one day I received a letter, by post, from Sister Bernadette.

Enclosed in the envelope was a further letter addressed to 'Celine'. Sister Bernadette wrote, 'I am enclosing the treasure that you have been waiting for.' I opened the envelope marked 'Celine', which had no address. It had contained a letter, which read:

My very own darling little Celine,

It is very hard for me to find time and to get an empty room, to write to you, undisturbed. Your father has never been told of your existence. If he found out now, it would break up his marriage and destroy the family. I pray for you every day and I pray that I shall hold you in my arms before I die. Now that you are sixteen years of age, you still need guidance. Go to Sister Bernadette for advice. She knows the world and will give you good advice.

Signed,
Your ever-loving mother

I had been really thrilled to receive this letter. I wanted to show it to everybody. As far as I was concerned, it proved that I had a mother who loved me. In my excitement, I showed it to Nonie. After reading it, she asked, 'What is your mother's name?' I said that it was Doreen. Casually, and with a certain vagueness, Nonie said, 'The only Doreen that I ever heard of is married to Jimmy's first cousin in Janesboro, in Limerick. But I don't think that it could be her, as she has nine children.' At one small moment in time while I was 16, I almost found out who my father was.

If only I had realised, how close I was to that knowledge. But even then, people like me could not ask questions. I could not have rocked the boat anyway. I was the housemaid, with a history and the baggage to prove it.

The next visitors that arrived to see my new exhibits were Harry's brother Paddy and his wife Kitty, along with her sister. I felt embarrassed that Kitty's sister was there. I felt that the whole family situation was my shame. I had been telling everybody that my parents were dead for years. It was coming as a bit of a shock to some people to find that they were suddenly resurrected, especially people who had been at my wedding.

This resurrection was of truly biblical proportions. Both of them were now alive and well, having been dead and buried for so long. I had prepared Paddy Roberts but I did not want it to go any further, outside the immediate family. I felt so ashamed that I did not want Kitty's sister to know about it. I was embarrassed because the Roberts portrayed themselves as a very upright and morally conservative family, whereas I was ashamed of my birth. Paddy Roberts made some crack about the prodigal daughter but my parents didn't react.

My mother started by talking to Paddy Roberts about how 'some people should not be allowed to bring up kids'. My father joined in and agreed with her.

I sat there in shock as they then went on to expose some of my worst lies for all to see. My parents were leaving my pious in-laws in no doubt as to my upbringing and they began to talk about my past in detail. I was in shock and Harry, in his role of Catholic Church mainstay, said nothing. I had told my father and mother about my years of horror, in trust. I felt that they had a right to know. And here they were talking about me to the Roberts family, as if I was a stranger, exposing my past to their certain disapproval. How could my parents take such a high moral ground after condemning me to the cesspool of life? I was livid, seething and torn apart. I felt so betrayed.

Even though I was in my house, my home, surrounded by my loving children, I felt trapped. That evening I felt, once again, like nothing better than a little beggar girl.

I left the room because I had to get out of there.

I went to cook dinner. Cooking has always been my escape. I could create something from the debris of my life.

I was doing for other people what I wanted them to do for me. I wanted them to look after me. When I put the children to bed that night, I remember thinking that they were the only precious things that I had in my life. They were the only people in my life that I could really trust.

The next day my parents and I went shopping. At the Aer Lingus office in Regent Street we booked a ticket for me to return to Limerick to meet my siblings. I would fly back to Shannon with them on the following Sunday. I wanted to buy a pair of black patent shoes for my trip to Ireland. My mother offered to pay for my shoes but I refused to let her.

My father said, 'Let her pay for them, she owes you millions.' I ended up buying a cheap pair, which I would never have worn normally, so the bill would be cheaper for my mother. After the previous night's upset, that was all I could bring myself to accept.

SEVENTEEN

Sibling Rivalry

Sunday came and we all flew in to Shannon Airport. We went through the customs check unhampered. I was beginning to feel nervous. I did not know whom I was going to meet. As we approached the final door before we entered the arrivals hall, I hesitated. My father nudged me gently in the back and verbally pushed me forward with, 'Go on girl, sure it is only your very own family, what are you afraid of?'

I emerged into the usual large arrivals area, to see the usual sea of faces, each searching for their own particular person. As I stepped through the door, I was approached by a small group of four people, two male and two female. They had detached themselves from the larger throng. A small noisy over-excited army engulfed me.

My father caught up behind me. He introduced me collectively to the party as, 'Here is the long-lost sister.' He then introduced my brothers and sisters to me individually.

It was a very emotional experience. There were a lot of tears from me.

It was so unreal. It was like this family was together and I was on the outside. I did not feel part of a family. When we were getting into a car, my new-found sister Eileen said, 'Come and get into the back with me, Sis'. I felt chuffed. I felt included for the first time. I felt she was including me in the family.

It was an emotional whirl.

I kept experiencing different reactions to my arrival.

We went to my brother's house. His name was Tommy O'Sullivan Junior. I met his wife Marion. Also at his house was another sister called Avril. She was wearing a tartan outfit and I thought she looked very elegant. I thought that she did not like the idea of my being there. Of all my siblings, I felt Avril disliked the idea of, 'the secret existence of an illegitimate older sister', being exposed. In time, however, Avril and I became quite friendly.

In general, I found that while I was welcomed to the family, I was not introduced on a large scale to their friends and neighbours. I felt that this was a sign that, deep down, they were still ashamed of me. Their friends and neighbours would always have known Eileen as the eldest of the family, but now they would have to explain to everyone that I was the eldest. Explaining this fact to everyone would have involved many other gory details, so, I expect that they thought better of it. Thinking about it, if the tables were reversed, I would have probably done the same. Even still, the lack of a full acceptance hurt.

After dinner at Tommy Junior's house, I was taken to my parents' home at Janesboro in Limerick. When we got to the area, they made me guess which house was theirs. I guessed the wrong one. It wasn't at all what I had anticipated. I expected it to be a large private house in its own grounds. The picture I had built up over a week of knowing my father was of a place with kennels for dogs, which I had confused with stables for horses.

When I actually saw it, I was shocked. I was ushered inside an end-of-terrace council house.

My father said, 'Welcome home.'

There were so many people there. I was introduced to all my siblings' wives and husbands and their respective children. I was overwhelmed. One woman emerged from the crowd when she saw me, and said to my mother in a loud voice for the entire world to hear, 'Doreen, how could you deny her, shure she is the spittin' image of you.'

My mother responded by looking daggers at her. The woman turned out to be called Tess. She was married to my father's younger brother, Frank. I got the impression that my mother did not like Tess very much.

I was to learn later that my mother was very fond of Frank. She told me that when Frank sang at parties, he used to sing a special song to her. He used to sing the song 'Good Night, Irene' to her, but he used to change the words to 'Good Night, Doreen'. I said that Frank was nice and thought no more of it. Frank treated me like a little girl. As time went on and I was flying in and out of Shannon, he would be waiting for me before I boarded the plane. He would always give me a box of chocolates and kiss me on both cheeks.

On the Saturday night, a family party was held. My father did not like alcohol in the house, but he bought a bottle of Black Tower white wine for me because he knew I liked to drink wine. My entire new family were present. I had met all my nine siblings over the week, four female and five male. From the eldest to the youngest they were Eileen, Avril, Tommy Junior, John, Marcus, Niall, Rosaleen, Michael and Thelma. All were at the party and we had a singsong with no alcohol. I was happy in their midst, and I enjoyed the feeling. I felt some sense of belonging at last.

On one of the nights we went to Buttevant with my parents and Tommy Junior, to visit Kit and Tony. Kit said to me, 'I've lost my little family.'

'No, never!' I said, and I really meant it.

After the party, I flew home to London. I wanted to be at

home with my children, but, at the same time, I wanted to
be in Limerick with my parents. I wanted to be a child with
them. I wanted them to make a fuss of me. I thought that it
would be different, I thought that I would be introduced to
their friends and neighbours, but I wasn't. My visit was very
closed and restricted to close family.

* * * *

It was November 1983. Back in London, I wrote to my
family. In my letter I said that 'I felt love in every part of
their home'. I did not know what that meant. But I thought
that it was the right thing to say. I wanted to be acceptable
to them. I was still at it. I had found my family, they had
welcomed me and yet I was still unhappy about myself. I still
felt unacceptable. Was it to dominate my life forever?

Life in London did not return to normal this time. I was
on the phone to my parents, well in truth, my father, at
every opportunity. He also called me very often. A lot of
letters were written by both my parents. They were loving,
in word and nature. I was amazed by the letters, especially
those written by my mother.

In contrast, I was ashamed of my own writing. My
mother suggested that it was because I was not brought up as
well as her other children. It brought back another memory
when on a visit, years later, I had met Sister Claude, my old
teacher. I had said I was sorry I'd missed so much school and
asked her if she had known what was happening to me. She
said, 'I knew you were being dragged up in there.' I knew she
was right. I felt embarrassed about my lack of education and
agreed with my mother. I even blamed myself for my bad
writing.

Christmas came and I wanted to buy a lot of presents for
my new family. I thought that by buying presents for
everyone, I would be more acceptable to them. Top of the

list was my father. I bought him an expensive sheepskin coat. They were very fashionable at the time. I also bought many gifts for my mother and something for each of my nine siblings. I bought something for each of my married siblings' children. It cost me a fortune. I wanted everyone to love me, so I didn't care. I got a few presents back for the boys, but that was it. I felt a bit disappointed.

I was still having health problems. I went to see a gynaecologist in January 1984. As soon as I was examined internally, I began to haemorrhage. They said that cauterisation would not be an option anymore. They advised a hysterectomy. I was booked in for February 26, 1984. I would not be able to have any more children. This was a devastating piece of news for me. On the way home from the examination, I was so upset that I rang my parents to let them know. I knew that, with my history, it had to happen sometime, but it was still an awful shock.

On the Sunday before the operation, my father and my youngest sibling, Thelma, arrived in London. She was 17. My father had told me that she wanted to train as a nurse. I was never asked to help but it was implied that I would be able to open particular doors in the world of trainee nursing for her.

I thought that this was what families did for one another, so I set about getting her a suitable position as a trainee nurse. I had set up interviews at St George's Hospital, in Tooting and West Park Hospital, in Epsom. I coached her in what to expect and what the suitable replies would be. She was accepted for both and opted for West Park.

When my father heard this, he was very pleased. He asked me to look after her, so that she would make a good nurse. That meant that she had to come and live with Harry and myself. I never questioned her coming to live with us, and Harry didn't mind. I assumed that was how families worked. It was like when my father asked me if I could find him some grapefruit spoons for one of my auntie nuns. It brought me right back to memories of the orphanage and serving the priest his breakfast and how hungry I used to be, but I felt had to help him find the spoons. He was my father after all.

Thelma was due to begin her new job on Monday. As it was her first day, I had arranged for Harry to drive her to work in the morning and to collect her in the afternoon, when she was finished for the day. All went smoothly until he returned in the afternoon to collect her. She was not there. When he went looking for her he was informed that she had 'gone home'. When he got home, it turned out she had quit, because it was not what she had expected.

After all the trouble I had gone to, she had served less than one day. She was firm, 'I am not going back, and that is that!'

My father was going home on the following Sunday and a friend of ours who owned a pub, came by the house to meet him. He offered her a job in the kitchen of his pub and Thelma accepted. My father must have told my mother about her daughter's change of career plans, as some days later I had an irate phone call from her. Mother informed me that, 'they did not educate Thelma to work as a skivvy in the kitchen of a dingy London bar.'

I went in for the hysterectomy. Once again my father decided what was right for me. He decided that it would be best if my mother came to look after my children, with Thelma's help, while I was in hospital. He said that it would bring my mother closer to me. Usually I would have asked Kit to come over and look after Harry and the boys. That is what had happened during my past sojourns in hospital and there were no problems whatsoever. I should have been more assertive and told my father that I could make my own plans. Once again I thought that was what fathers did, so I went along with the arrangement.

There was consternation between Harry and my mother. Two days after my operation, she rang me at the hospital. She was complaining that Harry had borrowed some money from her, and that she wanted it back immediately. I thought that it must have been a fortune that he had borrowed. Two days later she rang again with the same complaint that he still had not paid back the loan. She would not tell me how much money was involved.

The next day I took an early discharge from the hospital, against their best advice. Five days after having a hysterectomy, I was at home. As soon as I got into the house, I sat both Harry and my mother down for a confrontation.

I asked, 'How much was the loan?'

'Nine pounds.'

I gave her the money.

It transpired that Harry had been short nine pounds for petrol and had asked her if she could loan it to him. I suppose Harry meant 'a permanent loan' and promptly forgot about it. He probably had no intention of paying it back. It was just his way of asking for the nine-pound deficit, as the petrol was already in the car. I don't think he expected it to start World War Three!

I was supposed to be resting in bed but the war continued downstairs. She complained about the food. He had white bread and she wanted brown bread. He had corn flakes and she wanted porridge.

I was upset. What she really wanted was someone to look after her!

She caused further disruption by telling my neighbours about how my father and herself were going to build a nursing home for me to run as a business, as they wanted me to have some security in my life. She said my husband was only an uneducated wastrel, without any prospects whatsoever. While my life was based on many lies, I considered those lies as necessary for my survival. I never told lies just for the sake of projecting a snobbish image of myself.

Instead of helping me convalesce, my mother's presence made me feel worse. I was so mixed up. Then Thelma thought she should show me a letter she had got from a friend which said that my mother should not be forced to accept me. I was very hurt. I'd had hopes that together we could change the past, but of course, we couldn't. I began to realise that the years of damage could not be undone.

EIGHTEEN

Buying Acceptance

My new-found family caused another uncharacteristic change in my behaviour. Over my life I have always had to provide for myself. Nobody has ever given me anything. I have had to be aware of and careful with my financial expenditure. I don't like saving but I never allowed my money to run amok. But now, if any of my new-found family said that they wanted something, I would buy it for them.

Avril said, in a throwaway remark, that she needed a new carpet for her home. I sounded her out on what type and colour she would prefer. I bought one in London and had it shipped to her home in Limerick. My parents needed a TV, as they only had a black and white set. I had a small portable colour TV at the time, so that was delivered to Limerick. Videos had just come on the market. My parents said that they would like one, so I sent them a video recorder. They mentioned that they did not have a three-piece suite of furniture, so I had ours consigned to Limerick. On one occasion when they were at my house they admired my stair carpet. 'Do you want it?' I asked. It was duly whipped off the stairs and shipped to Limerick.

My subconscious reasoning for my irrational behaviour at the time was that if I could give them what they wanted, they would accept me and allow me to be part of their family. I would have done anything to be an acceptable part of that family. Anthony still remembers when his BMX bike was shipped off to his cousins in Limerick. Harry didn't seem to mind. The only time he got really angry was when he had found out about the nursing home story.

I wanted to be important to them and I wanted them to say to their neighbours and friends, 'This is my daughter or sister or aunt,' whichever particular title applied. I really wanted to hear those words being said by my family to someone who was not a family member. I just needed them to be proud of me. But it never really happened.

I felt that they were ashamed of me and, no matter what I did, I would never be acceptable to them. Within that family I felt an affinity with certain individuals, but as a group, I always was made to feel like an outsider. I should have been considered one of them. Yet that was not to be.

I was their own flesh and blood yet I was considered as something lower than them. I felt less than human. Just because my parents were not married when I was conceived and born, decisions were lightly made which changed my life utterly, especially compared to the life of my full natural brothers and sisters. All different kinds of things kept bringing this home to me. I can remember first having my hair washed with shampoo at Kit's home, when I was 12 years of age. Imagine never having had your hair washed with shampoo. It is something everyone in my family took as a basic human right from the day that they were born. I did not know what shampoo was until then. I had never even been properly clean. While I lived with my foster-parents, sometimes I used to wash myself in a pond at the corner of a field near the house. The pond had formed at the juncture of two streams, that flowed along the boundary of the property. The pond feature was probably designed to allow cattle or other domestic animals to get a drink or to wallow in. The bottom of the pond was muddy but you only sank a few inches into it. In springtime I remember it was full of tadpoles but in summer it was always full of green algae. That pond was my only washing facility until I was 12 years of age. The more I talked to my brothers and sisters about their childhoods, the more I would think no shampoo, no toothpaste and no toothbrush. Washing was just one example. Even though only a few miles separated me from my siblings physically, our daily lives were worlds apart.

My relationship with my new-found family, and in particular my mother, began to deteriorate. When my father was over with me and we were trying to entice the non-too-enthusiastic Thelma into a career in nursing, my mother wrote a letter to my father, which he showed me. It was a detailed letter about how much she missed him. In fact much of the detail was about how much she missed him, especially sexually, in bed. She was angry that he was still in London. He phoned her to try to calm things down but it didn't help. I felt that her anger was really directed towards me. She was furious, mainly because my father and Thelma had not called her.

My father put Thelma on the phone to talk to her. When Thelma said hello, she called her 'Mud'. Afterwards when I mentioned it, she told me that it was a nickname. She told me that they all had nicknames for each other, Tommy was 'Toss', Eileen was 'Shinny' – it was no big deal.

It was to me. I was jealous.

I was insanely jealous.

I wondered if I would have a nickname, but of course, I didn't.

I asked Thelma, 'What will my nickname be?'

She just laughed.

I also realised during this conversation that all my siblings had second or even third Christian names, such as Thelma Dolores Ellen. But I had only one – Celine. Instead

I'd had a few different surnames. I realised that I would never be part of that family unit.

And the jealousy set in again.

Compared to what I had growing up, they had a perfect life. They had food, clothes and beds to sleep in. Every time that I felt excluded, it brought back horrible memories for me. They never had to steal food. I was always hungry because I was barely ever fed. I had to take food whenever and wherever I could get it.

In summer I could eat raw vegetables that were being cultivated in the surrounding fields. I ate raw potatoes, swedes, turnips, cabbages and onions, anything I could get. Later in the year I could rely on mushrooms from the fields, while blackberries, strawberries and raspberries all grew wild in the hedgerows. In winter and other times I could always rely on the bounties of the Catholic Church. At the worst of the worst, when I was really starving, I would go to the Catholic Church in Kilmallock and eat the wax candles. These were always in good supply. They were on sale for a penny, to people who wanted to 'light a penny candle' for a special intention.

I think that by lighting a candle people were led to believe that it would give them a special intercession with God. He was supposed to look more favourably on their request if they bought a penny candle. I can still taste the candle wax to this very day. I realise now that I was very lucky not to be caught eating the candles. I would probably have been arrested and brought to court but not taken away from my foster-parents. I would have been killed if they had found out. It was bad enough knowing that God and Our Lady were watching me and could come and get me. I believed that they were real and could throw you into hell. I used to look up at the stained glass windows, with all the saints looking down and I knew they were watching me being bad, eating the candles.

Although I did not know it, my reputation was probably not great at that time. I was called a lot of different names by the local children and adults alike. I was not held in very high esteem. People would call me, 'ride', 'prostitute' and 'whore' among others. I didn't really know what the words meant but I knew from the vicious way that they were said to me, they were not good.

By the age of ten years my body had acclimatised itself to abuse and its attendant pain. I felt no pain or feeling in the lower half of my body. If men wanted to abuse my body, then they went ahead and did it, as long as they had the approval of my foster-mother. I realised after a while that the men gave my mother money for 'fucking' me.

I found that if she got paid for letting somebody 'fuck', then she treated me with a type of fondness. 'Good on ya, ya little ride ya,' she would say, as she pushed me out of her way or gave me what could be considered a playful whack on the back of the head, as she was counting the money. A push was about as much as I could expect in the way of affectionate physical contact from her. She was so nasty most of the time that I could not afford to go near her to try to get some affection. However, I found that she could be even nicer if I gave her money that I had 'earned' from my own enterprise rather than from her contacts.

I found that some of the men who wanted to 'fuck' me were even quite pleasant before the event and some even after the event. If they met me in the street they studiously ignored me. But if they met me somewhere where there were no other people, then they would talk to me and say nice things to me. They would make me feel special. But then it always had to end with them saying that they were going to 'fuck' me.

When I was 12, a man whom I only knew as 'the workman from Hannon's farm', in Kilmallock, used to give me a ten-shilling note if 'you let me fuck you in the churchyard'. This happened many times over the summer in the long grass near the evergreen trees beside the thick town wall, behind the astonishingly large church in Kilmallock. I remember lying on my back as he had sex with me and thinking that the steeple of the church was so high that it must touch the sky. When he was finished, he was always very nice to me. He smoothed down and brushed my crumpled clothes. He always gave me a ten-shilling note, reminded me not to tell anyone about us and told me when to meet him again, behind the church.

When I used to give my foster-mother the ten-shilling note, she would really be pleased with me. 'Ten bob, begor, that miserable auld so-and-so has it bad, what did the clergy ever do to him, good geril yerself.' But I did not know what I was doing. How could a ten-year-old girl turn around and say no? Of course, giving my foster-mother money usually turned out the worse for me. I would be sent to Meade's Pub for Guinness and whiskey. This would mean a party where everyone would get drunk. Back in the days when my foster-father was alive, he would get really drunk. When he got drunk, he would get aggressive and beat anyone who was near him. He never hit my foster-mother because he was afraid of her. She was well able to stand up for herself. If he had hit her, she would have hit him back twice as hard. He could only beat on somebody who could not defend themselves. I was beaten so often with the leather belt from the bellows beside the fire that I could only lie in pain, often for days, before I could move again. I gradually learned to take my cue from Spot the dog. When they began to get drunk, Spot would slink away and hide. He knew something was different and became uneasy. This was our time to head for my sleeping area. There Spot and I curled up together and hoped that they would forget about us. As they got progressively drunker, Spot would disappear altogether. He used to squeeze himself under a low cupboard where nobody could reach him. I was not so lucky. Of course, after my foster-father died, a party meant the same men calling to the house and I was never left in peace.

One major consequence of meeting all the members of my family was that I began to have these 'flashbacks'. I rarely used to have them before that. I suspect that meeting my siblings and feeling so much jealousy caused these flashbacks to my horrific past. I could not help but compare my unhappy childhood to what I perceived as the idyllic childhood experienced by my siblings. These flashbacks that I experience to this very day can fill me with depression. Depending on the severity of the painful memory, it can take me days to recover. With all of my heart, I long to be free of these nightmares of my past.

After I had my hysterectomy, my father phoned me every night in hospital. When I went home, he called me every night as well. This caused a rift between my father and my mother. During one of the conversations, I told him that I was feeling worse at home with my mother and Harry fighting.

Immediately he said, 'Come on home to Limerick and you can recuperate for six weeks.'

While I had by now realised that he was far from being the perfect father, I was still in awe of him. He was still the personification of my fantasy father-figure and of how I had visualised him to be, over all the years of not having a father. I respected him so I reluctantly decided to take up his offer and go to Limerick for six weeks of recuperation in the bosom of my family. I really wasn't sure about going. I was ceding control to someone whom I did not really know and I was uncomfortable with that aspect of it.

I informed Mother of the travel arrangements. She wanted to go as soon as possible. She could not wait to get away from Harry and the house and London. Ronan and I, along with my mother, were to go to Limerick. Harry was to stay in London and look after Anthony, who was still at school. As I was under strict instructions from the hospital not to do any heavy work, I had to travel as an invalid. I bought tickets for Ronan and myself. The three of us headed for Heathrow to fly to Shannon.

As we prepared to board the plane, mother was off-loaded. She was flying on a stand-by ticket. She was furious. As Ronan and I were being wheeled down the boarding chute to the plane, my last view of my mother was of two uniformed security men trying to restrain an irate, screaming woman. I was too unwell to care. I pretended that I did not know her. I knew that my father would be waiting for me at the other end of the flight, so I kept going.

My father collected us at Shannon and took us home to Janesboro. I told him what had happened to Mother. He was not bothered about it. 'She knows what to expect, she will get a seat eventually.' When we got home, I was put to bed to rest. Rosaleen, my sister, became real pals with Ronan.

The next day passed and there was no sign of Mother. It was a beautiful quiet day. The following day a hurricane blew in the front door. Mother was back.

She was really angry with everyone. When she was offloaded, she had to get a taxi back to my house from Heathrow. She got back to the house and knocked on the door. When the door opened, she barged past a bewildered Harry. She demanded that Harry would have to give her a lift back to the airport the next day. He made some excuse that he was unavailable. There was no way he was going to drive her to the airport, after the abuse he had been put through. Harry is a generous person in most respects, but he would have given anyone else in the world a lift to the airport before he would have driven my mother to Heathrow that day. She had to return to the airport by taxi.

As Shannon is a small destination in the world of aviation, there are few flights that go there each day. They are usually full. So stand-by is a bad way to get there. It may be cheap but you can get left behind. It wasn't so much the time involved that bothered my mother, but it was the ignominy of having to admit to or being seen as a cheapskate.

She could not get a flight the next day. She had to go back to Harry again by taxi. She barged past Harry once again. He had not expected to see her because if he had realised that she could not get a flight for a second time, he would not have opened the door to her. She did not ask for a lift to the airport for the following day, as I think she knew that she would not get one. She got a seat on a flight on the third attempt.

Once she was installed in her own home, she took to her bed. She never got out of her bed to help me. Every morning my father would go off to work, thinking that my mother was looking after me. I had to light the fire each morning. I had to cook for Ronan and myself and anybody else that was there. When she did get up she complained that Ronan and I were eating them out of house and home. She flew into rages about our eating habits. I tried to explain to her that she was taking too many prescription drugs, particularly Valium. I thought this was the reason for her irrational behaviour towards me. She was on uppers and downers and so many tablets, that it was unbelievable. I was concerned, but she saw it as interference.

Once again I was getting no help and my health was getting worse. I weighed just over six stone at this time.

I thought I was going to die and I wanted to go back to London. Every time that I said this to my father, he would persuade me to stay by saying that my mother wanted me to stay and that she loved me. When he was at home, she pretended that we were the best of friends. One time, in his presence, he told my mother and I to hug each other. In that embrace I knew that she did not want to be anywhere near me. I could feel her physically cringe when I hugged her.

With all the physical work that I had to do, I was exhausted. There were so many rows between my mother and I. It was obvious to me that she did not want me there. My father wanted to believe that my mother wanted me to be there. He saw my mother from a different point of view. He could think no ill of her.

While I was in Limerick, some gypsy caravans parked in a field nearby. One day some gypsy children came to the door with a small tin can and asked my mother for some water. Mother refused to give them water and ran after them brandishing a brush. I was shocked and I was angry. 'How could you refuse somebody a drink of water?' I screamed at her. She just looked through me and said nothing.

Ronan used to talk and play with the gypsy children. They used to have great fun together. He used to think that they were very funny, the way they used to say, 'Waaather'. They used to copy his English accent. One evening, in front of some neighbours, Ronan asked my mother for a 'cup a tay'. She was so embarrassed that she nearly died of shock, but Ronan got such a reaction from her that he kept it up for days. I used to hear the deep belly-laughs from them all and think that it was so innocent. I used to look at the gypsy children and think how badly dressed and unkempt they looked. They were weather-beaten and looked like they never washed themselves.

I suppose I saw myself in those children and, in her response to them, my mother's rejection of me.

After three weeks of misery I plucked up the courage to return to London.

NINETEEN

No Celebration

When I got back to London, I was so relieved. I was thrilled to see Anthony. Ronan was also very happy to be home with his dad and his brother. It felt strange to be back, but I was glad to be in my own home. Thelma was still there and part of me wanted her to stay but another part would have liked to get back to just the four of us. It wasn't so bad because she'd got a new job and wasn't in the house that often.

Life went back to normal. I did not have to cope with a hysterical mother who did not want me in her sight.

My father was uncomfortable with my coming back to London after only three weeks, as he knew I was off work for six weeks. He still had tunnel vision regarding my mother. He phoned me about twice a week and I called him more often. Much more often! My phone bill became appreciably high. Consequently we ran short of cash to pay some of the domestic bills.

Margaret Thatcher and her Conservative government had introduced the controversial poll tax. There was a lot of opposition to paying it at the time, from all corners of the political spectrum. It was just another bill as far as I was concerned, and I wanted to pay it. I had no argument with any British government, be they Tory or Labour. Whatever any of them did was all right by me. I was not particularly interested in politics as I had enough going on in my life, just to survive. But I would not hear a bad word said against whatever political party was in power or against the Royal Family.

As far as I was concerned, the British establishment had treated me very well. They had accepted me unconditionally and they did not ask about my parental status.

I was made to feel welcome in Britain. I was treated with respect from the very first day that I turned up on its shores searching for a new life.

But in this instance there was no cash to pay the poll tax. After a 'board meeting' between Harry and I, it was decided that Harry would ask his brother Paddy for a loan so that we could pay the tax. Harry rang him up and explained the situation. Paddy agreed to meet Harry under the railway bridge on our road and give him the money. When Harry came back with the money, he said that he'd had to endure a lecture from his brother. Paddy had told him that he knew that the money was not for the poll tax, but because I was making far too many phone calls to my father in Ireland.

I was raging. Somebody visiting or babysitting had told him. They could quite easily have seen a phone bill lying around the house or Harry may have told them that I was calling my father a lot.

It was then I decided that I had to leave that house. I decided that I wanted a change. I wanted a new house. Harry just went along with the decision to move while I started to look for somewhere else to live. I put the house on the market. I justified it to myself by saying that it was not my real choice to live there in the first place. The Roberts had left a bad taste in my mouth. I wanted to shake myself free of them as much as I could.

Harry and I looked at an end-of-terrace house in Surrey.

We both decided that it would be suitable, so we made an offer of £46,000 and it was accepted. Our old house sold for £43,000 shortly afterwards.

I was happy to move out and we all, including Thelma who was still with us, moved into the new house on December 8, 1984. No changes had to be made to Anthony's school or Ronan's nursery arrangements.

I just wanted some peace and quiet in my life.

* * * *

After things had settled down a bit and I was starting to feel better, we went to Ireland to visit Kit and Tony. Going to Thelma's 21st party in Cloughaun GAA Club was also on the cards. Thelma had got caterers from Shannon Airport for the party and there was going to be a big crowd. We had come over by ferry with the boys and I picked Thelma up at the airport on the Friday. We brought her up home and my father came out to welcome us all, but my mother stayed at the door. I was helping the boys get out, as Thelma went ahead into the house. She was hugging and kissing my mother and the boys were waiting behind her. My mother completely ignored them, even though poor little Ronan, who was only four and a half and was looking for a kiss. I didn't say anything, but I was furious. My father made us a cup of tea but we all felt uncomfortable. I told Anthony to take Ronan to Auntie Avril's as we were staying there that night and she lived nearby. We left ourselves soon afterwards.

I went out that night with all my sisters for a drink at The George Hotel. It was quiet enough but I was glad to be there. It made me feel part of the family.

The next day I went shopping before the party. All the children were being looked after in Avril's house. That night I got into my new clothes and we went up to the GAA Club.

Everyone was in the bar watching the Barry McGuigan fight. My mother and father were greeting people at the door but I think my dad was more interested in the fight. I ignored my mother because of the day before. I just didn't want to talk to her. She didn't react. We went on into the main hall and helped ourselves at the buffet. We were sitting with some of my brothers and it felt a bit strange to be out in public with them all for more or less the first time.

I was starting to relax a bit when my father brought my mother over to try to force a reconciliation, but I could see she wasn't interested. She said she didn't want to talk to me. I'd had enough and saw red. I said I didn't want to talk to her either, as she had hurt my children, who had done nothing to her, and that I wouldn't put up with it. I was really angry. She had thrown me on the scrap-heap and had made it plain that she wished I'd never been born, but I wouldn't allow her to hurt my children. She hated it. She forgot all about her pose as 'a grand lady' and lunged at me to slap me in the face. Niall, my second youngest brother, jumped up and pulled her back. He hustled her away before I could even say anything.

My Uncle Frank came over, put his arm around my shoulder, and said, 'The last generation didn't sort it, but the next one will.'

I was fuming and said, 'Over my dead body. This is not going to be passed to another generation.'

Later that night my father talked me into going out to the car, with both him and my mother, to try to talk things through. It was a disaster. My mother slapped me across the face and he was crying. We were all so angry. I said things I didn't even mean, like, 'I'll make you regret you ever had me.' Nothing was resolved and I just wanted to go home.

It was the beginning of a breakdown in communications. There was less and less contact after that.

* * * *

Once we got back to London I just decided to focus on my own family, as they were the ones I could really trust. We all went back to our normal routines. It was actually relaxing to go back to work and just do everyday things like taking Anthony to school. My life seemed to be getting back to normal, but then my father rang up and suggested that they both come over for the weekend, to see their two daughters. I think my father really wanted to try to patch things up. I didn't really want Mother to come over but at the same time I was so grateful that they were making the effort. So I said I'd be delighted if they came over. Nobody had told Thelma what happened at her birthday so she just thought it was a normal visit. Ronan got really excited at the idea of his grandparents coming over to see *him* again. I tried not to think about how mother had ignored him the last time and just kept agreeing that we'd have a great time.

Harry, Ronan and I went to Heathrow Airport to collect them. Ronan was off school that day because he was not well. He had what I thought was a tummy upset.

He seemed fine when we were greeting them but then he fell asleep in the car on the way home. That did not strike me as unusual or significant in any way. He often slept in the car and I just thought he was tired from all the excitement. When I mentioned to my mother that Ronan was a bit sick, she responded, 'Why didn't you tell us and we would not have come?'

To myself I said, 'That is why I didn't tell you, because I wanted you to come.' Despite everything that had happened at Thelma's 21st, I still longed for their acceptance.

We tried to do some tourist things on Saturday but there was a bit of an atmosphere and Thelma ended up having to work, which didn't help. We got through it somehow and at least Ronan was feeling better.

On the Sunday we all went to mass and then on to a market to buy Christmas presents. The day went really well.

Ronan was completely back to normal and the boys were delighted with the presents from their grandparents.

My parents returned home to Ireland the next day. In a way I was relieved to see them go, but in another way I wanted them to stay. All things considered, the weekend had gone really well and it had helped to get us all back talking to each other. We had even tentatively spoken about planning a visit to Ireland. I thought that things were looking up.

Later on that week, when I was taking Ronan home from school one evening, I noticed that he was dragging his right leg a little bit. 'Did you fall at school, or did anyone kick you or hurt you?' I asked immediately.

'No,' he said. I thought that he was walking 'funny'. I asked him if he wanted a piggyback.

He said, 'No.' He was a very independent little boy. He just walked on in front of me as usual. The next day he seemed fine and was walking perfectly.

It seemed to be a one-off and over the next few weeks we got caught up in the madness before Christmas. I was really looking forward to it because that Christmas I was not working. On Christmas Eve Anthony was serving midnight mass, so I wanted us all to go as a family because it was Anthony's big night. That included Thelma, especially as I wanted her to take photos of us all together. But she didn't turn up. I was really upset because it was one of my few Christmas holidays off duty and it would have been lovely to have photos as a memory of Anthony's special night. It was just one of those nights. I had bought a new outfit for Ronan but he would not wear it. He wanted to wear a pair of corduroy pants that my sister Eileen had bought for him. Eventually we all set off, without Thelma, but with Ronan's new pants. I remember praying to let my brother Tommy Junior and his wife Marion have a baby because I was so lucky to have two children. I was asking God to let them have at least one.

Christmas Day arrived and the boys had got everything they wanted from Father Christmas. I saw the wonderment in Anthony's and Ronan's eyes as they opened all their presents. It was really lovely to see their faces. I wished that I had a movie camera to capture their excitement.

We went to our good friends for Christmas dinner. While we were there, Ronan got a little bit sick. He vomited and I thought that it was strange because he had not eaten much Christmas dinner. Besides that, Ronan always loved his food. He was even known to ask for seconds!

The next day, Boxing Day, he vomited again. I became really worried because it was so unlike Ronan, as he never used to get even a cold. Even then I put it down to all the different bits and pieces he had eaten, like sweets and chocolate, but I was concerned because he didn't have diarrhoea, which would have indicated an upset stomach – I knew that the two usually go together.

When Christmas was over I decided enough was enough, and I took him to the doctor for a check-up. The doctor said that it was just a bug and that it would probably clear up. But the vomiting did not stop fully. He would vomit one day but maybe not the next. Then he started to vomit in the mornings. I immediately brought him back to the doctor. He was due to go back to school, so I was anxious that any illness would be cleared up, as I did not want him to miss classes.

The doctor decided to send him to the Infectious Disease Unit at St George's Hospital. I asked the doctor if he thought it might be a virus. 'When do children not get viruses?' he replied, with an air of tiredness about him. He thought that he had another panicky mother on his hands.

I went off to St George's with Ronan. They kept him in overnight and checked him over as much as possible. They did not consider that he had anything infectious so they moved him to 'Pygmy Ward', the paediatric unit, for further examination. I stayed in with him.

The next afternoon I left him playing in the ward, while I went home to get him some clean pyjamas.

When I arrived home, I called Kit and told her that Ronan was in hospital. She was surprised. 'Shure, he'll be grand, isn't he a real tough little man,' she assured me.

When I returned to the hospital the doctor was waiting to see me. He said to me, 'While you were away, Ronan walked into a door. It was as if he had not seen the door, have you ever noticed such behaviour before, Celine?'

'No,' I replied, trying to remain calm. But it was as if he touched a panic button in my brain. I looked across at Ronan who was in a bed beside the doctor. He suddenly looked very pale to me and he had a tiny nosebleed.

They decided that he should be transferred to Great Ormond Street Hospital for Children because he should have a scan done on his brain. Once I knew that he was having a brain scan, I knew that it was very serious. I rang my mother.

She said to me, 'I went through that with all of my children.'

'You may have been through it but not with ALL of your children,' I thought. Even in the middle of the crisis it hit me that she did not think of me as one of her children. I really needed some support but she was very offhand with me. It was her way of dismissing me. She was so snappy with me, that I quickly ended the call.

Next morning after work, I took my baby for his scan. Harry had gone into work like normal and we had sent Anthony back to school, as we didn't want to worry him. The scan did not show any abnormality, so the paediatrician said that maybe Ronan had had a small stroke.

I was not convinced and I was also puzzled. I was getting very frightened as well. By the end of the day Ronan was dragging his right leg noticeably. His co-ordination was not as good on his right side as on his left. When they were doing his neurological checks, his finger-to-nose co-ordination was not as accurate on his right side as it was on his left. It was slower. He was discharged after a week and they said that he would be okay.

As I brought him home, I was unhappy about the findings and the dismissals. For a boy who loved his food, he was not eating as well as he used to. I also found that his speaking volume was lower. He did not have the same strength in his voice.

Harry had asked our parish priest to call and see Ronan. I wanted him to bless Ronan. I think that the priest thought that I was being hysterical. Maybe I gave him the impression that I thought that he had some magical powers of healing. I felt that he was unsympathetic, especially when he left without giving Ronan a blessing.

As the days went by and Ronan didn't go back to normal, I felt that everyone thought that I was overly concerned. Harry's brother even said, 'Oh, he'll be grand, when the fine weather comes, he'll be able to kick a football. His leg will get stronger.' But I thought, 'Ronan has never been sick, not even the flu, even though he was always trying to take his clothes off when he was younger.' He was always stripping off his clothes. He hated wearing them. Even if we were at someone else's house, if he thought that I was not looking he would start stripping off his clothes. Other kids used to dive on him and try to stop him when they saw him start to strip, so he became expert at doing a full strip in an extraordinary short space of time.

There was no change during the week at home. I took him back to the doctor and he contacted Great Ormond Street. They said, 'Bring him to outpatients.' They did the usual full range of blood tests but there was nothing conclusive from the results.

'It must be a virus that has attacked the brain. It could take a long time, but he will get better,' they surmised.

I took him home again.

Next day his temperature rose significantly. It remained like that for 90 minutes. Then all of a sudden it dropped back to normal. It stabilised at normal and remained there.

I was not one bit happy.

He seemed like a very sick little boy for an hour and a half and then, in the twinkling of an eye, he became a normal little boy. He behaved as if nothing had happened. I gave him Phenegran, a mild children's sedative. After that day his temperature stabilised. There were no more fluctuations. But then his sleep patterns changed.

He would sleep for an hour. He would be awake for an hour.

He would sleep for six hours. He would then be awake for six hours, almost to the minute.

He would sleep all day and then he would remain awake throughout the night.

This was into the third week – the end of January 1986. I was a wreck, both mentally and physically. I could not interpret the symptoms. They were random and disparate. I rang the doctors' surgery. The receptionist said, 'Bring the child to the surgery.'

'There is no way I am bringing my son to the surgery in his condition. Is there any doctor there that knows what he is doing? Is there any doctor there that knows anything about children, because my child is very ill and nobody believes me or understands.'

She said that she would arrange for a doctor to visit the house. He arrived at our house about an hour later and began to carry out all the usual checks.

I stopped him before he finished. I said, 'Just sit there and watch my son walking.'

I made Ronan walk across the floor in front of him.

He said, 'I totally agree with you, Mrs Roberts, there is something seriously wrong with him.'

I thought, 'For the first time, here is a doctor who agrees with me about my son's condition. Here is someone who is prepared to empathise with a mother's experience.'

He referred him back to Great Ormond Street.

This was on a Thursday.

They agreed to take him in on the Saturday morning.

When I told Ronan that he was going back to hospital, he just said 'Okay Mum, but I want my Thomas the Tank pyjamas this time.'

By the time we got to the hospital, Ronan's condition had deteriorated. He was very sluggish. The day before, he had asked me to make him some gingerbread men. I was not able to bake them, as I had no ginger. When he was installed in his hospital bed, in a gown because of his condition, I rushed to Harrods' department store to buy him gingerbread men and fresh orange juice. I rushed back to the hospital and he ate them all. Later on, his swallowing became impaired.

He was still up and about the ward at this stage, but he was slow and dragging his leg. When they were checking him, they still said that they could not find anything wrong. They even repeated the brain scan.

Nothing showed up.

They asked me about his right eye, because they found it dilated. I said that I had noticed that his writing had altered. They got a teacher to assess it. She reported that she did not see any change!

I was stupefied. I felt it was not a fair assessment. I knew my son's writing like nobody else could.

One whole week passed, running more tests, doing X-rays and waiting for results. Ronan was getting tired of being in hospital and even all the visits from Harry, Anthony and Thelma, and me staying with him as much as possible, didn't cheer him up.

On a Friday morning they decided to take him to theatre because he always had a trickle of blood from one nostril. They thought that he might have some adenoid trouble. When he came back, they had removed some adenoid tissue but generally had found everything in good condition.

That afternoon Lucy came, and that evening our friends Barry and Angela Molohan arrived. They all told me to go home and have some rest. Harry had given up trying to get me to leave.

I just said, 'No.' I knew that there was something very wrong. I was panicking in my head. We did not have a diagnosis and I knew he was seriously ill. We were not getting anywhere with the results. We were no further on. We still had no definite diagnosis.

It was fairly obvious to me, by now, that it was something cerebral. The consultant also thought the same. He recommended a three-dimensional MRI scan of the brain. This was because of the type of intermittent morning vomiting, coupled with the other outwardly visible neurological signs. After he had the scan, it took a few hours for the results to be interpreted. When the diagnosis arrived it was definitive. Ronan had an inoperable brain tumour. It was the size of a golf ball and growing. I was told that no surgeon would attempt to remove it due to its inaccessible location.

On receiving this news, the survivor in me took over once again.

The staff had provided me with an armchair-type cot bed beside Ronan. I think they knew without me telling them that I was not going to leave him, not for one minute. At night, to be comfortable, I took off my blouse and sat there in my skirt and slip watching Ronan. One night around midnight, he opened his eyes and a tear formed in his left eye and fell on to his cheek.

I said, 'It's all right darling, Mummy's here and I am not going home. Go to sleep.'

There was something about the way he looked at me. It filled me with fear that something was going to happen. It was as if he was confirming my own fears that something major was wrong.

He appeared to go back to sleep.

About an hour later, he turned over slowly on to his back. Then from a prone position at the top of the bed, with his head on the pillow, he did a complete somersault through 180 degrees, rising about two feet in the air and landing at the bottom of the bed, with his head at the end-rail.

He was still asleep, as if nothing had happened.

It happened so quickly.

Throughout my entire nursing career, I had never seen it happen before.

I was really scared and I called a nurse over. Four nurses and a doctor came. They all agreed that he'd had some kind of fit. They left and said to me to continue to observe.

About two hours later, I realised that his breathing had changed. I put on my blouse.

I realised that he had just had a cardiac arrest and I called the nurse again. She was an agency nurse and I realised that she lacked experience of cardiac arrest procedure. I helped her to put an airway into my own son. I was able to help her for a while. It was as if I had isolated myself.

I began to panic for a doctor to come and, after what seemed like an interminable wait, one arrived. They started working on Ronan. A care worker took me to another room. I prayed to Our Lady of Lourdes to let my son live. I prayed so hard for my son to be born; here I was, six short years later, praying to God and his Holy Mother to let him live.

I wanted so desperately for him to live.

They brought him around and put him on a respirator.

On that Friday night, they injected him with Vincristian, a standard chemotherapy drug.

I was still staying at the hospital but I was in a separate

room by this stage. Harry was staying at home with Anthony and my parents, who had flown over once I told them the diagnosis.

On the Saturday morning, when I went in to see Ronan, he was much brighter. His big beaming smile was back. He was alert. I thought, 'My God, the drug is working.' But the effects were only to last for a few hours.

Later, everybody was there again. Kit and Tony had come over and were a great support. Mother and Father were arguing with each other in the corridor. It really got to me. I did not know what they were arguing about and I wasn't interested.

Over the weekend, lots of my friends came to see Ronan. Breeda Conway knew someone who had a piece, a relic of a mitten of Padre Pio and asked him to bless Ronan with it.

I was grateful for any help, however tenuous, but by then I knew that it was not going to work.

On Saturday night, Michael Roberts, Harry's brother, stayed the entire night by the bedside.

Sunday came.

My cousin Terence and his fiancée Niamh came directly from the airport to see Ronan. He was able to tell them that he was going to get a puppy. He did not know whether to get a large one or a small one.

One of the consultants came to see me. He said, 'You have some very difficult decisions to make. My family will pray for you at church today.'

Strangely, it was more than my family said to me. I wondered how many of them were going to pray for my son or me on that Sunday, in February 1986. My parents were not praying. I could hear them laughing and arguing again out in the corridor. I had two mass cards from my two brothers, John and Tommy Junior, but that was all.

Monday, February 10. Early in the day, my friends Peter and Angela were there when Ronan wanted something. He couldn't speak properly and was trying to make signs. I knew that he wanted cake and custard. I remember asking a nurse if we could put some in his mouth and then take it out again. She was so nice about it and went to ask the staff nurse. The staff nurse said not to give him anything.

Harry, Paddy, Kit and my parents got together in consultation. It was decided between them that, 'Any decisions to be made, it's up to you.' After talking with the consultants, it was decided that in the event of another cardiac or respiratory arrest, he would not be resuscitated.

It was the most difficult decision of my life.

I had been making decisions all my life, but no decision had ever been this tough.

I felt very alone.

Before making the decision I asked for guarantees of life. There were none.

I asked about a timeframe. Six months? Four months? I wanted the longest time possible.

They were talking in terms of weeks.

That Monday night it was fairly obvious to me that Ronan was not going to survive. He pointed to some cards on the wall and indicated that he wanted them to be taken down. Two of them were mass cards. One was of St Joseph and the child Jesus. The second one was of Our Lady with roses spread around her feet. When he was holding the card with Our Lady on it, I asked him, 'Is this lady very special?'

'Yes,' he said

'Am I as good as her?' I asked.

'No.'

'Can I ever be as good as that lady?'

'No.'

'Ronan, do you want to go home?'

'No.'

'Can I go wherever you are going?'

'No.'

'Can I ever go where you are going?'

'Yes,' he said.

With that, I just broke down in tears. I could not hold back the flow. The tears streamed down my cheeks as if they were eroding them.

My heart was broken.

I was inconsolable.

The muscles in the back of my throat were constricted so hard that I could hardly breathe between long racking sobs. I wanted to go with him. At that point I wanted my life to be over. But for some perverse reason, I had to live on.

Ronan had told me so.

I was not to give up.

Of all the many and cruel things that had happened to me during my life, this was the worst. No physical pain had hurt like this. Of all the times that I had wanted to end my life, I was surely justified on this occasion.

But Ronan had said, 'No.'

I wondered why I had to endure so much punishment in this life.

Sometime later, it must have been around midnight, the chaplain, Father Gallagher, silently came in to me. He suggested that I freshen up. I went to an area where parents and relatives gathered to make a cup of tea and sit down. I asked someone for a cigarette. I have no idea why I did that. I must have thought that they provided some solace at times like these. During my work I had seen many relatives of patients go for a much-needed smoke, from which they gained some obvious satisfaction. All that happened to me was that I coughed and spluttered. The smoke that I did inhale just made me feel dizzy.

I went to the ladies' to wash my face and threw the cigarette down the toilet. That was the first and only cigarette that I have ever smoked.

I could not stay away from Ronan. I went back to him immediately.

This was the first night that Harry was staying at the hospital with me and he went to bed.

I was there alone with Ronan. He was a bit restless. At four in the morning I took him out of his bed to sit in my lap.

I had a white blouse on. I opened the blouse so that he could feel closer to my skin and feel safer.

I talked to him.

I told him how much I had wanted him to be born.

I told him how much I loved him.

I told him how much his big brother loved him.

I told him how much his dad loved him.

He died in my arms at a quarter to five in the morning.

TWENTY

Loss of My Life

I was numb.

I held my dead son in my arms for a while.

I could not let him go, physically.

I could not let him go, emotionally.

The nurse came back and I sort of mouthed the words, 'He is gone.'

No sound came.

But she knew and asked, 'Where is your husband?'

I was unable to answer or to even lift my head in response. She found him after some time. He came into the room and stood at the opposite side of the bed from where I was sitting with our dead son in my arms. I lashed out verbally at him and shouted, 'You couldn't even stay awake with me, even for one night. Our beautiful Ronan is dead.'

He didn't say anything.

I then put Ronan on the bed and Harry kissed his forehead. The nurse had taken away all the tubes and said that she wanted 'to lay him out'. I said that I did not want him removed from the ward before his brother had seen him. I asked Harry to call home and tell Thelma what had happened. I did not want her to tell Anthony the bad news. I wanted to tell him myself.

It was 6 am.

While Harry was phoning, I washed Ronan with the nurse. I put white socks on him. He wanted his Thomas the Tank pyjamas, but he never got to wear them because of all the equipment and tubes. I dressed him in the Thomas the Tank pyjamas with tears silently cascading down my cheeks. I thought, 'Little did you know that when you asked for them, you would be dead before you got to wear them.'

Between sobs, I would try to steady myself. I would blow out long exhalations of air to obtain some form of breathing. I put a little toy monkey that Thelma had given to him under his right arm and under his left arm I put a little toy dog that Maria had given to him. As I looked at him, I had a flashback to my first day in the orphanage in Limerick, when I looked at my brown leather handbag with my name on it for the last time.

I realised then, that Ronan was never mine to keep.

He was only ever on loan to me.

I had to give him back.

I thought that Thelma and my parents would bring Anthony into the hospital immediately, but they did not arrive until 9 am. I had no idea what delayed them, but I was anxious to tell Anthony about his brother. When Anthony came in, I was waiting to talk to him.

The first thing he said to me was, 'I knew Ronan would get better. He is all right isn't he?'

'No darling, he is not all right. Ronan is gone to Heaven. I am going to take you to see him now. He is going to feel different. He is going to feel cold when you touch him.'

I took Anthony in to see his little brother. My parents were in the room already. Thelma was there with Harry. My parents both held me briefly. Harry did not touch me or try to comfort me in any way. He might have been afraid to.

Anthony said, 'He is so cold.' That is why I had wanted Thelma and my parents to bring Anthony into the hospital as soon as possible. I did not want Anthony to feel the coldness. I wanted Ronan to still be warm.

They took Ronan to the hospital chapel. We left the hospital to go home at midday. Before we could go home we had to go to an office in Camden to register the death. I did all the necessary form filling.

I felt alone, empty and numb. Another part of me had died.

Harry said, 'He is better off in Heaven.'

That was not the way I saw it. I wanted him back.

If I could not have him back, I wanted to be where Ronan was.

We finally reached home. Michael Roberts was probably the most upset. He cried for Ronan. I had never seen a member of the Roberts family cry until that day, and I have never seen one cry since.

People appeared from everywhere. Friends came and neighbours too.

My GP came round to see if I needed him, even though he politely said that he did not want to intrude on my private time. It was very good of him, but I decided that I was not going to take any form of medication.

I was hard.

I was tough.

I would get through without it.

Someone asked me if I wanted a drink. I thought that if I started drinking, I would never stop. I resolved not to have any alcohol while this entire crisis was going on around me. I had survived on sandwiches, supplied by my friend Angela and her husband Peter, while I was in the hospital. They even used to take away my washing. I only left Ronan to wash and change my clothes. I couldn't stay away for long.

During the day Harry and his brother Paddy went to the local graveyard, Streatham Cemetery, and bought a burial plot. Paddy paid Harry £1000 towards burial expenses. I was very grateful. They also secured an undertaker to take Ronan from the hospital to a funeral parlour, and from there, to the church.

Eventually I went to bed in a single bed in Ronan's room, because my parents were in our bedroom and Thelma was in the small bedroom. Harry and I had been sleeping in the single bed. Ronan and Anthony slept in bunk beds in their own room. Harry was already asleep when I went in. I lay down exhausted. I was in a bed for the first time in about two weeks, because I had been with Ronan all the time. I felt totally drained in every sense.

I cried for all the losses of my life. Long muscle-wrenching sobs racked my body.

I had wanted to comfort Anthony and find out how he was really feeling about the loss of his brother but I couldn't. I couldn't feel anything except my own pain. It was the worst pain of my entire life.

The week was just a blur of people coming and going.

On Saturday I cleaned the house from top to bottom with Thelma. I gave my mother money to buy whatever food was needed.

On Sunday, Harry's sister Alice, my brothers Tommy and Niall, along with Miriam Cooke, arrived from Ireland. Kit and Tony didn't stay for the funeral. Kit said they'd visit later when everything had died down.

We went to the funeral parlour to collect Ronan's remains. Angela's sister Peggy said the rosary there. I had never gone to the undertakers to see Ronan 'laid out'. I couldn't. I was not able to see him like that.

He was there for almost a week. The reason that he was there for so long was that in London you have to wait for a slot for burial, as there are so many funerals taking place at the same time. When I got there and saw him in the coffin, I thought that his head was too low. I asked for another pillow, which they placed under his head.

One of Harry's bosses arrived, holding his young son in his arms. When the young child saw Ronan in the coffin, he asked his father, 'Is that the baby Jesus, Dad?'

I wanted to scream. I just smiled and acted as if it meant nothing and did not bother me. I was good at acting.

I walked out before they closed the coffin. I just couldn't take anymore. But as I walked out I couldn't avoid hearing the sound of them closing it. It felt as if they were tightening the screws into my heart.

We all left the funeral parlour together. Ronan was brought to the church for six o'clock mass at St Michael's Church, Clapham. After a brief service at the church, more people came to the house. My neighbours kept everyone fed with sandwiches. Most of the women and nearly all of the men went to the pub, which was also close by. I tried to keep busy by preparing food for after the funeral the next day. Angela cooked many legs of lamb, which I spent the evening carving. All the food was brought over to the church hall for the next morning.

That night, after having been to the pub, Terence O'Regan came back to the house before the others. He knew that things were difficult between my parents and I. He said to me, 'Why do you put up with their behaviour? Why can't you block it out?'

'They are my parents and I have waited a long time to have them in my life. I love them,' I said.

But I was all mixed up in my mind, because as I was saying that, I was thinking, 'Is the death of my child, the price I have to pay for finding my parents? If I had known that it was the price I had to pay, I would never have begun the search. If it was the price that I had to pay for finding my parents, it was not a fair trade.'

Nothing could ever be worth the price of my child's life.

Crazy thoughts were flying around in my head. I even

wondered when he was dying, did the gypsies curse him, because my mother had refused them water?

Next morning, it was Monday, February 17th, 1986. I got up after a mainly sleepless night. I had maintained my resolve not to take any medication or alcohol. It had been snowing overnight and a light, icy residue remained on the ground. Angela gave me a sheepskin coat to wear to keep out the cold. I left everybody in the house and went to the church. I wanted to be with Ronan on my own.

It was not to be.

When I got there, my friend and colleague Lily O'Donohue was already there with her husband Paddy. They both hugged me. I thought that they were some of the very few people who could really understand what I was going through, because they themselves had lost their only son. His name was Tony and he was their only child. He died suddenly at the age of twenty from a brain haemorrhage.

I didn't notice who arrived next.

Suddenly my pew at the front of the church was full.

Suddenly the entire church was full of people.

I did not get my private moment alone with my baby.

The service began.

Thelma read the lesson. The priest said that the Roberts were no strangers to suffering. He meant it in the context of my having lost two other unborn children and my having had a lot of surgery. As he said it, I remember thinking, 'If only you and the entire congregation really knew all of the suffering I have had to go through.'

He probably said a lot of nice things about Ronan, but I didn't hear them. I wanted to be with Ronan. As soon as the service began it was over. Michael Roberts, Tommy Junior and Niall, friends Peter Lynch and Peter Sweeney, carried the small mahogany coffin, containing my young son's dead body, to the hearse for the short journey to his final resting place, at Streatham Cemetery. I had asked Harry and Paddy to choose a burial plot with trees close by.

Ronan loved climbing trees.

When I first saw the spot, there were not any proper trees around it. It wasn't what I would have picked myself. That part of the graveyard seemed neglected and old. I was upset about that but I did not say anything about it to anyone.

We had two funeral cars, with Harry, Anthony, my parents and myself in the leading one, following the hearse. When I reached the place that my baby was to be interred, for time immemorial, I felt that I did not want to see it.

I wanted to run away and hide.

I did not want to face it. It was just all too horrible, too cruel. I did not want to have to bury my baby. I just kept thinking, 'Why? Why isn't it me?'

He had so much to live for. I had so much to escape from, so many memories to leave behind, why couldn't I have died? I couldn't understand it.

Everyone was saying to me that I had to live and be strong for Anthony and Harry. I wanted to say, 'I don't want to live for myself, how could I want to live for anyone else?' But no one would want to listen to me.

I remained emotionally destitute but silent.

The same men carried the coffin from the hearse to the grave. The undertakers lowered the coffin down into the grave, as the priest led the large crowd in some prayers. I couldn't identify the prayers. When the prayers were over, the undertaker laid the wreaths around the grave. It was a large amount of flowers. There were 125 wreaths in total.

I felt that I was no longer able to stand so I went to the funeral car and got in.

Nobody got in with me and no one followed me.

I sat there alone.

Anthony came next. I said to him, 'Whatever are we going to do without him, darling?' He did not reply. We just both cried in reply. We returned to the church hall. I only stayed for a short time and then I returned to the house.

Later that afternoon, I returned to the grave with Tito, my friend Zelda's husband. He had been unable to come to the funeral earlier as he had to give a lecture. It looked different because they had covered it up with all the flowers. Tito said, 'If a child dies in Goa, where I come from, they put just white flowers on the grave.'

The next day my parents went home. They were the last to go. Then everyone was gone.

But people continued to come and see me all that week.

I went back to work on the following Monday. But it was not like previous times that I had gone back to work after a disappointment. I could not turn off the pain and bury it. It was never to be the same. I could not just cut myself off. I could never forget my baby. Every thought, every minute of the day, I saw Ronan.

I was a nurse. I was a professional. I did the job. But my life would never be the same again.

Father Bernard wrote me a letter. He was in the United States at the time and in it he said, 'I wish I was there to hold you.'

I remember just wishing somebody had been.

TWENTY-ONE

A Soulmate and a Wedding

I finally stopped working nights in May. I thought that I should stop running away from Harry. Some part of me thought that I should have a normal life. I took a job working in the Ambulance Escort Unit. I took it because the hours were more regular, from 8 am to 4 pm or from 9 am to 6 pm. We took patients from one hospital to another for specialised treatments.

It was a difficult time for me. I was very fragile emotionally. I remember an episode when my ambulance driver was angry that a patient was not ready for collection. I felt, 'What is the matter? What is five minutes extra?' I remember bursting into tears and being angry with the driver and shouting at him. I'm sure he was glad to go off-duty that day. It was bad enough when the patient was late, but to have the escort-nurse rounding on him as well.

I felt very mixed up. I worked at that job for two years. I kept my head down and tried not to disturb anyone. I tried to work a routine job, in a routine life, without annoying anyone. I wanted to distract myself from the memory of Ronan. I turned so far into myself that I became depressed.

In June 1988 I got a phone call from Tony in Buttevant

to say that Kit was in hospital. I was extremely upset. I knew it was serious if Kit was in hospital. She wouldn't even go to a doctor. She asked Tony to take her to the doctor because she had found a lump on her breast. He sent her to hospital for tests and that is when Tony called me. She was diagnosed with cancer. She was sent home without surgery.

I went to see her by myself the following August. The first thing she said to me when I sat down beside her at the edge of the bed was, 'Yer auld one is dying, a Gra.'

She knew she was dying.

I knew she was dying, but I did not want to admit it to myself.

I only stayed two nights and Tony took me to the station at Charleville.

I stood there alone.

The conspiracy of silence between Kit and myself overwhelmed me. Both of us knew so much about each other and the difficulties of our lives, yet we never mentioned them.

She also felt that she was unacceptable. It was the last time I saw her alive, although we spoke many times on the phone over the next few months. She was taken to hospital for radio and chemotherapy but it was all too late. She was finally sent home again.

In her last phone call to me she was crying. That was not like Kit. She would be courageous and, rather than upset anyone, she would pretend that everything was fine. This time, between her tears, she was saying goodbye to me. After I put the phone down, my eyes welled up, the muscles in my neck constricted and I sobbed my heart out for two hours.

She died next day – it was Sunday, October 23, 1988.

I was almost 40 years old and one of the very few people to whom I felt acceptable in the entire world, was gone. I went to her funeral on my own, feeling numb throughout.

* * * *

My relationship with my father deteriorated. This was as a result of pressure put on him from my mother. If we met at any time, my mother always accompanied him. He could not relax in my company, as my mother disapproved of him even speaking to me.

He told me that he also had financial problems. With such a large family, it seemed like money was always a problem. I assured him that I would help him out. He told me how much he needed. It was a significant amount to me but made a big difference to him. I was pleased to help my father and my family because it made me more acceptable to them. I was still trying to fill that emptiness inside of me.

But it was evident from my father's letters to me that his quality of life was less than he desired. Even his dog racing and gambling did not hold the allure that they once did. I think he expected to have an easier life.

He did not want to have to cope with the problems arising between his wife, whom he loved, and his eldest daughter, whom he also loved, but in a different way. The problem was that his daughter and his wife did not form the expected third side of a stable family love triangle. My mother hated me and what I represented, and my father could not cope with that. She had closed a door on that part of her life for ever, and she never wanted to face it again. But every time she saw me, or my father mentioned my name, it triggered an angry reaction in her which was uncontrollable.

On one occasion when my father, as always accompanied by my mother, came to visit me, one of my friends saw the strain and pressure that my mother was causing me. She arranged for my mother to visit a psychiatrist. Mother caused a fierce commotion. She insisted that she was not mad. She was highly indignant that any member of the Cliffords should even be considered for a psychiatric consultation. She ranted and she raved that she would not lower herself to even admit such deviancy.

But my father was enthusiastic that she should go and keep the appointment. He eventually persuaded her to go, mainly because the consultation was in London and nobody at home in Ireland would know. It was just to be a one-off visit. Afterwards, I asked my mother whether the visit had helped her. She would not discuss it with me or anybody else, under any circumstances. And she never did.

I went to see the psychiatrist myself, subsequently. I wanted to find out why she didn't tell my father about my existence over the years. All he said to me was, 'Was there ever anything that you kept secret from someone else?'

'Of course there was,' I said.

'Well then,' he replied.

That was it. He would not entertain my questions any further. I had to resign myself to the fact that I would never get an answer to that question.

After living with us in Surrey for seven years, Thelma had bought her own flat in Croydon. She now had a good job and was obviously well able to support herself. My parents came over to stay with her for a ten-day visit. They never visited me, or my son or my dead son's grave, even though we were less than a ten-minute taxi ride away. I was not invited over to Thelma's to see them. That really hurt.

That visit was about six months before Thelma's wedding.

When Thelma became engaged to be married, I expected to participate in all the excitement leading up to the wedding of my sister. Instead, I was excluded from all the preparations, except that I was asked to make the wedding cake. I must have been good enough as a baker. That should have put me in my place. But I was so pleased to be allowed to do anything. I had placed my family on a high pedestal and I was grateful for any crumbs that fell from their table. They were much more important than me, and at least I had my uses.

I also indirectly paid for the wedding dress, with a good bit of luck thrown in. The local church had a monthly draw and I paid for Thelma's monthly ticket. It was only one pound per month. That year her name was on a winning ticket. She won £300 and that paid for the wedding dress.

I used to feel that my father was exploiting me, through Thelma. I suppose I put myself in the way of being used. Yet I always felt protective of her and she was part of my real family, who was living with me. It was what I always wanted, a family to protect. I was so proud to have a family member living in my house. I never asked, nor expected anything from her. To her credit, she did help with the housework and, together with my son Anthony, she bought me my first dishwasher.

Harry, Anthony and I were invited to the wedding to be held in Adare, County Limerick, in April 1991.

We took our usual route to Ireland by car and ferry, as we had to transport the wedding cake, all four tiers. One tier was a special heart-shaped sponge, as Thelma did not eat heavy fruitcake.

At the church, I found things very difficult, as it reminded me of my own wedding day. This was the first family wedding I had attended, along with my parents and siblings. The church was a small beige-painted purpose built edifice, which stood out starkly against the dull drab working-class Janesboro background.

My father and mother walked their daughter Thelma down the aisle to the altar. I thought back to how my wedding day ought to have been. I really should have had my parents there. They should have been at my wedding, instead of the bogus family that I had to arrange.

I sat behind my parents in the church. As they came in, my father said 'Hello' only to the three of us in general. My mother just gave me a look, as if to say, 'Why are you here?'

As the ceremony began, I thought, 'Thelma has no baggage like me, no fears to deal with on her wedding day.' I started to feel excluded.

For Thelma's wedding I had bought a Moschino dress from the Ritz Boutique in Wimbledon. It cost me £725. Even my underwear was designer. It was a La Perla Body, so that no lines showed through the dress. It alone cost £95. I had French La Bourje tights from Harrods. My shoes and bag were from Russell and Bromley and cost £450. The outfit was finished off with a Norwegian natural blue fox jacket from a Knightsbridge furrier, which cost me £2200. All complemented by a navy hat, which was put together for me by Beverly Haynes, one of Jean Muir's designers. I was dressed to the nines. Knowing how well and expensively my mother dressed, I thought that if I could wear good quality and expensive clothes, I would fit in, be acceptable and be good enough to attend an O'Sullivan wedding.

When I first arrived at the church, the first three people I met were my auntie Eileen, my father's sister, and her two daughters. Eileen had a turquoise suit and hat, with perfectly matching accessories. Both of her daughters were dressed equally smartly.

I immediately felt that I could never match up to them or ever be as good as them. I felt that all my expensive dress-wear was in vain. And then I encountered my mother, dressed in what looked like a £1000 creation. I felt terrible.

I felt I was an outsider, looking in. That is where I had always been.

The church ceremony went smoothly. The priest made the usual harmless and inoffensive wedding speech to the bride and groom. He then handed over to the local parish priest who was assisting him, to say a few well-chosen words. After wishing the bride and groom well, he thanked Tom and Doreen for being such strong Catholics and such upright members of the local community. He thanked them for their extraordinary generosity to the local church and clergy, and for 'always giving that bit extra' as a financial contribution. When he said that, I remembered how, as their child, in another church, not 20 miles away, I had eaten the penny wax candles because I was starving from hunger due to a lack of food.

You see, everything for me was a potential trigger. And yet, there was conflict. I was also proud of my father and mother, particularly as Harry's brother and his wife and my friend Majella were at the wedding. The ego side of me wanted them to see my fabulously dressed family. I wanted them to see my cousins – the priests, and my aunts – the nuns and doctors. That was what the ego part of me was proud to claim a relationship to. That was what I thought I wanted. I wanted to belong, at any price. I thought that this family were ideal. But I now know that the 'real me' was questioning, 'How could this family not know and care about me and the life of degradation and deprivation that they had consigned me to?' Inside my head, there was this constant internal dialogue of conflicting emotions taking place.

When the local priest got up and spoke in such glowing terms of my parents' family responsibility and their more-than generous financial contributions to the Catholic Church, I began to seethe with anger. I wanted to go up to the altar, take the microphone from the priest and tell everybody present that it was all hypocrisy really, because

I was the daughter that they abandoned to squalor and the ruination of my life. I wanted to ask all the parents present how they would have felt if it had happened to their young daughter.

I wanted to include my auntie nuns, the relatives that sent me the First Communion dress that I was so brutally raped in. My 'auntie nuns' knew I existed. Every Mercy nun that knew me and spoke to me, referred to them. They must have known where I was. They could have got to me somehow. Instead they chose to ignore me.

That day at the wedding I wanted to expose them as contributors and knowing collaborators. It was all organised through the medium of the Catholic Church, by its priests and nuns, albeit at the behest of my natural family.

But once again I held my peace. That is what I did best, remain silent and tell no one. Little did Thelma realise how close she had been to having her wedding ceremony controversially hijacked by her new sister.

After the photographs, we headed off to the reception. My sister Avril was matron of honour and my other sister Rosaleen was a bridesmaid.

As Thelma had lived with me in London, I thought that she had accepted me as her sister. I thought that she would want me to be an integral part of her special wedding day. I was even instrumental in her meeting her husband, because his sister Majella and I were friends when I lived in Belfast. As their romance progressed, I suppose, in a way, I took it for granted that I would be matron of honour at her wedding. But then, one day, my friend Anna had told me that Thelma was having Avril and Rosaleen. I felt really hurt and betrayed, firstly because I was excluded and secondly, because I had heard the details second-hand.

Thelma had phoned me at work soon afterwards and I

said to her, 'Anna told me you are having Avril as matron
of honour and Rosaleen as a bridesmaid.'

She said, 'That's right, they are my sisters. I grew up
with them.'

It was just as if she had stabbed me. It wasn't because
she had not chosen me as a bridesmaid, it was purely the
fact that she regarded them as her sisters and did not see
me as an equal sister. I was really hurt but I never showed
my feelings. I suppressed my pain and my anger and
continued to play their game. That is what it was for me at
this stage – mind games.

We arrived at the Woodlands Hotel for the reception. My
mother and father were lined up in the foyer greeting all
the arrivals.

Except me! Neither shook hands with me. Neither
said any words to me. I didn't know why.

I attempted to greet my mother with a kiss, but she
averted her head and instead gave me one of her cutting
stares. While standing in the foyer I asked Harry to get
some drinks and to include my mother in the round. She
declined his offer, in a sharp voice. As Harry headed for
the bar, he shot me a glance which said, 'Don't ever ask
me to speak to that woman again.'

I tried everything to talk and be friendly with her that
afternoon. But it didn't work. I thought she looked
miserable that day. She looks miserable in all the
photographs. I followed my mother around if I thought
that she was going to be in a photograph. If she posed for
a photo, I would stand behind her.

I was not going to let her forget me and she was not a
bit pleased.

But bad and all as I felt, I acted my way through the
day, as if I had not a care in the world. I socialised with my
siblings. I had in-depth conversations about trivialities

with aunts on my father's side. I spoke more to the groom's family whom I had known for quite a long time, from my Northern Ireland days. His mother was lovely and was happy to see her son married.

After the reception and the dancing was over, when the bride and groom were leaving the hotel to go on their honeymoon, I found myself standing beside my mother, I remarked to her, 'You have lost a lot of weight.'

'Yes I have,' she answered.

The tone of her reply was not as sharp as previously, so I felt she had mellowed or thawed out a little. I felt it was progress, no matter how small, as we hadn't spoken to each other since the night of Thelma's 21st birthday. I felt to some degree that I was to blame for the lack of communication. After Ronan's death, I was back in survival mode, and contact with my parents or the fact of their existence in my life, became merely incidental. That short verbal exchange was the sum total of my conversation with my mother during the entire wedding. But I was pleased and prepared to accept any tolerance, however small.

We were both, to some degree, to blame for the great breach that now existed between us.

Next morning, as I was packing to leave the hotel, I had a phone call from my father.

He asked me if I would go down to their house, or 'call up home' as he put it.

I said, 'I don't think so. I don't think that is a good idea, do you? My mother didn't want to speak to me yesterday; why would she want to speak to me today? I am not going over there to be abused and shouted at.'

He persuaded, 'Oh forget about yesterday, your mother does want you to come and visit.'

So I agreed to go. I had nagging doubts about going there and I was really nervous.

As I think about it now, I ask myself, 'How many people feel nervous about visiting their parents in their own house?'

I eventually arrived at the house and my father told me to hug my mother. As I approached her, she recoiled as if something horrible was about to touch her.

I pulled back.

Her eyes were looking daggers at my father. He threw his arms up in the air, turned on his heel and walked away. Then she looked at me and in the blink of an eye, we agreed a silent truce. I understood, in a strange way, how she felt because I knew how it felt to touch someone, when you did not want to be touched.

Tea and sandwiches were laid out in the front sitting room. That had never happened before. The atmosphere was formal, yet quite civil and almost friendly. We even discussed my birth and my mother described how she got rheumatic fever after I was born. This was when she was living with her Uncle Jack, who took pity on her plight. He must have been the person who paid the £100 for her release from the home for unmarried mothers. She could not have stayed with Uncle Jack if she had an illegitimate baby hanging out of her. She was not allowed to return to her mother's house at Clarina. She was good enough to stay at Uncle Jack's house as long as she pretended that she did not have an illegitimate baby. But me, the illegitimate baby, regarded by the family as the dregs of the earth was not eligible for such careful consideration.

My father said that he used to go up there and take her for slow careful walks, until she regained her full health. I wanted to ask her what she had told my father about her six-month absence. Where did he think she had been for six months? He must have asked her.

Did she tell him a lie or the truth?

If she told him a lie about where she had been for six months, did he believe her?

Did he have his suspicions about why she had to leave for six months?

Did it suit him, not to know where she was for six months?

If she told him a lie, and he believed her, it may have suited them both not to pursue the matter any further. But if she told him the truth, then he knew about me. He would have known about me all along. Of course, I have no answer to these questions, as I never asked them.

I did ask her about her time in the home for unmarried mothers, in Bessboro, where I was born, but she dismissed my question with a wave of her hand and a look of annoyance. She would not give me any glimpse into her life while she was pregnant with me. She would rather talk about when my father was young. I feel there was a great sexual attraction between them.

Her health problems were a large topic of conversation and she would expand on them at length. By this stage, it was too late. I could not feel any empathy for her problems because she had been the cause of all of mine. Also, my mother, while mellowing, remained detached.

After the tea and sandwiches, I accompanied my father to the local shop for the daily paper. He brought up the subject of finance once again. I steeled myself for another touch for a loan of some kind. He asked me if I had sorted out my finances. He said that he was aware of the problems I had regarding all the money that I had spent on them.

As usual, I said that I had the problem sorted. What I did not tell him was that I was heavily in debt to the bank and would be paying off loans for many years. Thanks to my considerate bank manager, he had tidied up all my financial affairs neatly and spread my repayments over a long-term loan. This took the worry and stress off my shoulders.

After making me feel secure about my finances, my father then told me that he himself was having further financial problems. He told me that he had taken out a large loan and was unable to finance the repayments.

I volunteered to help. He didn't even have to ask if I would help. I said that I would help him with his monthly repayment and so I took on an extra financial burden that I could not afford. I realised that with all the expensive clothes that I had for the wedding, I must have been setting myself up for such a request. I sent him a cheque by post every month.

We were based in Buttevant for the rest of the week of the wedding. I felt back in my family fold, but it was not the same without Kit. Yet I was happy there. There was no rancour or bitterness. No arguments.

I did see my parents once more during the week. I took them out to eat at The Texas Steakhouse in Limerick.

The entire meal was very civilised. I had changed.

I was not going to let my parents play such an important role anymore.

The death of my son had shattered my life.

We returned to Buttevant where Tony had packaged the top tier of the wedding cake for the return trip to London.

Back in London, I found it difficult to cope with everything and anything. I couldn't function properly and things didn't get better. One day, when Harry's brother was in the house, I announced in all seriousness that I was unable to cope. I said that I was going to seek help through the aid of a counsellor.

With equal solemnity and in a low voice, in case anyone

might hear him, Paddy Roberts said, 'Ohhhhh, you don't want to be goin' an tellin' your business to those kind of people.'

But this time I was determined to do what was right for me.

TWENTY-TWO

His Departure

From the time of the wedding, an arid period developed between my parents and myself. I had found a counsellor and possibly our sessions affected my relationship with them, but there were no more long conversations over the phone, on either side.

I was still helping my father out. We kept this secret between ourselves. But, little by little, I began to realise that my father seemed to be spending the money. I was upset about the fact that he had tapped me for financial help, for a loan that I had no evidence that he was in fact repaying. I stopped buying things for them that I thought they might like.

I next saw them in August of that year, when Harry's brother Michael died in an industrial accident at his workplace. He was buried in Ireland and we went there for the funeral.

My parents also came to the funeral. We took them out to dinner one night. Everything went smoothly, Mother was calm and Father seemed happy enough. We did not have a lot of time with them and we politely said our goodbyes. No hugs or touching this time.

I didn't know that this was the last time that I would see my father alive.

If I had known, I certainly would have been more tactile. We spoke by phone infrequently after that.

A few months later, on a Sunday evening, November 3, 1991, after I returned from church, Harry said that Marion, Tommy Junior's wife, had phoned. I thought that it was strange, because Marion never called me. I called her back and she said, 'Your father got bad at mass this evening.'

I knew from her voice that she was really upset. She said that he was in hospital and she gave me the telephone number. I rang it immediately. I got through to accident and emergency and they asked me to hold on. I had to listen to upbeat rock music, while I tried to stay calm.

The sister eventually came on the phone. I could tell from her responses that it was serious.

'Did he have a cardiac arrest?'

'Yes.'

I posed a negative question, 'He didn't make it then, did he?'

'No.'

I was so shocked and upset, I just felt the phone slide out of my hand.

Anthony was in the hall beside me, deciphering my one-sided phone call. He realised what had happened. He hit the wall so hard in anger that he broke a bone in his hand. The sister put me on to my mother.

She said to me, 'Oh, my darling has gone.'

She was very upset.

I felt sad for her and for myself.

I felt that there was so much unfinished business between my father and me.

I felt cheated. I had never got any answers. I had never found out things that I wanted to find out. I wanted to talk to them both about how it all went disastrously wrong for us.

I wanted to talk about the euphoria of meeting them and the breakdown of our relationship. I wanted to explain my feelings of inadequacy, of being unacceptable and of not fitting into their family. I would never get to say those words now.

I rang Thelma and told her. I expected her to be hysterical at the news because she was the 'apple of his eye'. I was surprised at her reaction, but then I realised she must have been in shock.

Anthony and I flew to Ireland as soon as we could. Tommy Junior met us at Shannon. It transpired that my father was at evening mass when he had a heart attack. He was dead on admission to hospital.

Tommy Junior and Avril went to the undertaker to make all the arrangements for his burial. I went to a florist to order wreaths. I wrote, 'Sadly missed by your eldest daughter, Celine.' But in my heart I wanted to say that I felt cheated, that our time together was so short and because my mother was so bitter. I felt she had not allowed us to develop a proper father-daughter relationship and now that could never be.

Each grandchild threw a yellow rose into his grave, including Anthony. Anthony adored his grandfather. They often used to talk about maths and numbers together. He really looked up to him. All those kids loved my father.

As the days passed, I realised that his death was not as earth-shattering as I would have expected. It did not impact on my life to any great extent. What was going around my head were the unanswerable questions, the nagging doubts. I wanted to take a lock of his hair, but the opportunity did not present itself, so I don't have a personal memento.

On the day he died, I was not the same person that tracked him down and found him. When I first laid eyes on him, for the first time in my life, as he walked towards me at the airport, he looked like a god to me. He was so special. Although his death would be an enormous loss in my life, there was no loss that could compare to the death of my son. At the same time, my father's death did feel very final. This was the end. I could not question it any more. If any more questions did arise, my opportunity or window in time was gone.

In the cemetery he was buried next to his younger brother, Frank. He once told me that they had been great pals and had done everything together, up until the time they got married.

I didn't cry that day, not even as the grave was being filled in. As we walked away, I looked back at the grave and thought that I should be crying but I couldn't. No tears would come.

All the mourners went to Cloughaun Football Club where refreshments were available and everyone who knew him spoke well of him. To the large crowd, even in death, I was not introduced to anyone as his daughter. It was as if I was still to be hidden.

Once when he introduced me to his cousin he said, 'This is Celine, this was our love-child that we kept hidden away.' He had kind of laughed as he said it. It was as if he was trying to explain my long absence and my sudden appearance, and that it was all at once acceptable. But to me it was not acceptable. I was not just hidden away; I was consigned to a life of degradation from which, as a small child, I could not escape.

My father was gone. My mother and my siblings had the closeness of the family to support each other but I felt excluded.

After the funeral I went back to my mother's house. She allowed me to undress her, get her ready for bed and generally look after her. It was the first time I thought that she might accept me. It was as if a heavy weight had been lifted off her shoulders.

It felt very strange indeed. I stayed in my brother Tommy's house and went home a few days later. I wondered what the future would hold for my mother and I now.

TWENTY-THREE

New Answers

After Ronan's death and then my father's, I really tried to bring some normality into my world. I just wanted to be doing normal, everyday things – like looking after Anthony and Harry, and working normal hours. But instead, I thought that I was going off my head.

Then Tony, who used to ring quite often after Kit's death, died suddenly one day. We were all so shocked. I was not prepared for his death at all. I screamed and screamed when they told me he was dead, 'Tony is dead and they bought me my first shoes.' I was hysterical. His death was one of the deaths that really shocked me. He had gone for a walk with his dog, come back and sat down to have a rest. His sister found him dead just afterwards. I couldn't stop screaming. I was back there again in Charleville, with the first new shoes I had ever owned.

I couldn't stand it. Everything felt bad. My finances were disastrous. The sex side of my marriage was depressing me. I hated it. Previously when I was working nights, it was to escape the sex. I didn't see it as Harry's fault. He had a strong sexual appetite and, while I tried to accommodate him, I was unable to enjoy it. Now that I was not working nights, he wanted sex daily.

I had to get away. I decided to further my education. I

applied to do a foundation course at King's College, University of London. I was adamant to prove that I was not the stupid child that the nuns at the Mount Industrial School had said I was, when they denied me any further education at the age of 13 years. They said I was only good for peeling potatoes and carrots, and cleaning toilets.

I was accepted to do the course. With the sound of those educational judgements still ringing in my ears, I presented myself in the university halls for the first time. It was a big, old building and instead of a sense of awe, I had a feeling of pride as I walked the corridors. I was not nervous. How far I had come. From having no education as a child, I now wanted to be part of a university.

It felt good.

Even the language was different and alien to me. During the first lecture, the professor discussed how he would be giving us salient points, references and bibliographies. The terminology excited me. I wondered what the meaning of those new words could be. I couldn't wait to get home and look up the meaning of a 'salient' point.

I was to bury myself in a university degree course in gerontology for the foreseeable future. I loved it. I could be me. It became my focus. I really used to study whenever I had spare time, be it late into the night or on my days off from work.

It became my sanity. I needed it because I was continually ambushed by my past. One time I was back in Waterford for a visit and I was at a dance with Harry. A friend came up to me and said they wanted to introduce me to a man and his wife from my home in Limerick. It was his eyes I recognised. It was the neighbour who had raped me all those years ago. He didn't even look uncomfortable. I pretended everything was fine, but when Harry came over to meet them I was terrified he would invite them for a visit. I got through it somehow, but when we were walking away

Harry asked me, 'Aren't you going to give them our address?' We'd had other people over to stay in London and he thought it was the same thing. I just said no and kept walking. I've never been back in Waterford for a proper holiday since then, only for a day here and there.

I really loved studying for my degree and in a way I was almost disappointed when I graduated in 1993. I had done my finals and passed with credit. I had my presentation at Birkbeck College, University of London.

On the day, I was allowed to have two guests present. Anthony was one guest and I decided that I had to have my mother present. It was probably a subconscious urge for me to demonstrate to her how well I had done in life. I also wanted her to know firsthand of my academic achievement, above that of any of her other children. It was to prove to her that, despite her abandonment, I had proven myself to be better than any of them. I had come from a feeling of no worth to a feeling of proving myself beyond my wildest dreams. I wanted her there because I wanted her to be proud of me.

The day arrived but she was so bewildered over the whole event, I made no impact whatsoever. I felt that because she always dressed so elegantly, and certainly rose to every occasion, she might buy something new for my graduation. But she didn't. In fact she almost dressed down for the occasion. She wore an old outfit, which she had often used for shopping trips.

The entire ceremony was way above her head. When the formal part was over, at a small reception I introduced her to one of my professors. As they talked briefly, I sensed her trying to take the glory of my triumph as she told the professor how she had educated 'all her children'. She was not proud of me; she was just playing one of her games. I did not mind, I was well used to it by then. I knew Anthony was proud of me and I realised that she would never be, no matter what I achieved. But deep inside, one other person was proud of me. I was sort of shocked to experience it. I was proud of myself. It was a very new experience for me.

After my conferring, my mother never stayed at my home again. I think it was because she did not have to monitor what I said to my father any more. When my father was alive, it was as if I was a serious threat to their relationship. In case I came between them, in any possible way, she had to supervise him. She was not going to allow us to be alone together. If we did escape her vigilance and have a few moments together, she was not far away.

After my father died, I never stayed in my mother's house again. It was as if anyone to whom I was acceptable was gone. There was no reason for me to go there again.

Whenever my mother or my siblings came to London, they all stayed at Thelma's place. She was living over the pub they ran as a successful business. It reinforced to me that they were all part of a family and I was not.

A two-year period passed when I did not see my mother. We had no contact by phone either. Then one Friday in May, 1996, I was out shopping in the West End. When I returned home there was a message on the answer phone from Thelma to say that my mother had had a heart attack. In her message she made light of the fact, by saying that it was probably one of her pleas for sympathy. Even at this stage I was not used to Thelma's sense of humour. She had left the phone number of the hospital in Limerick. I rang the hospital immediately and introduced myself as a ward sister, using my confident self-assured ward sister's tone of voice. I wanted no beating around the bush, or being left on hold, this time.

'Has she had an arrest?'

'Yes.'

'You obviously got her back then?'

'Yes.'

'My mother has had a previous history of heart trouble. Should I come home?'

'Well, you and I both know that you should be thinking about it.'

'That is all I want to know, thank you.'

I searched the travel agents frantically for a flight to Shannon. There were none available. There was one available to Dublin, so I took it.

Before I left for the airport I rang my cousin Tommy O'Sullivan, who lived in Malahide on the outskirts of Dublin, and told him what had taken place and why I was flying to Dublin. Tommy was a cousin on my father's side of the family. He said that he would collect me at the airport and that I could stay at his house until the following day.

During the journey to Dublin my head was in a 'tizz'. It was full of 'what if she dies and I am not there'. I had a million questions and here I was to be stuck in Dublin overnight.

I remembered an old saying that Kit used to use, 'If "ifs" and "ands" were pots and pans, there would be no need for tinkers.'

Tommy met me and wanted to take me home to his house.

'No, I will get a cab from Dublin to Limerick,' I said

'That is all the way across the country, it will cost a bloody fortune.'

'I don't care what it costs, I am going to Limerick tonight.'

He must have realised that he was dealing with a hysterical woman, so without giving out to me, he calmly said that he would drive me to Limerick himself. I have never forgotten that generosity and have always found him and his family to be very accepting of me. I had done nothing to deserve their acceptance, but once I appeared on the scene I felt whole-heartedly acceptable to their family.

We arrived at St John's Hospital Limerick at 3 am. Tommy Junior and Avril, my sister, were there. When my mother saw me she was somewhat disoriented. She thought that I was over in Ireland on holiday. She was a bit phased out with everything that had happened.

When I saw her, I knew that it was the end. She had a myocardial infarction. In other words she had suffered a major heart attack. She was very frail-looking and had no fight left in her. There would be no going back, no getting well for her.

We all left the hospital at 4 am. My cousin Tommy drove off back to Dublin and I went to stay the night at Tommy Junior's house.

The next day, Saturday, Darren my nephew was being confirmed in the Catholic Church. It was a big family occasion and everyone was invited but I didn't go. Instead I went to the hospital and stayed with my mother. She drifted in and out of sleep all day. I had polite small talk with her. She was not well enough to have any deep conversations. I had loads of questions to ask her. I wanted answers.

One of the times as she drifted off, she mumbled, 'Ronan is with me.'

You never saw such speed. I sprang out of my chair to her side, 'What, where, where?' I realised she was hallucinating and sat down in my chair, with a slow exhale of breath.

Her cardiologist came to see her.

I said to him, 'My mother looks very precarious. She is very erratic.'

He said, 'You're right, she has been bad for a couple of years.'

I wasn't prepared for how ill she really was.

I said to him, 'This is it?'

He pursed his lips and silently nodded assent.

During one of her lucid moments I asked her if she would come and live with me in London where I could look after her. She said she would. I felt she was being her usual self. She would say anything to get out of a difficult situation.

I asked her if she wanted to talk about anything. I asked

her if she wanted a priest. My perception of what she might want to talk about and hers might have been different.

The priest came.

She asked to see him alone. He left without speaking to me. She never told me what she had said to him. I never saw him again. The Irish clergy were never very empathetic towards me.

I left her for a short time and joined the other family members for lunch at the confirmation celebrations. After eating, I went straight back to the hospital. I felt that I wanted to be with her until the end. I knew that she would die. It was only a matter of a few short hours and I did not want her to die alone.

About 7 pm that evening, I went back to Tommy Junior's home to freshen up before the long night vigil to come. While I was at his house, I was informed that Avril had phoned to say that the nurses at the hospital had said that our mother needed rest.

I wanted to get back to the hospital but Tommy Junior thought that it was better not to go. I went along with that decision, grudgingly. I was sure that she was going to die in a few short hours.

My head began to race. Were my siblings conspiring against me, to prevent me from being with my dying mother? Why didn't they want me to be there? Did they not realise that I would know what a dying person would need? As a nurse, I know that when someone is just about to die, it can make such a difference to have someone there with you as you slip out. Rest was little use to her at this stage. I wasn't going to prevent her from resting; I just wanted to be with her when she died. Was I the only one who knew that she was dying? Maybe they thought that I might be a bit hysterical or over the top.

I went to bed, but no sleep came. At 4 am, the phone

extension in my room rang. I grabbed it immediately. It was the hospital. They told me that my mother had died. I was raging. I felt that Avril, alone, or in collusion with some of my siblings, had prevented me from being where I wanted to be. I should have been assertive, jumped in a cab and gone back to the hospital. I wasn't with her when she died because I didn't want to antagonise my siblings. I kept it all in and told Tommy Junior and Marion she was dead and we went to the hospital.

I remember thinking, 'Oh God, she is gone.'

I was angry that she had brought ten children into the world and that she had died alone.

I came out of the ward, rushed down the stairs on my own and shouted, 'It is all so bloody unfair.'

I wanted more time, to say what there was to say.

I told her that I loved her, many times.

I wanted her to tell me that she loved me.

She never said it.

Her body was taken to the undertakers on Sunday evening. She was buried next to my father at Mount Oliver's Cemetery, on the Tuesday.

I came home to London on the Wednesday. I took the whole week off work to recover.

How did it affect me?

One thing was certain – my mother had not won this time.

EPILOGUE

Onwards and Upwards

Since the death of my parents, there has been a form of closure to a part of my life. But in the slamming of one door, truly another one has opened.

I am trying to look forward emotionally but in order to progress, I have to look over my shoulder at my past. In doing so, it has thrown up a mountain of questions to which I do not have the answers. With the help of counselling, I am embarking on a confrontational retrospective journey down a not-so-pleasant memory lane.

Most of the sequences, which I recall, have to be analysed, truthfully. I cannot run away and hide emotionally from them and pretend that they did not happen.

I still have not come to terms with events that led to my being given to such an evil, ageing foster-mother. As I think of eating the wax candles in the church and stealing food almost every day of my childhood, it reminds me of a life of misery and neglect, abuse and starvation. I didn't have the innocence of a happy childhood.

I went back to visit the church beside Meade's pub at Bulgaden one time and I found a plaque on the wall by the holy water font. It was commemorating a parish priest who had died many years before my time there. It read:

Earnestly pray for the repose of the soul of
Rev. James Walsh
Thirty-nine years Parish Priest of Bulgaden and Ballinvana
who by his Piety, Eloquence and Zeal
put vice to shame
and confirmed the well disposed
He dept. this life Dec. 24 1858
Aged 77 years
Have Mercy on me O Lord according to Thy Great Mercy

It was strange to think that the area had a problem with 'vice' almost 100 years before my childhood experiences. I just wished that someone had been there when I needed help. The area is now a community alert area. From my point of view it was too late. The community never took any notice of what was happening to me. I hope that they are more 'alert' now.

To face that pain is not easy. I am unable to 'lay those ghosts to rest'. The sexual abuse haunts me. Night after night, I see the faces of my abusers. As nightmares, the acts are replayed in the cinema of my head, to an imprisoned audience of one.

I cannot escape.

I feel angry inside.

I struggle to find words to describe the tangible fear and horror that a young child experiences when a frenzied male adult is raping her delicate body. In cases of child sexual abuse, it always surprises me when adults think that young children do not try hard enough to stop an adult sexually invading their body. It is a commonly held perception that children should fight their abuser. What strength has a child against a fully adult man, who is so emotionally deficient that he can leave the broken and internally damaged body of a young seven-year-old-girl, lying on the dirty ground, waiting for someone else to rescue her?

Today these men are reviled as paedophiles, but when they arrived at our house, they presented themselves as the most charming of men. Some of them were pillars of the local community. When they paid my foster-mother for my services, she was at her most pleasant to me. This behaviour has disturbed me throughout my entire life. How could any woman force another female, especially a young child, to indulge in this type of depravity? It was the behaviour of someone who suddenly realised that they had a considerable asset in their possession, and had to maintain it for its future earnings potential.

I am not yet free of the horrors of the sexual abuse. I don't even know if that freedom is available to me, ever. From where I am now, it is difficult to generate any optimism on that front.

How did society allow these things to happen to me? Many people knew that it was happening and yet they allowed themselves to turn a blind eye. As long as it was happening to someone else or someone else's child, they simply did not care.

My 'auntie nuns' are players in my life that I have difficulty with. When I found my immediate family, members of that extended family began to appear. Some of the first members of my father's family to contact me and 'welcome' me to the family were my 'auntie nuns', his two sisters. I received many letters from them, as if they had always been unaware of my existence.

When I asked them directly, 'Were you aware of me as your niece at any time?' they denied any knowledge. I don't believe them. I think they said it because if they admitted they knew about me, they could have rescued me. They were in positions of power, but they chose not help me. As Mercy nuns, they were an active part of the management of a very powerful institution. They were part of a religious order that indulged in institutional child abuse and treated its occurrence as normal behaviour. I find this difficult to come to terms with. Having witnessed such hypocrisy and denial from the clergy of the day, from close quarters, I could never respect them. So it is with disappointment that I have to treat any lofty excuses from my 'auntie nuns' as suspect, pious testaments. They alone know the truth and they have their own God to answer to.

While at first I considered my father to be a god, his status as a deity declined rapidly for me. He was unable to control my mother. I thought that he was going to solve all my problems with her, but he was always trying to please her first, rather than me. While he accepted me unconditionally, he also wanted my mother to accept me. He was frustrated that he could never achieve a mother-and-daughter harmony between us. But he never delved deeper to see why my mother could not love me. I found him to be a weak man in the end.

My mother provides the greatest turmoil in my head.

The questions keep coming.

Even when she was alive, she would not extend any quarter to me.

She hated me.

She went to great lengths to distance herself from me.

Initially she must have felt safe. I was not a threat. After our first meeting at the convent, she was probably happy enough that I would not cause her any problems. She probably felt very smug after our second meeting at the trade fair. Her secret was safe. But when I appeared again, with my own family in tow, wanting to meet my father, alarm bells started to ring for her. I was a loose cannon.

Her darkest secret was in danger of being exposed and for that, she would never forgive me. I now wonder why, when she had married my father and had nine other children with him, couldn't she tell him about me? After the intimacy of nine children, how could they have secrets from one another? Maybe she did tell him!

They got married about one year after I was born.

Why didn't they come and get me then?

Did my father know about me but pretended not to know, when he was confronted?

Did they both decide to leave me to my own fate and never rescue me from hell?

Could my mother not tell him about me because he was not my father?

Was someone else my father?

Tom O'Sullivan accepted me as his daughter, why couldn't my mother accept me?

She never gave in.

I just wanted her to love me. I was definitely her daughter. Even as an adult, there was no denying me. Physically, I was just like her. I was the image of her. I think that is why Tom accepted me so readily. He saw me as a young Doreen.

Finally, I find it difficult to accept that the Irish state and its public services allowed such abuse to occur undetected. Of course, it is not only the state but also society itself that is responsible for allowing those awful abuses. Irish society refused to admit that such practices existed, while many actually knew it to be true.

I was there.

Those men were there.

The people where I lived were there.

They knew what was happening, otherwise why did the ISPCC get involved?

I am only now beginning to feel good about myself and to look back at some of the things I have achieved. When I finally passed my RGN exams I was awarded the Florence Nightingale medal for my high achievement in the exam. It was presented to me at Southwark Cathedral. That day I felt that I had fulfilled my promise to Father Bernard and Mrs Cooke in some way. I was so proud of that medal with my number and name on it, and I still wear it with pride to the Florence Nightingale memorial service at Westminister Abbey every year. Then, in 1982, I was asked to be the sole representative of all the Irish nurses working in the UK, as part of an 'Irish contribution to Britain' delegation, to make a presentation to the British Prime Minister who was Margaret Thatcher at the time. I presented her with a symbolic nurse's cap. She was very pleasant to our delegation and arranged to have us shown around. Imagine me seeing all around 10 Downing Street! I felt really important and overwhelmed at the same time. I felt I had come a long way.

In 2002 I was accepted by Brookes College, Oxford, to do my Masters in neurology and rehabilitation. Being accepted at Oxford finally proved to me that the nuns in the industrial school were wrong when they told me I was stupid.

I have also made some changes.

Harry still lives in the same house and we remain married. However, we lead separate lives. I asserted myself and obtained that freedom. He is the father of my son and, in that respect, I would not want to see him hurt.

I am still very close to my brother, Tommy, and his family. We are in regular contact, to this day. Many of my other siblings have drifted from me. My son Anthony, his wife and my beautiful grandchild are my family now.

And of course there is not a day in my life that I don't think about my beloved Ronan. I miss him so very much but I know I will see him again one day.

After so many years of 'acting' that everything was all right, of telling different lies to different people, just to survive and appear normal, I am glad that I decided that I had to change. I needed help. I was so tired of simply 'coping' with my past.

When I decided to go for counselling, I had never spoken about my life, truthfully, to anyone before. It wasn't easy to face up to the reality of my life, but now I have been able to put some perspective on it.

And down through the years, while I may have wanted or coveted what other people had, I never wanted to be anyone else. I just wanted to be me.

Now, I want to find the REAL me!

With that goal in mind, I set out once again – a survivor.